MIGRATING

om Microsoft®

WINDOWS NT
SERVER 4.0
to **WINDOWS
SERVER™ 2003**

A Guide for Small and Medium Organizations

The Microsoft Windows Server Team

PUBLISHED BY
Microsoft Press
A Division of Microsoft Corporation
One Microsoft Way
Redmond, Washington 98052-6399

Library of Congress Cataloging-in-Publication Data

    Migrating from Microsoft Windows NT Server 4.0 to Windows Server 2003 / Microsoft Windows Server Team.
       p. cm.
    Includes index.
    ISBN 0-7356-1940-9
    1. Operating systems (Computers)   2. Client/server computing.   3. Microsoft Windows NT server.   4. Microsoft Windows server.   I. Microsoft Windows Server Team.

    QA76.76.O63M52478   2003
    005.4'4769--dc21   2003043004

Printed and bound in the United States of America.

1 2 3 4 5 6 7 8 9   QWE   8 7 6 5 4 3

Distributed in Canada by H.B. Fenn and Company Ltd.

A CIP catalogue record for this book is available from the British Library.

Microsoft Press books are available through booksellers and distributors worldwide. For further information about international editions, contact your local Microsoft Corporation office or contact Microsoft Press International directly at fax (425) 936-7329. Visit our Web site at www.microsoft.com/mspress. Send comments to *mspinput@microsoft.com*.

Acquisitions Editor: Martin DelRe
Project Editor: Julie Miller

Body Part No. X09-45934

Table of Contents

Acknowledgments

Microsoft would like to thank the following people for their contributions:

Writers: Jim Bevan, Ross Carter, Kathleen Cole, Judy Cowan, Douglas Goodwin, Deborah Jay, Merrilee McDonald, Chris McKitterick, and Letha Radebaugh

Editors: Lara Ballinger, Ann Becherer, Chris Clements, Laura Graham, Anika Nelson, Anne Taussig, Scott Turnbull, and Julia Ziobro

Content Architect: Kathleen Cole

Project Manager: Paulette McKay

Lab Management: Robert Thingwold and David Meyer

Publishing Team: David Hose, Jody Ivy, Richard Min, Mark Pengra, Autumn Sheppard, Gabriel Varela, and Erica Westerlund

Technical Reviewers: Chris Adams, Charles Anthe, Calvin Choe, Richard Costleigh, Joseph Davies, Michael Dennis, Brian Dewey, Chris Edson, Levon Esibov, Keith Hageman, Elliot Lewis, Andreas Luther, Tim Lytle, Jay Paulus, Florin Teodorescu, Sakura Thompson, Mark Williams, and Jill Zoeller

Special thanks to Martin DelRe for his support and sponsorship. Without his contribution, the publication of this book would not have been possible.

Introduction

Migrating your environment from the Microsoft® Windows NT® Server version 4.0 operating system to the Microsoft® Windows Server™ 2003 operating system offers tremendous advantages in system performance, security, and features. This book provides clear, concise migration information targeted to the unique needs of small and medium-sized organizations, including migration information for the following server roles: domain controller, DHCP server, WINS server, remote access server, file server, print server, and Web server.

The chapters in this book are designed to provide the simplest and most reliable migration path or paths for each service, as well as all the steps required to support an end-to-end migration for each. This information is useful for organizations that are migrating their entire network or that are migrating individual services to a server running Windows Server 2003, and that have the following characteristics:

- Between 10 and 1000 network users.

- A single Windows NT 4.0 domain environment, which they plan to migrate to a single Windows Server 2003 Active Directory® directory service domain.

- Three or fewer physical locations.

- Servers currently running Windows NT 4.0 that meet the hardware requirements to run Windows Server 2003, or plans to purchase these servers.

For information about migrating servers on larger networks, for more complex scenarios, or for services not covered in this book, see the *Microsoft® Windows Server™ 2003 Deployment Kit*, which is available on the Web at http://www.microsoft.com/reskit.

In This Book

Chapter 1 in this book provides information for planning your migration process in order to meet the goals for your organization. Because most services that run in a Windows NT 4.0 environment can run on a single server, this chapter also provides information about server consolidation. It is important to review this chapter before you begin your migration process.

If you are not upgrading your entire environment to Windows Server 2003 at this time, you can choose to migrate individual services to a new Windows Server 2003 member server that you introduce in your environment, or you can upgrade your domain controllers to Windows Server 2003 Active Directory but continue to run some services on Windows NT 4.0 member servers.

Chapters 2 through 6 in this book describe how to migrate a service from a server running Windows NT 4.0 to a Windows Server 2003–based server. Some chapters also describe how to upgrade a service in place, if it is currently running on a Windows NT 4.0–based server that meets the hardware requirements to run Windows Server 2003. Chapter 7 describes how to move from a system policy–managed environment to a Group Policy–managed environment. Each of these chapters is designed to be stand-alone and can be used independently of the other chapters.

1

Planning the Migration

Small and medium-sized organizations can migrate from a Microsoft®
Windows NT® version 4.0 operating system environment to a Windows
Server™ 2003 operating system environment to take advantage of Windows
Server 2003 features. Careful planning is important to ensuring that the migra-
tion proceeds smoothly and quickly. This chapter describes how to assess your
current Windows NT 4.0 environment, make decisions about your new
Windows Server 2003 environment, and plan the sequence of steps required to
perform the migration.

In This Chapter:

1

Overview of Planning the Migration

Before you migrate your organization from a Windows NT 4.0 domain to a new Windows Server 2003 Active Directory directory service domain, it is important to evaluate your existing domain controllers and member servers, plan your migration process, and design your new Windows Server 2003 domain. Planning for a migration to Windows Server 2003 involves the following steps:

- Selecting a migration path
- Assigning server roles
- Designing the new Windows Server 2003 domain
- Planning for test and recovery

To illustrate the migration process from Windows NT 4.0 to Windows Server 2003, Chapters 1 and 2 in this book describe how a fictitious manufacturing company, Fabrikam, Inc., plans and deploys Windows Server 2003 in its environment.

Fabrikam has 300 employees; approximately 270 of these employees work at the Seattle headquarters, and another 30 work in the field. Fabrikam plans to open an office in Boston, which will be part of the Seattle-based network, and relocate 20 employees to that location. The IT department for Fabrikam consists of an IT manager and a network and user support person.

The Fabrikam environment consists of the following:

- One domain, named Fabricorp, which is running Windows NT 4.0.

- Three servers: the PDC, which is running on new server hardware purchased six months ago, a BDC, and a member server, both running on older server hardware.

- The WINS name resolution service on the internal network, and internal DNS as well as DNS services provided by an Internet Service Provider (ISP).

- Remote Access Service, file service, and print services running on the Windows NT 4.0–based servers.

- Several different client operating systems, including Microsoft® Windows® 98, Windows® 2000 Professional, and Windows® XP.

The Fabrikam IT department established the following goals for their migration:

- Upgrade the Windows NT 4.0 domain to a Windows Server 2003 Active Directory domain.

- Consolidate services onto two servers, both running Windows Server 2003.

- When the Boston office opens, create a new Active Directory site and place a new domain controller in Boston.

Figure 1.1 shows the current Windows NT 4.0 environment.

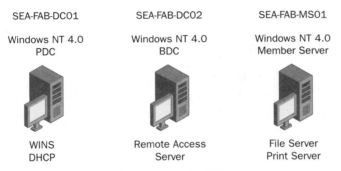

SEA-FAB-DC01   SEA-FAB-DC02   SEA-FAB-MS01

Windows NT 4.0   Windows NT 4.0   Windows NT 4.0
PDC   BDC   Member Server

WINS   Remote Access   File Server
DHCP   Server   Print Server

Figure 1.1   Current Environment for Fabrikam

Server Roles   A server role is a dedicated function that a computer running one of the Windows Server operating systems provides remotely to network clients. Server roles can be combined on a single server. The server roles that are important to small and medium-sized organizations include:

- Domain controller

- DHCP and WINS

- File and print

- Remote access

- Web

Terms and Definitions

Before beginning a server migration, it is important to be familiar with the following terminology.

Server   A computer running Windows NT 4.0 or a later Windows server operating system that is connected to a local area network (LAN). Each server is configured to perform one or more services for network clients.

Client   Any computer (workstation or server) that is connected to the LAN and that requests data, files, or account information from a server to complete a function.

Server role   A service performed by a server to support network client needs; for example, a server might have a role of file server or Web server. A server can execute one or several server roles.

Source server   A server from which a server role is migrated.

Target server   A server to which a server role is migrated.

Selecting a Migration Path

Before you migrate your environment from Windows NT 4.0 to Windows Server 2003, you must select the migration path the best meets the needs of your organization. The size of your organization, your existing hardware, and the operating system that you are currently running impact the migration path that you select.

Organizations that include fewer than 75 network devices might want to consider using the Microsoft® Small Business Server network operating system Small Business Server network operating system instead of Windows Server 2003. Small Business Server delivers e-mail, secure Internet connectivity, business intranets, remote connectivity, support for mobile devices, and file and printer sharing on a single server.

For more information about migrating to Small Business Server, see the Small Business Server Web site at http://www.microsoft.com.

Evaluate Your Existing Hardware

If you have any domain controller in your current environment that is capable of running Windows Server 2003, then plan to upgrade this domain controller in place to establish your Windows Server 2003 Active Directory domain. To do this, the domain controller must be the PDC; if it is not currently the PDC, you must promote it to be the PDC before you upgrade.

Evaluate your existing hardware to identify which servers you can upgrade to Windows Server 2003 and which servers do not meet the recommended hardware requirements. To do this, first document the RAM, CPU, and disk space on each server in your environment, and then compare this information to the Windows Server 2003 System Requirements link on the Web Resources page at http://www.microsoft.com/windows/reskits/webresources.

Based on this evaluation, determine whether you need to purchase new server hardware.

Table 1.1 shows the server hardware configuration information for Fabrikam, Inc.

Table 1.1   Fabrikam Server Hardware Configuration

Existing Server	Operating System	RAM	CPU	Disk Space	Upgradeable to Windows Server 2003 Domain Controller?	Upgradeable to Windows Server 2003 Member Server?
SEA-FAB-DC01	Windows NT 4.0	2 GB	1 x 850 MHz	10 GB	Yes	Yes
SEA-FAB-DC02	Windows NT 4.0	256 MB	1 x 400 MHz	4 GB	No	Yes
SEA-FAB-MS01	Windows NT 4.0	256 MB	1 x 400 MHz	2 GB	No	No

The PDC, SEA-FAB-DC01, meets the requirements for a Windows Server 2003–based domain controller, so it will be upgraded in place.

The BDC, SEA-FAB-DC02, does not meet the recommended requirements for a Windows Server 2003–based domain controller. Fabrikam will use it as the Windows NT 4.0 rollback server if a problem occurs during the in-place upgrade process. Because two domain controllers at minimum are required, they will plan to deploy a new computer, SEA-FAB-DC03, as a domain controller running Windows Server 2003.

The member server, SEA-FAB-MS01, does not meet the recommended hardware requirements for a member server. The services running on this server will be migrated to SEA-FAB-DC03, and SEA-FAB-MS01 will be retired. Fabrikam's new environment will consist of two servers, SEA-FAB-DC01 and SEA-FAB-DC03.

If the server that holds the PDC role in your environment does not meet the hardware requirements, you can transfer the PDC role to a BDC that does meet the hardware requirements and upgrade the new PDC to Windows Server 2003. If none of your Windows NT 4.0 domain controllers meet the Windows Server 2003 hardware requirements, in order to upgrade in place, you must install a Windows NT 4.0 BDC on a computer that does meet the hardware requirements for a domain controller that is running Windows Server 2003 and transfer the PDC role to it.

You can also add a Windows Server 2003–based member server to a Windows NT 4.0 domain at any time before you upgrade to Windows Server 2003 Active Directory. Windows Server 2003–based member servers can operate within a Windows NT 4.0 environment. However, you cannot install

Active Directory on the member server to make it a domain controller, until after you have upgraded the Windows NT 4.0 PDC.

If the PDC is running other services, such as WINS, DHCP, file and print, or Web server, you must also determine whether to upgrade those services in place or migrate them to other servers before upgrading the PDC. If the PDC is running Remote Access Service, you must migrate the service to a server running Windows Server 2003 before you upgrade the PDC. For more information about assigning server roles to server hardware, see "Assigning Server Roles" later in this chapter.

Figure 1.2 summarizes the process for evaluating your current hardware to determine which server, if any, in your current environment you will upgrade to Windows Server 2003 to establish your new Windows Server 2003 domain.

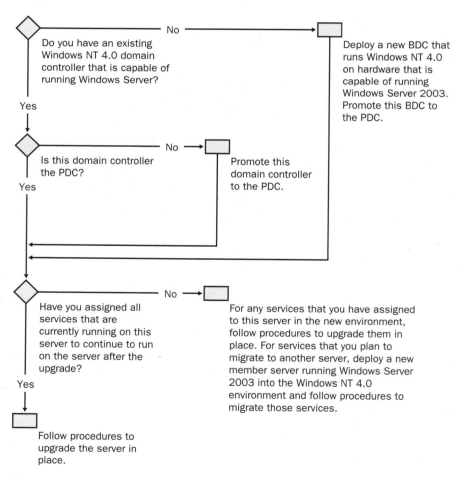

Figure 1.2 Evaluating Your Existing Hardware

Determine Supported Operating System Upgrades

Identify the Windows NT 4.0 platforms that are running in your environment and determine whether an operating system upgrade to Windows Server 2003 is supported, or whether you must perform a clean operating system installation.

You can upgrade the following Windows NT 4.0 platforms to Windows Server 2003, Standard Edition directly:

- Windows NT 4.0 Server, Standard Edition
- Windows NT 4.0 Terminal Server

> **Important**   All versions of Windows NT 4.0 must have Service Pack 5 or later installed before you upgrade to Windows Server 2003.

You do not need to reinstall applications on platforms that you can upgrade directly to Windows Server 2003; however, be sure to verify with the vendor of the application that it can run on Windows Server 2003.

If you have computers in your environment that are running operating systems that you cannot upgrade directly to Windows Server 2003, such as the Microsoft® Windows NT® 3.51 operating system, you must do one of the following:

- If you need to retain applications that are located on those computers, verify that those applications will function on and are supported by Windows Server 2003, and then upgrade the computers to run an operating system that you can upgrade to Windows Server 2003.

- If you do not need to retain applications that are located on those computers, perform a clean installation of Windows Server 2003 on those computers.

Assigning Server Roles

As you plan your migration from a Windows NT 4.0 environment to Windows Server 2003, it is important to plan your future server role assignments. This involves completing the following steps:

- Documenting the servers in your current environment and the services that each server provides.

- Assigning the server roles in your new environment, and documenting those assignments.

- Performing basic capacity planning to verify that you have sufficient capacity on your servers to host the assigned server roles.

- Evaluating the existing network configuration, including IP address and network adapter information for each server.

Document Servers and Services in Your Current Environment

Identify the servers in your existing Windows NT 4.0 domain, and document the services that each server provides. Be sure to identify servers that provide the LAN Manager Replication (LMRepl) service, Remote Access Service, and file service, because you will need to perform tasks prior to upgrading to ensure the continued functionality of these services and access to resources for clients.

You can create a simple table to document your servers and services. Table 1.2 shows the servers and services documentation for Fabrikam, Inc.

Table 1.2 Servers and Services in the Current Environment for Fabrikam

Server Name	Server Role	Services
SEA-FAB-DC01	PDC	WINS, DHCP, LMRepl export server
SEA-FAB-DC02	BDC	LMRepl import server, RAS server
SEA-FAB-DC03	BDC	New BDC deployed on upgradeable hardware.
SEA-FAB-MS01	Member server	File server, print server

For more information about the effect of upgrading to Windows Server 2003 Active Directory on WINS, DHCP, the RAS service, and the LMRepl service, see "Upgrading to Windows Server 2003 Active Directory" in this book.

Assign Server Roles in the New Environment

To assign server roles in your new environment, first assign the domain controllers in your existing environment roles in your new Windows Server 2003 domain. Then, decide where to place other services in the new domain.

Domain Controller Roles

Assign the existing Windows NT 4.0–based domain controllers roles that they will assume in the new Windows Server 2003 domain after the upgrade is complete. Assign one of the following three roles to Windows NT 4.0–based domain controllers in a Windows Server 2003 domain:

■ **Windows Server 2003–based domain controller**. Assign the role of Windows Server 2003–based domain controller to the Windows NT 4.0 PDC and to any BDCs that meet the appropriate hardware and software requirements.

■ **Rollback server**. Assign the role of rollback server in the Windows Server 2003 domain to a Windows NT 4.0 BDC that does not meet the Windows Server 2003 domain controller hardware requirements.

■ **Windows Server 2003–based member server**. Assign the role of member server in the Windows Server 2003 domain to a Windows NT 4.0–based BDC that does not meet the Windows Server 2003 domain controller hardware requirements.

It is helpful to document this information in a table. List in the table the Windows NT 4.0–based domain controllers in your domain, whether they meet the hardware requirements for Windows Server 2003, the current role of the domain controller, and the role for the domain controller after you upgrade the domain.

Fabrikam documented their domain controller role assignments as shown in Table 1.3.

Table 1.3   Domain Controller Role Assignments

Domain Controller Name	Meets hardware requirements?	Role before upgrade	Role after upgrade
SEA-FAB-DC01	Yes	Windows NT 4.0 PDC	Windows Server 2003 domain controller
SEA-FAB-DC02	No	Windows NT 4.0 BDC	Rollback server
SEA-FAB-DC03	Yes	Windows NT 4.0 BDC	Windows Server 2003 domain controller

Server Roles

Decide where to place all services on both domain controllers and member servers after you migrate your environment to Windows Server 2003. This decision depends on whether your existing server hardware meets the requirements to run Windows Server 2003. Generally, if a server on which a service is running meets the hardware requirements, you can either upgrade it in place or migrate it to another server; if the server on which the service is running does not meet hardware requirements, you must migrate the service to or reinstall the service on a different server. You can also choose to migrate services to different servers to consolidate them on fewer servers, or, alternatively, to separate them.

Server Role Assignment if All Windows NT 4.0 Domain Controllers Meet Hardware Requirements   If your Windows NT 4.0–based domain controllers are running other services, such as DHCP, WINS, File and Print, or IIS, then determine whether you want to upgrade these services in place on the existing hardware, or migrate them to one or more separate domain controllers or member servers. If a server is running the Remote Access Service, you must migrate the service to a server running Windows Server 2003 before you upgrade the domain controller. For more information about migrating these server roles to Windows Server 2003, see the following chapters in this book:

- "Upgrading and Migrating WINS and DHCP Servers to Windows Server 2003"

- "Migrating File and Print Servers to Windows Server 2003"

- "Migrating to Dial-up and VPN Remote Access Servers Running Windows Server 2003"

- "Migrating Web Sites from IIS 4.0 to IIS 6.0"

Server Role Assignment if the PDC Does Not Meet Hardware Requirements   If the PDC does not meet hardware requirements, deploy a new Windows NT 4.0 BDC on new server hardware. You can then promote the new BDC to the PDC, and this computer will become your first Windows 2003 domain controller.

If you have other server roles running on the original PDC, such as DHCP, WINS, File and Print, RAS, or IIS, then develop a plan to migrate these roles from the original PDC to the server of your choice in your Windows Server 2003 environment. For more information about migrating these server roles, see the following chapters in this book:

- "Upgrading and Migrating WINS and DHCP Servers to Windows Server 2003"

- "Migrating File and Print Servers to Windows Server 2003"

- "Migrating to Dial-up and VPN Remote Access Servers Running Windows Server 2003"

- "Migrating Web Sites from IIS 4.0 to IIS 6.0"

Server Role Assignment if a BDC Does Not Meet Hardware Requirements   After you deploy your first Windows Server 2003 domain controller, you can install additional new Windows Server 2003 domain controllers and member servers. You can then migrate any services on the original BDC to the first Windows Server 2003 domain controller or to the new server of your choice.

Example: Server Role Assignments for Fabrikam   Fabrikam assigned their server roles as shown in Table 1.4.

Table 1.4   Server Role Assignments

Server Name	Meets hardware requirements?	Role before upgrade	Role after upgrade
SEA-FAB-DC01	Yes	Windows NT 4.0 PDC, WINS server, DHCP server	■ Windows Server 2003 domain controller ■ DNS server ■ WINS server ■ DHCP server ■ File server, print server
SEA-FAB-DC02	No	Windows NT 4.0 BDC, RAS server	Rollback server
SEA-FAB-DC03	Yes	Windows NT 4.0 BDC	■ Windows Server 2003 domain controller ■ DNS server ■ WINS server ■ DHCP server ■ Routing and Remote Access Server ■ File server, print server
SEA-FAB-MS01	No	File server, print server	None, server not upgradeable

One of the goals for Fabrikam is to consolidate all services on two servers in Seattle. Because two domain controllers are required, both servers were assigned the domain controller role. To achieve both redundancy and standardization, both servers were also assigned the roles of DNS server, WINS server, DHCP server, file server, and print server. On SEA-FAB-DC01, WINS and DHCP were already running, so they will be upgraded in place. The services that were running on servers that will not be upgraded (RAS, file, and print) were assigned to be migrated to SEA-FAB-DC03.

Plan for Server Capacity

Domain controller capacity planning for smaller organizations is straightforward. For a single domain with up to 2999 users and one location, you will need two domain controllers, each with a Uniprocessor 850 megahertz (MHz) or higher CPU. If you have more than one location, you will need an additional domain controller for each location.

If you have other services running on the domain controllers, you might want to add more CPU, RAM, or disk space to improve performance. File servers have capacity requirements that vary depending on the data in your organization. For information about planning for file server capacity, see "Migrating File and Print Servers to Windows Server 2003" in this book.

Example: Sequence of Migration Tasks for Fabrikam   After they assigned server roles to server hardware and established their capacity requirements, the IT department for Fabrikam listed the sequence of tasks to be performed in order to place the server roles. These include the following:

- Purchase one new server with sufficient capacity to run the services assigned to SEA-FAB-DC03.

- Deploy SEA-FAB-DC03 as a new member server running Windows Server 2003 in the Windows NT 4.0 environment. (They will install Active Directory on this server after they upgrade the PDC, making it the second domain controller in the Windows Server 2003 domain.)

- Migrate the Remote Access Service currently running on SEA-FAB-DC02, and the file and print services currently running on SEA-FAB-MS01, to SEA-FAB-DC03.

- Upgrade the domain to Windows Server 2003 Active Directory, following the sequence of tasks in the "Upgrading to Windows Server 2003 Active Directory" chapter in this book.

The Fabrikam IT department chose to deploy their new server, SEA-FAB-DC03, as a member server in the Windows NT 4.0 environment, rather than waiting until after the upgrade to deploy it. This allowed them to migrate the Remote Access Service from the BDC, SEA-FAB-DC02, and take the BDC offline as their rollback server. It also enables them to gain experience with the administration tools in Windows Server 2003 before they upgrade their domain.

Evaluate the Existing Network Configuration

Evaluate the existing network configuration for your Windows NT 4.0 domain to determine whether it is sufficient for your new Windows Server 2003 domain. Some network adapter drivers that are included with earlier versions of the operating system are not distributed with Windows Server 2003. If you attempt to upgrade a Windows NT 4.0–based server to Windows Server 2003 and a network adapter is installed for which a driver is not provided, your network information might be lost or detected incorrectly during the upgrade.

> **Note**   You can install device drivers that are not included on the Windows Server 2003 operating system CD from the vendor's Web site.

Identify the type of network adapter that each server in your domain uses. Also, include the TCP/IP configuration information for each server, including IP address, subnet mask, and default gateway. You can run the ipconfig command at the command line to determine IP address, subnet mask, and default gateway. For more information about the ipconfig command, type **ipconfig /?** at the command line.

To determine whether the network adapter is supported by Windows Server 2003, see the Windows Server Catalog link on the Web Resources page at http://www.microsoft.com/windows/reskits/webresources.

Table 1.5 shows the network configuration information for Fabrikam.

Table 1.5   Fabrikam Server Network Configuration

Domain Controller Name	Network Adapter	IP Address	Subnet Mask	Default Gateway
SEA-FAB-DC01	Netgear FA310TX Fast Ethernet Adapter	172.16.12.2	255.255.252.0	172.16.12.1
SEA-FAB-DC03	IBM Netfinity 10/ 100 Ethernet Adapter	172.16.12.3	255.255.252.0	172.16.12.1
SEA-FAB-MS01	3COM Etherlink III LAN PC Card (3C589) (Ethernet)	172.16.12.14	255.255.252.0	172.16.12.1

Designing the New Windows Server 2003 Active Directory Environment

Before you begin your migration process, it is important to design your new Windows Server 2003 domain. This involves creating an Active Directory logical structure design and planning for DNS.

Design the Active Directory Logical Structure

Active Directory allows administrators to organize elements of a network (such as users, computers, devices, and so on) into a hierarchical, treelike structure of containers. The largest Active Directory container is called a *forest*. Within forests, there are *domains*. Within domains there are organizational units (OUs). This is called the logical model because it is designed independently from most physical aspects of the deployment, such as the number of domain controllers required within each domain and the network topology.

This book describes how to deploy a single global domain design, which is the easiest to administer and the least expensive to maintain. The single global domain design consists of a forest that contains a single domain. This domain contains all of the user, group, and computer accounts in the forest. In a single domain forest, all directory data is replicated to all geographic locations that host domain controllers. You do not need to create a forest or domain design when you upgrade from a single Windows NT 4.0 domain to a single Windows Server 2003 Active Directory domain.

You might want to design a simple OU structure for your single global domain, particularly if you plan to use Group Policy to help manage your environment. You can do this either before the migration, or at a later time. For more information about applying Group Policy to an OU structure, see "Migrating to Group Policy–Based Administration" in this book.

Plan for DNS

Windows Server 2003 uses DNS for name resolution rather than the Windows Internet Name Service (WINS) NetBIOS name resolution method that Windows NT 4.0–based networks use. It is still possible to use WINS for applications that require it; however, Active Directory requires DNS. Active Directory uses the name resolution services provided by DNS to enable clients to locate domain controllers and enable the domain controllers hosting the directory service to communicate with each other. To plan for DNS, you need to select a DNS domain name, and determine how to configure the DNS Server service on domain controllers.

Select a DNS Domain Name

Before you begin using DNS on your network, decide on your DNS domain name, based on the following guidelines:

- If you have a Web presence (for example, if an ISP hosts your site called www.fabrikam.com), reuse this name and add a prefix to create the DNS name for your Windows Server 2003 Active Directory domain (for example, fabricorp.fabrikam.com).

■   If you do not have a Web presence, consider whether you plan to have one in the future. If you do plan to have a Web presence, then register the name before you install Active Directory. If you do not have a Web presence, then you do not need to register the name.

> **Note**   To register a name, you must register your second-level domain name (such as fabrikam.com) with an authorized DNS domain name registration authority. Your ISP can often perform this function and obtain a name on your behalf, usually for an additional fee.

Determine How to Configure the DNS Server Service on Domain Controllers

The process for designing DNS to support Active Directory varies according to whether your organization already has an existing DNS service or whether you are deploying a new DNS service. This chapter discusses three starting scenarios:

■   No existing DNS.

■   No internal DNS, with DNS services provided by an ISP only.

■   Internal DNS and DNS provided by an ISP.

If one of the following scenarios describes your current DNS infrastructure, then see "Deploying DNS" in *Deploying Network Services* in the *Microsoft Windows Server™ 2003 Deployment Kit* (or see "Deploying DNS" on the Web at http://www.microsoft.com/reskit) for more information:

■   An internal DNS namespace, used only on your own network.

■   An internal DNS namespace with referral and access to an external namespace, such as referral or forwarding to a DNS server on the Internet.

No Existing DNS   An organization has no existing DNS infrastructure if the following are true:

■   The organization does not have any existing DNS servers in the network infrastructure.

■   The organization does not have any clients that access DNS servers. This means that the organization does not rely on an external source, such as a network service provider, for DNS services.

If this is true for your organization, you can allow the Active Directory Installation Wizard to configure an internal Active Directory-integrated DNS on the PDC automatically. To configure DNS on the PDC and subsequent domain controllers, follow the procedures in the "Upgrading to Windows Server 2003 Active Directory" chapter in this book.

No Internal DNS, DNS Provided by an ISP Only   If you do not have an internal DNS, but your ISP provides DNS services, then you can allow the Active Directory Installation Wizard to automatically configure an internal Active Directory-integrated DNS on the PDC. Your ISP does not need to make any changes. To configure DNS on the PDC and subsequent domain controllers, follow the procedures in the "Upgrading to Windows Server 2003 Active Directory" chapter in this book.

After you complete these procedures, you will have both an internal DNS and DNS provided by an ISP. The first domain controller that you deploy will automatically be configured to host the DNS zone that corresponds to the DNS name of the domain. To install and configure DNS in your environment, it is recommended that you do the following:

- Install the DNS Server service on every domain controller. This provides fault tolerance in the event that one of the DNS servers is unavailable. In this way, domain controllers do not need to rely on other DNS servers for name resolution. This also simplifies the management environment because all domain controllers have a uniform configuration.

- Configure domain controllers that are running DNS to use either forwarding or root hints for recursive name resolution, depending on which method your existing DNS service uses. When you follow the sequence of procedures in the "Upgrading to Windows Server 2003 Active Directory" chapter, the Active Directory Installation Wizard automatically configures recursive name resolution.

Internal DNS and DNS Provided by an ISP   When creating a DNS server configuration when you integrate Active Directory with an existing DNS namespace, it is recommended that you do the following:

- Install the DNS Server service on every domain controller. This provides fault tolerance in the event that one of the DNS servers is unavailable. In this way, domain controllers do not need to rely on other DNS servers for name resolution. This also simplifies the management environment because all domain controllers have a uniform configuration.

- Configure domain controllers that are running DNS to use either forwarding or root hints for recursive name resolution, depending on which method your existing DNS service uses. When you follow the sequence of procedures in the "Upgrading to Windows Server 2003 Active Directory" chapter, the Active Directory Installation Wizard automatically configures recursive name resolution.

- Configure the first domain controller that you deploy to host the DNS zone that corresponds to the DNS name of the domain. To do this, you do not need to make any changes to the existing DNS structure. You simply need to create a delegation to your Active Directory zone from your existing DNS hierarchy. For more information about creating this delegation, see "Upgrading to Windows Server 2003 Active Directory" in this book.

Planning for Test and Recovery

Before you begin your migration process, it is important to have a test plan and a recovery plan in place.

Develop a Test Plan

Develop a plan for testing your in-place domain upgrade procedures throughout the in-place domain upgrade process to ensure that they have completed successfully and to determine whether the process of upgrading Windows NT 4.0 domains to Windows Server 2003 Active Directory was successful.

Table 1.6 lists the Active Directory configurations that you must test and the tools that you can use to test each configuration. For more information about the options that are available for these tools, see "Active Directory support tools" in Help and Support Center for Windows Server 2003. For more information about specific configuration and functionality tests that you can perform before and after the Active Directory installation, see the Active Directory link on the Web Resources page at http://www.microsoft.com/windows/reskits/webresources. Search under "Administration and Configuration Guides" and download the *Active Directory Operations Guide*.

Table 1.6 **Active Directory Configuration Test Components**

Configuration	Tool	Purpose
Active Directory service	Dcdiag.exe	Tests for successful Active Directory connectivity and functionality. Confirms that the domain controller has passed the diagnostic tests (such as connectivity and replicated objects). Each test must return a "passed" result.
	Netdiag.exe	Diagnoses networking and connectivity problems by performing a series of tests to determine the state of your network client and whether it is functional.
Active Directory replication	Repadmin.exe /replsum	Returns all replication events taking place between the forest root domain and other Active Directory domain controllers. This must return a successful replication event with all inbound and outbound replication partners.
BDC replication status	Nltest.exe /bdc_query:*domainname*	Shows connection status for all the BDCs. This must show "status = success" for each domain controller within the domain.

After you confirm that the Active Directory configuration is correct, you need to verify that Active Directory is functioning correctly. Table 1.7 lists the Active Directory functions that you need to test and the methods that you can use to perform the tests.

Table 1.7 **Active Directory Functionality Test Components**

Function	Test	Method
New user creation	Create a new user on the Windows Server 2003–based domain controller.	Log on with administrator credentials and use Active Directory Users and Computers to verify that the new user was created successfully.
New user object replication	After replication to BDCs takes place, determine whether new user is replicated to BDCs.	1. Type **Net User** at a command prompt on a Windows NT 4.0–based domain controller, and then verify that the new user account exists. 2. Modify a property of an existing user and verify that the modified property replicates with the user.

Table 1.7   Active Directory Functionality Test Components

Function	Test	Method
Successful logon request	Verify that users can log on successfully.	1. Disconnect the Windows Server 2003–based domain controller to confirm that the Windows NT 4.0–based domain controller is validating the user logon request. 2. Verify that you can log on successfully by using the new user account credentials from each client computer. 3. Verify that all client operating systems in the upgraded domain and the domains that it trusts can log on successfully. 4. Repeat step number two over trust relationships where the trusting domain controller has a secure channel with the Windows NT 4.0–based and Windows Server 2003–based domain controllers in the trusted domain.
Successful resource access	Verify that the user can access important resources.	1. Access e-mail resources. 2. Access roaming profiles. 3. Access printers. 4. Resource permissions belonging to the user and a group.

Develop a Recovery Plan

Create a recovery plan for use if the domain upgrade process does not go as planned. Select a Windows NT 4.0 BDC to be used as a rollback server. Synchronize the BDC with the PDC and take the rollback server offline in the event that it must be promoted to a PDC to restore the domain to its original state. Although you are unlikely to need the offline domain controller, it is recommended that you take one offline as a precautionary step if the Security Accounts Manager (SAM) account database on all domain controllers becomes corrupt.

Include the following in your recovery plan:

■   The steps needed for recovery.

■ The estimated time that can elapse before recovery must take place. When elements of the upgrade process test unsuccessfully, you might spend unanticipated amounts of time identifying and correcting errors. Establish clear guidelines for the time period after which the deployment team must restore operations for end users.

Restoring the Domain to its Original State   If your upgrade process fails, you can roll back a Windows Server 2003 Active Directory domain to its original state as a Windows NT 4.0 domain. You can roll back the deployment to its original state in one of two ways:

> **Note**   The first recovery method is preferred for restoring a domain to its original state. Use the second recovery method if the SAM database on all domain controllers becomes corrupt.

1. Remove (either by disconnecting the network cable or turning off) any Windows Server 2003–based domain controllers from the domain.

2. Promote a Windows NT 4.0 BDC to become the PDC.

3. Synchronize all Windows NT 4.0–based domain controllers.

4. Test Windows NT 4.0 server operations and domain validation.

5. Resolve the issues that caused the domain upgrade to fail, and begin the upgrade process again.

   – or –

1. If a failure occurs after performing the steps above, remove all Windows Server 2003–based domain controllers from the network and promote the Windows NT 4.0 BDC that is designated as the rollback server to become the PDC.

2. Perform a full synchronization of all Windows NT 4.0 BDCs.

3. Test Windows NT 4.0 server operations and domain validation.

4. Resolve the issues that caused the domain upgrade to fail, and begin the upgrade process again.

> **Important**   You must take all Windows Server 2003–based domain controllers offline before you promote the rollback server to become the new PDC. If any Windows Server 2003–based domain controllers remain online in the domain, the promotion of the BDC to a PDC will not work.

Additional Resources

These resources contain additional information related to this chapter.

Related Information

- "Restructuring Windows NT 4.0 Domains to an Active Directory Forest" in *Designing and Deploying Directory and Security Services* in the *Microsoft Windows Server 2003 Deployment Kit* (or see "Restructuring Windows NT 4.0 Domains to Active Directory Forest" on the Web at http://www.microsoft.com/reskit) for more information about restructuring domains when upgrading from Windows NT 4.0 to Windows Server 2003.

- "Designing the Active Directory Logical Structure" in *Designing and Deploying Directory and Security Services* in the *Microsoft Windows Server 2003 Deployment Kit* (or see "Designing the Active Directory Logical Structure" on the Web at http://www.microsoft.com/reskit) for more information about the Active Directory logical structure.

- "Designing the Site Topology" in *Designing and Deploying Directory and Security Services* in the *Microsoft Windows Server 2003 Deployment Kit* (or see "Designing the Site Topology" on the Web at http://www.microsoft.com/reskit) for more information about Active Directory site topology.

- "Enabling Advanced Windows Server 2003 Active Directory Features" in *Designing and Deploying Directory and Security Services* in the *Microsoft Windows Server 2003 Deployment Kit* (or see "Enabling Advanced Windows Server 2003 Active Directory Features" on the Web at http://www.microsoft.com/reskit) for more information about enabling functional levels.

- "Deploying DNS" in *Deploying Network Services* in the *Microsoft Windows Server 2003 Deployment Kit* (or see "Deploying DNS" on the Web at http://www.microsoft.com/reskit) for more information about deploying DNS.

2

Upgrading to Windows Server 2003 Active Directory

You can upgrade a Microsoft® Windows NT® version 4.0 domain to the Windows Server™ 2003 Active Directory® directory service in order to improve the security and scalability of your network infrastructure while reducing administrative overhead. This chapter provides step-by-step instructions for upgrading the primary domain controller (PDC) and backup domain controllers (BDCs) in a single Windows NT 4.0 domain to a new Windows Server 2003 Active Directory domain.

In This Chapter:

Overview of Upgrading to Windows Server 2003 Active Directory

Small to medium-sized organizations that are currently running Windows NT 4.0 can take advantage of Active Directory features by upgrading their environment to a Microsoft® Windows Server™ 2003, Standard Edition; Windows Server™ 2003, Enterprise Edition; or Windows Server™ 2003, Datacenter Edition Active Directory domain.

When you perform an upgrade of a Windows NT 4.0 domain to Windows Server 2003, Active Directory, you can use your existing server hardware if it meets the requirements to run Windows Server 2003, or you can introduce new server hardware. Whether you use existing or new hardware, upgrading has no adverse effect on your Windows NT 4.0 production environment.

Upgrading a Windows NT 4.0 domain to Windows Server 2003 Active Directory involves the following steps:

■   Completing pre-upgrade tasks.

■   Upgrading the PDC.

■   Upgrading additional domain controllers.

■   Completing post-upgrade tasks.

If your organization includes more than one physical location, you will also need to create Active Directory sites, and part of your upgrade process will involve configuring the site topology.

If you are consolidating multiple Windows NT 4.0 domains into a single Active Directory domain by using a restructuring tool such as the Active Directory Migration Tool (ADMT), see "Restructuring Windows NT 4.0 Domains to an Active Directory Forest" in *Designing and Deploying Directory and Security Services* in the *Microsoft® Windows Server™ 2003 Deployment Kit* (or see "Restructuring Windows NT 4.0 Domains to an Active Directory Forest" on the Web at http://www.microsoft.com/reskit).

Considerations for Upgrading to Windows Server 2003 Active Directory

A single domain design is the easiest to administer and the least expensive to maintain. The single domain design consists of a forest that contains a single domain. This domain contains all of the user, group, and computer accounts. In a single domain forest, all directory data is replicated to all geographic locations that host domain controllers. You do not need to create a forest or domain design when you upgrade from a single Windows NT 4.0 domain to a single Active Directory domain.

Before you begin to upgrade your Windows NT 4.0 domain, it is important to become familiar with the factors that can affect the upgrade process.

PDC Offline Operations

During the process of upgrading the operating system on the primary domain controller (PDC) from Windows NT 4.0 to Windows Server 2003 and installing Active Directory, client operations such as logon and resource access will continue to function because these services are provided by backup domain controllers. However, because the PDC is offline during most phases of the upgrade process, typically between one and three hours, operations that require data to be written to the domain will not succeed. For example, users will not be able to change their passwords and administrators will not be able to create, delete, or unlock user accounts. Administrative tools, such as User Manager for Domains or Server Manager, can be used only in read-only mode on backup domain controllers in the domain. In addition, you will not be able to create new objects, such as users and groups, while the PDC is offline.

Client Authentication

If your organization includes client computers that are running Microsoft® Windows® 2000 or Windows® XP operating systems in the domain, it is recommended that you upgrade all Windows NT 4.0–based domain controllers as quickly as possible. This is because all Windows 2000 and Windows XP clients will only use Windows Server 2003 domain controllers for logon after you upgrade the PDC.

Service Compatibility

Until you upgrade all workstations and servers to Windows 2000 or later, continue to run your environment in the pre-Windows 2000 compatible access mode. This mode allows services that run in the context of the Local System account, such as Remote Access Services (RAS), to operate properly. To enable the pre-Windows 2000 compatible access mode, you can do one of the following:

- While installing Active Directory on the upgraded Windows NT 4.0 PDC, on the Permissions page of the Active Directory Installation wizard, select **Permissions compatible with pre-Windows 2000 Server operating systems**.

  – or –

- Add the Everyone group and the Anonymous Logon group to the Pre-Windows 2000 Compatible Access built-in group by using Active Directory Users and Computers or the command line.

To add the Everyone group to the Pre-Windows 2000 Compatible Access Group by using the command line, at the command line, type

```
net localgroup "Pre-Windows 2000 Compatible Access" Everyone /add
```

To add the Anonymous Logon group to the Pre-Windows 2000 Compatible Access Group by using the command line, at the command line, type

```
net localgroup "Pre-Windows 2000 Compatible Access" "Anonymous Logon"
/add
```

> **Note**   After this update to the Pre-Windows 2000 Compatible Access group replicates, you must restart the Server service on all domain controllers.

After you upgrade all RAS servers, and when you no longer need backward compatibility with operating systems earlier than Windows 2000, remove the Everyone group and the Anonymous Logon group from the Pre-Windows 2000 Compatible Access built-in group. For more information about removing the Everyone group and the Anonymous Logon group from the Pre-Windows 2000 Compatible Access group, see "Eliminate Anonymous Connections to Domain Controllers" later in this chapter.

WINS and DHCP Services

If you have WINS or DHCP running on a domain controller, you need to consider the effect of the upgrade on these services. Both WINS and DHCP are designed to upgrade their databases automatically when you upgrade from Windows NT 4.0 to Windows Server 2003, so you do not need to perform any additional steps to upgrade these services after you upgrade the operating system. However, after you install Active Directory, you must authorize your Windows Server 2003–based DHCP servers in Active Directory before they will continue to lease IP addresses. For more information about authorizing DHCP servers in Active Directory, see "Authorize the DHCP Service" later in this chapter.

> **Note**   If your existing WINS services, DHCP services, or both, are on a PDC or BDC that you are upgrading in place, the WINS and DHCP databases are upgrade automatically when the operating system is upgraded. This might cause the upgrade of the domain controller to take additional time.

After you upgrade the server operating system to Windows Server 2003, test the WINS and DHCP services to ensure that performance meets the appropriate standards. If performance is not satisfactory, you can migrate the services to a different computer. For more information about migrating WINS and DHCP services to a different computer, see "Upgrading and Migrating WINS and DHCP Servers to Windows Server 2003" in this book.

LAN Manager Replication Service and File Replication Service

During the upgrade process, for a period of time one or more domain controllers might be running Windows Server 2003 while others are still running Windows NT 4.0. Windows Server 2003 and Windows NT 4.0 domain controllers use different file replication services. If you have files that are replicated between domain controllers, such as logon scripts, you will need to manage them separately.

Security Policy Considerations for Upgrading to Windows Server 2003 Active Directory

Server message block (SMB) packet signing and secure channel signing are security policies that are enabled by default on Windows Server 2003–based domain controllers. To allow clients running earlier versions of Windows to communicate with domain controllers running Windows Server 2003, you might need to disable these security policies temporarily during the upgrade process.

SMB Packet Signing

SMB packet signing is a security mechanism that protects the data integrity of SMB traffic between client computers and servers, and prevents man-in-the-middle attacks by providing a form of mutual authentication. This is done by placing a digital security signature into each SMB packet, which is then verified by the receiving party. Server-side SMB signing is required by default on Windows Server 2003–based domain controllers, which means that all clients are required to have SMB packet signing enabled.

Clients running Windows NT 4.0 with Service Pack 2 or earlier, and clients running the Microsoft® Windows® 95 operating system without the Directory Service Client Pack, do not support SMB packet signing. These clients will not be able to authenticate to a Windows Server 2003–based domain controller. To ensure successful authentication, upgrade these clients to a later version of the operating system or Service Pack. However, if you cannot upgrade your clients, you can allow them to be authenticated by configuring SMB packet signing on all Windows Server 2003–based domain controllers so that SMB packet signing is preferred but not required.

For more information about SMB packet signing, see "Microsoft network server: Digitally sign communications (always)" in Help and Support Center for Windows Server 2003.

For more information about configuring SMB packet signing on Windows Server 2003–based domain controllers, see "Modify Security Policies" later in this chapter.

For more information about the Directory Services Client Pack, see article 323466, "Availability of the Directory Services Client Update for Windows 95 and Windows 98" in the Microsoft Knowledge Base. To find this article, see the Microsoft Knowledge Base link on the Web Resources page at http://www.microsoft.com/windows/reskits/webresources.

Secure Channel Signing and Encryption

When a computer becomes a member of a domain, a computer account is created. Each time the computer starts, it uses the computer account password to create a secure channel with a domain controller for its domain. This secure channel is used to ensure secure communications between a domain member and a domain controller for its domain. Secure channel signing is required by default on Windows Server 2003–based domain controllers, which means that all clients must enable secure channel signing and encryption.

Clients running Windows NT 4.0 with Service Pack 3 or earlier installed do not support secure channel signing. These clients will not be able to establish communications with a Windows Server 2003–based domain controller. To ensure successful communication, upgrade these clients to a later version of the operating system or Service Pack. However, if you cannot upgrade your clients, you must disable secure channel signing on all Windows Server 2003–based domain controllers so that the traffic passing through the secure channel is not required to be signed or encrypted.

> **Note**   Unlike SMB packet signing, secure channel signing does not affect Windows 95 clients.

For more information about secure channel signing, see "Domain member: Digitally encrypt or sign secure channel data (always)" in Help and Support Center for Windows Server 2003.

For more information about configuring secure channel signing on Windows Server 2003–based domain controllers, see "Modify Security Policies" later in this chapter.

Completing Pre-Upgrade Tasks

Before you upgrade your Windows NT 4.0 domain to Windows Server 2003 Active Directory, you must complete the following pre-upgrade tasks:

- Relocate the LMRepl file replication service.

- Migrate the Remote Access Service.

- Prepare for file and print service upgrade.

- Enable the Windows NT 4.0 environment change freeze.

Relocate the LMRepl File Replication Service

The LMRepl service is used to replicate files such as logon scripts or policies between Windows NT 4.0 domain controllers. To maintain the replication of files in the NETLOGON shared folder from the Windows NT 4.0 export server to all other Windows NT 4.0 BDCs running the LMRepl replication engine during the in-place domain upgrade process, upgrade all servers that are hosting import directories before you upgrade the server that is hosting the export directory.

If the server hosting the export directory is the PDC, then you can do one of the following:

- Promote a BDC that meets the Windows Server 2003 domain controller hardware requirements to become the new PDC and demote the existing PDC to serve as a BDC hosting the export server.

    – or –

- Reconfigure the LMRepl export server on a BDC and remove it from the PDC.

To determine whether the PDC is hosting the export directory, open Server Manager, select the PDC, click **Computer**, and then click **Properties**. Click **Replication** and verify that **Export Directories** is selected.

To test the new configuration to ensure that LMRepl continues to work correctly, place an empty file on the export server and verify that the file is replicated to the import directories during replication. Next, delete the replicated file from the import directory, and then verify that the file is deleted during the next replication.

Migrate the Remote Access Service

If Remote Access Service (RAS) or Routing and Remote Access Service (RRAS) is running on the PDC, a BDC, or a member server running Windows NT 4.0, you must migrate the service before you upgrade the operating system on that server. Migrating the RAS or RRAS service involves documenting the current service configuration settings, then using those settings to configure Routing and Remote Access on a server running Windows Server 2003. For information about planning to migrate the remote access services, see "Planning the Migration" in this book. For information about performing the migration, see "Migrating to Dial-up and VPN Remote Access Servers Running Windows Server 2003" in this book.

Prepare for File and Print Service Upgrade

If the file service or the print service is running on the PDC, a BDC, or a member server running Windows NT 4.0, it is recommended that you migrate those services to a new server running Windows Server 2003. However, if you want to upgrade these services in place, perform the following steps before upgrading the operating system:

- If a file server contains multidisk volumes, verify that your backup software and hardware are compatible with both Windows NT 4.0 and Windows Server 2003. Next, back up and then delete all multidisk volumes (volume sets, mirror sets, stripe sets, and stripe sets with parity) before you upgrade, because Windows Server 2003 cannot access these volumes. Be sure to verify that your backup was successful before deleting the volumes. After you finish upgrading to Windows Server 2003, create new dynamic volumes, and then restore the data.

- If your paging file resides on a multidisk volume, you must use System in Control Panel to move the paging file to a primary partition or logical drive before beginning Setup.

■ When you upgrade a print server in place, you retain your existing print queues, drivers, and ports, minimizing the impact on users. However, you might encounter interoperability issues with your existing printer drivers. Before upgrading your servers, use the command-line utility Fixprnsv.exe, provided with Windows Server 2003, to help you identify any printer driver problems.

For more information about upgrading or migrating the file and print services, see "Migrating File and Print Servers to Windows Server 2003" in this book.

Enable the Windows NT 4.0 Environment Change Freeze

Before you upgrade the PDC in your Windows NT 4.0 domain to Windows Server 2003 Active Directory, you must freeze the Windows NT 4.0 environment to ensure that no other domain changes occur until after the PDC is upgraded. Freeze the Windows NT 4.0 environment when:

■ You have completed all of the updates to the Windows NT 4.0 domain and have replicated them to all domain controllers.

■ You have synchronized a BDC and have taken it offline for recovery purposes.

When you freeze the Windows NT 4.0 environment, no additional domain changes can take place until you upgrade the Windows NT 4.0 PDC to Windows Server 2003. Communicate to all appropriate individuals that changes to the environment, such as password updates, will not be accepted after a specific date.

Upgrading the PDC

To upgrade your Windows NT 4.0 environment to a new single domain forest, you must complete some or all of the following tasks:

■ Back up all domain data.

■ Delegate the DNS zone for the new Windows Server 2003 domain, if you have an existing DNS infrastructure.

■ Identify potential upgrade problems.

■ Upgrade the operating system of the Windows NT 4.0 PDC.

■ Install Active Directory.

- Authorize the DHCP service, if DHCP is running on the PDC.
- Configure the Windows Time Service.
- Enable aging and scavenging for DNS.
- Verify DNS server recursive name resolution.
- Perform post-upgrade tests.
- Modify security policies.

To help to illustrate the process for upgrading to a single domain forest, sample data for a fictitious company, Fabrikam, Inc., is provided within the context of the tasks that must be performed.

Back Up Domain Data

Back up your Windows NT 4.0 domain data before you begin the upgrade. This task varies according to the operations and procedures that already exist in your environment. It is recommended that you complete the following steps:

- Back up the PDC.
- Back up the BDC that you designated as the rollback server.
- Test all backup media to ensure that the data can be restored successfully.

> **Important**   Before you begin the upgrade process, store the backup media in a secure offsite location.

Delegate the DNS Zone for the Windows Server 2003 Domain

If your organization has an existing DNS infrastructure, review current network diagrams and DNS domain hierarchy diagrams. Also, review the existing DNS zone configuration, replication, and resource records that are used for delegation and forwarding. To configure the DNS zone for the single domain forest, the DNS administrator of your existing DNS infrastructure delegates the zone matching the name of the new Windows Server 2003 domain to the DNS servers that are running on the domain controllers in the single domain forest.

> **Note**   If you do not have a DNS infrastructure, or if your DNS services are provided by an ISP, you do not need to complete this step. Proceed to the next step, "Upgrade the Operating System of the Windows NT 4.0 PDC" later in this chapter.

In preparation for the deployment of the single domain forest, create a delegation for the DNS servers that will be running on the domain controllers in the Windows Server 2003 domain. Create the delegation by adding DNS name server (NS) and address (A) resource records to the parent DNS zone.

> **Note**   The delegation that occurs in this step references the first Windows Server 2003–based domain controller, which does not currently exist. The DNS service is installed and configured on the first Windows Server 2003–based domain controller in a later step. However, it is important to add this record before you install Active Directory on the PDC, because the Active Directory Installation Wizard will use the record to configure the new DNS zone that Active Directory uses.

To delegate the DNS zone for the Windows Server 2003 domain

1. Create a name server (NS) resource record in the parent zone. Use the full DNS name of the domain controller, as follows:
    forest_root_domain IN NS ***domain_controller_name***

2. Create a host address (A) resource record in the parent zone. Use the full DNS name of the domain controller, as follows:
    domain_controller_name IN A ***domain_controller_ip_address***

    For example, Fabrikam's PDC name is SEA-FAB-DC01, and its IP address is 172.16.12.2. During the Active Directory installation, Fabrikam will install the DNS Server service on this domain controller. In preparation for that step, the DNS administrator for Fabrikam created the following DNS resource records in the parent zone, fabrikam.com:

- **fabricorp** IN NS **SEA-FAB-DC01.fabricorp.fabrikam.com**
- **SEA-FAB-DC01.fabricorp.fabrikam.com** IN A **172.16.12.2**

Identify Potential Upgrade Problems

Before upgrading the operating system to Windows Server 2003, use the Winnt32.exe command-line tool to identify any potential upgrade problems, such as inadequate hardware resources or compatibility problems.

To identify potential upgrade problems

■ At the command line, connect to the I386 directory located at your installation source and type the following command:

```
winnt32 /checkupgradeonly
```

For example, if your installation source is the Windows Server 2003 operating system CD in the D: drive, navigate to D:\I386 and type the following command:

```
D:\I386>winnt32 /checkupgradeonly
```

The screen will then display the command prompt while the tool is running. It can take a few minutes for the Microsoft Windows Upgrade Advisor screen to appear.

Resolve reported problems before performing the upgrade.

Upgrade the Operating System of the Windows NT 4.0 PDC

To install the operating system on the PDC, insert the Windows Server 2003 operating system CD in the CD-ROM drive of the domain controller and select the option to install the operating system, or use an automated installation method. If the Windows Server 2003 media is shared on the network, run the Winnt32.exe command.

Complete the operating system installation by doing the following:

1. Verify that you are using a static IP address.

2. Use NTFS to convert the partitions if necessary. The installation of Active Directory will not succeed if you do not have at least one NTFS partition available on which to locate the SYSVOL shared folder.

3. Select **Upgrade** for the Installation type.

4. Configure DNS client settings by using the IP address of the closest DNS server for the **Preferred DNS Server** settings. If you have more than one DNS server, add the IP address of the next closest DNS server to the **Alternate DNS server** setting. If there are no other DNS servers, leave the alternate setting blank. These DNS client settings are temporary and will be changed during the installation of Active Directory.

5. Install Windows Support Tools, which are available in the \Support\Tools folder on the Windows Server 2003 operating system CD.

During the operating system upgrade the computer will restart three times. After you upgrade the operating system on a Windows NT 4.0 domain controller to Windows Server 2003, the computer is in an intermediate state, meaning that the computer is no longer a Windows NT 4.0–based domain controller, and it is not a Windows Server 2003–based member server or domain controller until Active Directory is installed. After the computer restarts for the last time, the Active Directory Installation Wizard appears.

Install Active Directory

Proceed immediately with the installation of Active Directory by completing the Active Directory Installation Wizard. The Active Directory Installation Wizard creates the Active Directory database and moves objects from the Windows NT 4.0 SAM to the Active Directory database. In addition, on the first domain controller in a new domain, the wizard completes the following tasks:

- Prompts the administrator to verify the installation and configuration of the DNS Server service.

- Configures DNS recursive name resolution forwarding by adding the IP addresses of the existing entries for **Preferred DNS server** and **Alternate DNS server** to the list of DNS servers on the **Forwarders** tab of the **Properties** sheet for the domain controller.

- Configures DNS recursive name resolution by root hints, by adding the root hints that are configured on the **Preferred DNS server** to the list of DNS servers on the **Root Hints** tab of the **Properties** sheet for the domain controller.

- Configures the **Preferred DNS server** to point to the DNS server that is running locally on the domain controller, and configures the **Alternate DNS server** to point to the closest DNS server.

- Creates two application directory partitions that are used by DNS. The DomainDnsZones application directory partition holds domain-wide DNS data, and the ForestDnsZones application directory partition holds forest-wide DNS data.

- Prompts the administrator to select the forest functional level.

Table 2.1 lists the actions required to complete the Active Directory installation wizard on a Windows NT 4.0 PDC, and lists sample data for installing Active Directory on the first domain controller in the single domain forest for Fabrikam, SEA-FAB-DC01.

Table 2.1 Information for Installing Active Directory on a Windows NT 4.0 PDC

Wizard Page or Dialog Box	Action	Example
Create New Domain	Select **Domain in a new forest**.	
New Domain Name	Type the full DNS name of the domain.	**Fabricorp.fabrikam.com**
Forest Functional Level	Choose **Windows Server 2003 interim**. This is the preferred level because replication is more efficient when you are operating at the Windows 2003 interim functional level than when you are operating at the Windows 2000 functional level.	Because Fabrikam does not plan to add any Windows 2000–based domain controllers to their forest at any time, they chose the **Windows Server 2003 interim** forest functional level.
Database and Log Folders	Type the folder locations specified by your design.	The design for Fabrikam domain controllers specifies that the database folder and log folder remain in the default location: **C:\Winnt\NTDS**.
Shared System Volume	Confirm or type the location specified by your design.	**C:\Winnt\SYSVOL**
DNS Registration Diagnostics	DNS Registration Diagnostics will indicate that it cannot find the name and address of the DNS server with which this domain controller will be registered. This is because the pre-created delegation record points to the local computer and DNS has not been installed on the domain controller at this point. Select the option to **Install and configure the DNS server on this computer and set this computer to use this DNS server as its preferred DNS server**.	

Table 2.1   Information for Installing Active Directory on a Windows NT 4.0 PDC

Wizard Page or Dialog Box	Action	Example
Permissions	Select the security level specified by your design: ■ Permissions compatible with pre-Windows 2000 server operating systems ■ Permissions compatible only with Windows 2000 or Windows Server 2003 operating systems	Because Fabrikam currently has services running on Windows NT 4.0–based servers under the context of the Local System account, they selected **Permissions compatible with pre-Windows 2000 server operating systems**.
Directory Service Restore Mode Administration Password	In the **Password** and **Confirm password** boxes, type any strong password.	

When you complete the Active Directory Installation Wizard, verify that all information on the Summary page is accurate, and then click **Finish**. After the Active Directory Installation Wizard finishes, you will be prompted to restart the computer. The installation will not be complete until the computer restarts.

For more information about installing and removing Active Directory, see the *Directory Services Guide* of the *Microsoft Windows Server 2003 Resource Kit* (or see the Directory Services Guide on the Web at http://www.microsoft.com/reskit).

After you install Windows Server 2003 Active Directory, enable Remote Desktop for Administration, formerly known as Terminal Services in Remote Administration mode, to enable administrators to log on remotely if necessary.

To enable Remote Desktop for Administration

■ In Control Panel, double-click **System**, select the **Remote** tab, and then select **Allow users to connect remotely to this computer**.

Example: Installing Active Directory on the PDC

Fabrikam completed the Active Directory Installation wizard on the Windows NT 4.0 PDC, SEA-FAB-DC01. Figure 2.1 shows the Active Directory Installation Wizard welcome screen.

Figure 2.1 Welcome to the Active Directory Installation Wizard page

The PDC becomes the first domain controller in a new domain in a new forest. Figure 2.2 shows the selection to create a new domain on the Create New Domain wizard page.

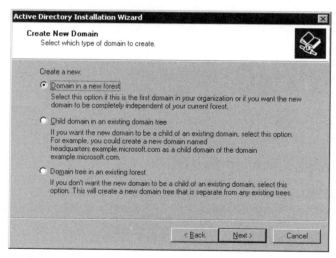

Figure 2.2 Create New Domain Wizard Page

The DNS name of the Fabrikam Windows Server 2003 domain is shown in Figure 2.3.

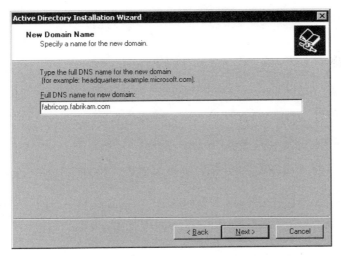

Figure 2.3   New Domain Name Wizard Page

Because Fabrikam does not plan to add any Windows 2000–based domain controllers to their forest at any time, they selected the **Windows Server 2003 interim** forest functional level, as shown in Figure 2.4.

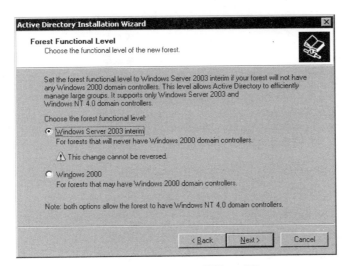

Figure 2.4   Forest Functional Level Wizard Page

The design for Fabrikam domain controllers specifies that both the database and log folders remain in the default location: **C:\Winnt\NTDS**, as shown in Figure 2.5. Smaller organizations can place both folders in the same location without affecting performance.

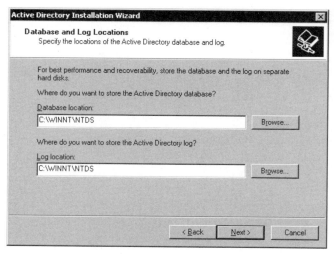

Figure 2.5   Database and Log Locations Wizard Page

The design for Fabrikam domain controllers specifies that the SYSVOL folder remain in the default location: **C:\Winnt\SYSVOL**, as shown in Figure 2.6.

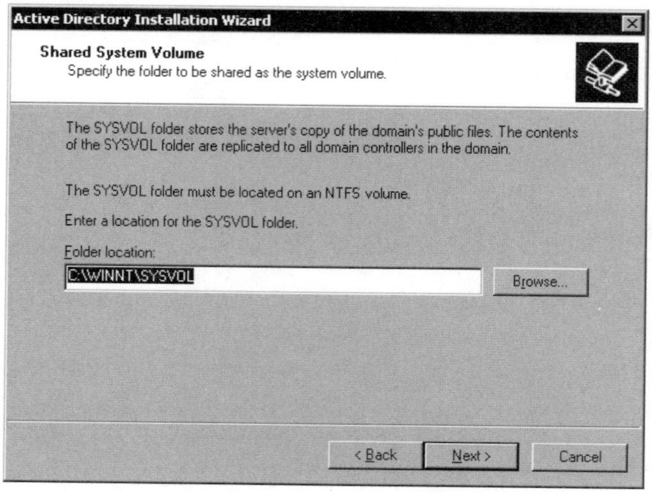

Active Directory Installation Wizard

Shared System Volume
Specify the folder to be shared as the system volume.

The SYSVOL folder stores the server's copy of the domain's public files. The contents of the SYSVOL folder are replicated to all domain controllers in the domain.

The SYSVOL folder must be located on an NTFS volume.

Enter a location for the SYSVOL folder.

Folder location:
C:\WINNT\SYSVOL

Browse...

< Back   Next >   Cancel

Figure 2.6   Shared System Volume Wizard Page

DNS Registration Diagnostics indicates that none of the DNS servers used by this computer responded. Fabrikam selected the option to **Install and configure the DNS server on this computer and set this computer to use this DNS server as its preferred DNS server**, as shown in Figure 2.7.

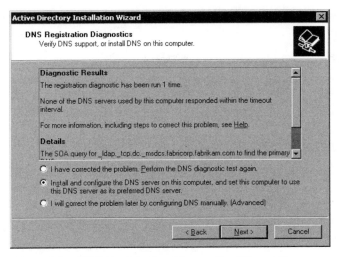

Figure 2.7   DNS Registration Diagnostics Wizard Page

Because Fabrikam currently has services running on Windows NT 4.0–based servers under the context of the Local System account, they selected **Permissions compatible with pre-Windows 2000 server operating systems,** as shown in Figure 2.8.

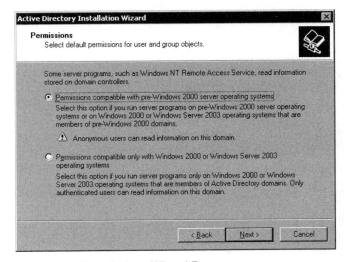

Figure 2.8   Permissions Wizard Page

Fabrikam set a strong Directory Services Restore Mode password, as shown in Figure 2.9.

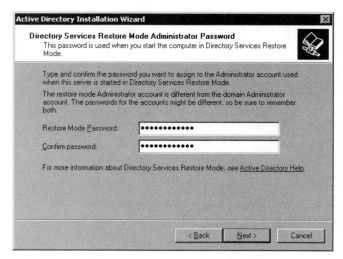

Figure 2.9 Directory Services Restore Mode Administrator Password
Wizard Page

The Active Directory domain controller has been created in a site called
Default-First-Site-Name, as shown in Figure 2.10. For organizations that have a
single physical location, no changes to this site assignment need to be made.
Organizations that include more than one physical location can create sites, and
move the domain controller to one of the new sites. For more information
about creating sites, see "Configuring the Site Topology" later in this chapter.

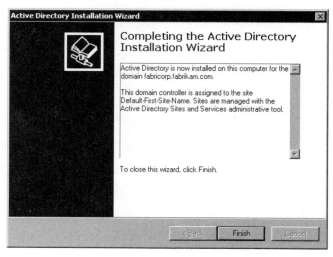

Figure 2.10 Completing the Active Directory Installation Wizard Page

Authorize the DHCP Service

If your PDC was also a DCHP server, you must authorize the server in Active Directory to allow it to lease IP addresses after the upgrade to Windows Server 2003 Active Directory.

To authorize a DHCP server in Active Directory

1. Log on to the domain controller by using an account that is a member of the Enterprise Admins group.

2. In the DHCP snap-in, right-click **DHCP**.

3. Click **Manage authorized servers**.

4. In the **Manage Authorized Servers** dialog box, click **Authorize**.

5. In the **Authorize DHCP Server** dialog box, type the name or IP address of the DHCP server, and then click **OK**.

Configure the Windows Time Service

It is important to configure the Windows Time Service correctly to meet the needs of your organization. The Windows Time Service provides time synchronization to peers and clients, which ensures that time is consistent throughout an organization.

Configure the first domain controller that is deployed to synchronize from a valid Network Time Protocol (NTP) source. If no source is configured, the service logs a message to the event log, and uses the local clock when providing time to clients. Although Internet NTP sources are valid for this configuration, it is recommended that you use a dedicated hardware device, such as a GPS, or Radio clock to ensure increased security.

If the first domain controller in the new Windows Server 2003 domain is removed at any time, you will need to repeat this operation.

To configure the Windows Time Service on the first domain controller in the domain

1. Log on to the domain controller.

2. At the command line, type:

    ```
    W32tm /config /manualpeerlist:peers /syncfromflags:manual
    ```

    where *peers* is a space-delimited list of DNS and/or IP addresses. When specifying multiple peers, enclose the list in quotation marks.

3. Update the Windows Time Service configuration. At the command line, type:

    ```
    W32tm /config /update
    ```

    – or –

    ```
    Net stop w32time
    Net start w32time
    ```

> **Note** When specifying a manual peer, do not use the DNS name or IP address of a computer that uses the forest root domain controller as its source for time, such as another domain controller in the forest. The time service does not operate correctly if there are cycles in the time source configuration.

For more information about configuring and deploying the Windows Time Service, see the *Directory Services Guide* of the *Microsoft Windows Server 2003 Resource Kit* (or see the Directory Services Guide on the Web at http://www.microsoft.com/reskit).

Enable Aging and Scavenging for DNS

In a new single domain forest, you need to enable aging and scavenging on Windows Server 2003–based domain controllers running the DNS Server service to allow automatic cleanup and removal of stale resource records (RRs), which can accumulate in zone data over time.

With dynamic update, RRs are automatically added to zones when computers start on the network. However, in some cases, they are not automatically removed when computers leave the network. For example, if a computer registers its own host (A) RR at startup, and is later incorrectly disconnected from the network, its host (A) RR might not be deleted. If your network has mobile users and computers, this situation can occur frequently.

If left unmanaged, the presence of stale RRs in zone data might cause problems, including the following:

■   If a large number of stale RRs remain in server zones, they can eventually take up server disk space and cause unnecessarily long zone transfers.

- DNS servers loading zones with stale RRs might use outdated information to answer client queries, potentially causing the clients to experience name resolution problems on the network.

- The accumulation of stale RRs at the DNS server can degrade its performance and responsiveness.

> **Caution**   By default, the aging and scavenging mechanism for the DNS Server service is disabled. Enable aging and scavenging only after you understand all parameters. Otherwise, the server can accidentally be configured to delete resource records that need to remain. If a resource record is accidentally deleted, users will fail to resolve queries for that resource record, and any user is able to create the resource record and take ownership of it, even on zones configured for secure dynamic update.
>
> For more information about how to configure aging and scavenging, see "Understanding aging and scavenging: DNS" in Help and Support Center for Windows Server 2003.

To enable the aging and scavenging features, and to configure the applicable server and its Active Directory–integrated zones, perform these tasks:

- Enable aging and scavenging on two servers that are running Windows Server 2003. These settings determine the effect of zone-level properties for any Active Directory–integrated zones loaded at the server.

- Enable aging and scavenging for selected zones at the DNS server. When zone-specific properties are set for a selected zone, these settings apply only to the applicable zone and its resource records. Unless these zone-level properties are otherwise configured, they inherit their defaults from comparable settings maintained in server aging and scavenging properties.

To set aging and scavenging properties for the DNS server

1. Log on to the computer that is running the DNS Server service by using an account that is a member of the local Administrators group.

2. In the DNS console tree, right-click the applicable DNS server, and then click **Set Aging/Scavenging for all zones**.

3. Select the **Scavenge stale resource records** check box.

4. Modify other aging and scavenging properties as needed.

To set aging and scavenging properties for a zone

1. Log on to the computer that is running the DNS Server service by using an account that is a member of the local Administrators group.

2. In the DNS console tree, right-click the applicable zone, and then click **Properties**.

3. On the **General** tab, click **Aging**, and then select the **Scavenge stale resource records** check box.

4. Modify other aging and scavenging properties as needed.

Verify DNS Server Recursive Name Resolution

DNS server recursive name resolution is configured automatically during the Active Directory installation process. If your design specifies a different configuration, you can use the DNS snap-in or Dnscmd.exe to modify these settings. Use the DNS snap-in to verify DNS server recursive name resolution based on the information in Table 2.2.

Table 2.2   Information to Verify DNS Server Recursive Name Resolution

Method	Configuration
Recursive name resolution by root hints	No additional configuration is necessary. When the DNS server specified as the Preferred DNS server during the installation process is correctly configured, the root hints are automatically configured. To verify the root hints by using the DNS snap-in: 1. In the console tree, right-click the domain controller name, and then click **Properties**. 2. In the **Properties** sheet for the domain controller, view the root hints on the **Root Hints** tab. Root hints are the recommended method to use for recursive name resolution in a Windows Server 2003 environment.

Table 2.2   Information to Verify DNS Server Recursive Name Resolution

Method	Configuration
Recursive name resolution by forwarding	Forward unresolved queries to specified DNS servers. To verify forwarding by using the DNS snap-in:
	1. In the console tree, right-click the domain controller name, and then click **Properties**.
	2. On the **Forwarders** tab, in the Forwarders list in the selected domain, verify that the IP addresses match those specified by your design.
	Use forwarders only if that is what your organization's design specifies. Root hints are the recommended method to use for recursive name resolution in a Windows Server 2003 environment.
No existing DNS infrastructure	No additional configuration is necessary.
	In this environment, if you want to configure internal DNS servers to resolve queries for external names, then configure this DNS server to forward unresolved queries to an external server, such as one in your perimeter network, or one hosted by an Internet service provider.

Perform Post-Upgrade Tests

After the Active Directory Installation Wizard completes, verify that the Active Directory installation was successful. Review the Windows Server 2003 event log for any errors.

Next, perform the tests that you defined in your test plan to determine whether the Active Directory configuration is functioning correctly. For more information about developing a test plan, see "Planning the Migration" in this book.

After you verify that the upgrade of the Windows NT 4.0 PDC and the instllation of Active Directory succeeded, complete the upgrade process.

Modify Security Policies

To ensure that clients running earlier versions of the Windows operating system can access domain resources in the new Windows Server 2003 domain, you might have to modify default security policies.

In order to increase security, Windows Server 2003–based domain controllers require by default that clients attempting to authenticate to them use SMB packet and secure channel signing. Clients running the Windows 95 operating system without the Directory Service Client Pack or Windows NT 4.0 with Service Pack 2 and earlier do not support SMB packet signing and will not be able to log on or access domain resources on the network. Clients running

Windows NT 4.0 with Service Pack 3 and earlier do not support secure channel signing and will not be able to establish communications with a domain controller in their domain.

The most secure way to enable these clients to log on and access domain resources on the network is to apply either the appropriate service pack or the Directory Service Client Pack. If you cannot apply either of these, configure all Windows Server 2003–based domain controllers to not require SMB packet signing and secure channel signing. To do this, disable the following settings in the Default Domain Controllers Policy:

- **Microsoft network server: Digitally sign communications (always)**

- **Domain member: Digitally encrypt or sign secure channel data (always)**

> **Important**   If you modify these policies, the default security policies in your environment are weakened. However, this is necessary to ensure that some clients running earlier versions of Windows can access domain resources. After all the clients in your environment are running versions of Windows that support SMB packet and secure channel signing, you can re-enable these security policies to increase security. It is recommended that you upgrade your Windows clients as soon as possible.

To make SMB packet and secure channel signing optional on Windows Server 2003–based domain controllers

1.   Open **Active Directory Users and Computers**, right-click the **Domain Controllers** container, and then click **Properties**.

2.   Select the **Group Policy** tab, and then click **Edit**.

3.   Under **Computer Configuration**, navigate to Windows Settings\Security Settings\Local Policies\Security Options.

4.   In the details pane, double-click **Microsoft network server: Digi-**

tally sign communications (always) and then click **Disabled** to prevent SMB packet signing from being required.

5. Click **OK**.

6. In the Details pane, double-click **Domain member: Digitally encrypt or sign secure channel data (always),** click **Disabled** to prevent secure channel signing from being required, and then click **OK**.

7. To apply the Group Policy change immediately, either restart the domain controller, or run the **gpupdate /force** command.

> **Note**   Modifying these settings in the Domain Controllers container will change the Default Domain Controllers Policy. Policy changes that are made here are replicated to all other domain controllers in the domain, requiring you to modify these policies only one time.

For more information about SMB packet signing and secure channel signing, see "Considerations for Upgrading to Windows Server 2003 Active Directory" earlier in this chapter.

For more information about security policies, see "Security options: Security Setting Descriptions" in Help and Support Center for Windows Server 2003.

Upgrading Additional Domain Controllers

After you upgrade the operating system and install Active Directory on the Windows NT 4.0 PDC, add another Windows Server 2003–based domain controller to the domain as soon as possible. This provides redundancy for any clients running in the environment.

You can add additional domain controllers to the Windows Server 2003 domain by upgrading Windows NT 4.0–based BDCs and installing Active Directory, or by adding Windows Server 2003–based member servers to the domain and installing Active Directory on the member servers.

To complete the process for upgrading additional domain controllers, perform the following tasks:

1. Upgrade the operating system of Windows NT 4.0 BDCs.

2. Install Active Directory.

3. Install DNS on additional domain controllers.

4.   Reconfigure the DNS Service.

5.   Add Windows NT 4.0 BDCs to the Windows Server 2003 domain if necessary.

6.   Perform post-upgrade tests.

Upgrade Windows NT 4.0 BDCs

You can upgrade any Windows NT 4.0 BDC to a Windows Server 2003–based domain controller as long as it meets the hardware requirements for a domain controller running Windows Server 2003. To determine whether your hardware configuration is compatible with Windows Server 2003, see the Windows Server Catalog link on the Web Resources page at http://www.microsoft.com/windows/reskits/webresources.

Before upgrading the operating system to Windows Server 2003, use the Winnt32.exe command-line tool to detect any upgrade problems. This tool reports potential upgrade problems, such as inadequate hardware resources or compatibility problems.

To identify potential upgrade problems

■   At the command line, connect to the I386 directory located at your installation source and type the following command:

```
winnt32 /checkupgradeonly
```

For example, if your installation source is the Windows Server 2003 operating system CD in the D: drive, navigate to D:\I386 and type the following command:

```
D:\I386>winnt32 /checkupgradeonly
```

The screen will then display the command prompt while the tool is running. It can take a few minutes for the Microsoft Windows Upgrade Advisor screen to appear.

Resolve reported problems before performing the upgrade.

To install the operating system on the computer, insert the Windows Server 2003 operating system CD in the CD-ROM drive of the domain controller and select the option to install the operating system, or use an automated installation method. If the Windows Server 2003 media is shared on the network, run the Winnt32.exe command.

To complete the operating system installation, perform these tasks:

1.   Verify that you are using a static IP address.

2.   Use NTFS to convert the partitions. The installation of Active Directory will not succeed if you do not have at least one NTFS partition available on which to locate the SYSVOL shared folder.

3. Select **Upgrade** for the Installation type.

4. On the first additional domain controller that is upgraded, configure DNS client settings by using the IP address of the PDC for the **Preferred DNS server** setting and do not specify an IP address in the **Alternate DNS server** setting.

    On all remaining domain controllers that are upgraded, configure DNS client settings by using the IP address of the PDC for the **Preferred DNS server** setting and use the IP address of the second domain controller upgraded for the **Alternate DNS server** setting.

    These DNS client settings are temporary and will be changed during the installation of Active Directory.

5. Install Windows Support Tools, which are available in the \Support\Tools folder on the Windows Server 2003 operating system CD.

During the operating system upgrade the computer will restart three times. After the computer restarts for the last time, the Active Directory Installation Wizard appears.

Install Active Directory on the Additional Domain Controllers

After upgrading the operating system on a Windows NT 4.0 additional domain controller to Windows Server 2003, the computer is in an intermediate state, meaning that the computer is no longer a Windows NT 4.0–based domain controller, nor is it a Windows Server 2003–based member server or domain controller.

The Active Directory Installation Wizard allows you to create an additional domain controller or a member server in the new domain. If you are installing Active Directory by replicating the directory data over the network or from another media source, select the **Member Server** option in the Active Directory Installation Wizard. This configures the computer to be a Windows Server 2003–based member server, allowing you to install Active Directory at a later time.

To install Active Directory on a Windows Server 2003–based member server

■ At the command line, type **Dcpromo**.

   – or –

Open **Administrative Tools**, and then click **Configure Your Server Wizard**. Select **Domain Controller (Active Directory)** to configure your domain controller. After the Configure Your Server Wizard finishes, the Active Directory Installation Wizard begins.

For more information about installing and removing Active Directory, see the *Directory Services Guide* in the *Microsoft Windows Server 2003 Resource Kit* (or see the Directory Services Guide on the Web at http://www.microsoft.com/reskit).

Table 2.3 lists information for installing Active Directory on additional domain controllers, as well as sample data for installing Active Directory on additional domain controllers in the Fabrikam single domain forest. Fabrikam will use the **dcpromo /adv** command to install Active Directory on a member server by copying directory data over the network from a domain controller.

Table 2.3 Installing Active Directory on Additional Domain Controllers

Wizard Page or Dialog Box	Action	Example
Additional Domain Controller or Member Server	Select whether you want the computer to become a member server or an additional domain controller for the domain.	Fabrikam will select Member Server. They will install Active Directory at a later time using the **dcpromo /adv** command.
Domain Controller Type	Select **Additional domain controller for an existing domain**.	When Fabrikam initiates the Active Directory Installation Wizard by using the **dcpromo /adv** command, this is the first wizard page that appears.
Copying Domain Information	Select either: ■ Over the network from a domain controller ■ From these restored backup files	Fabrikam will copy domain information from the first domain controller that is deployed, SEA-FAB-DC01, which is in the same location as the new one. Therefore, they selected **Over the network from a domain controller** to copy the information in the shortest time.

Table 2.3   Installing Active Directory on Additional Domain Controllers

Wizard Page or Dialog Box	Action	Example
Network Credentials	Type the user name and password of an account with sufficient administrative credentials to install Active Directory on this computer, and the fully qualified domain name of the domain in which the computer will become an additional domain controller.	
Additional Domain Controller	Type the full DNS name of the forest root domain.	**Fabricorp.fabrikam.com**
Database and Log Folders	Type the folder locations specified by your design.	■ Database folder: **C:\Windows\NTDS** ■ Log folder: **C:\Windows\NTDS**
Shared System Volume	Confirm or type the location specified by your design.	**C:\Windows\SYSVOL**
Directory Service Restore Mode Administration Password	In the **Password and Confirm password** boxes, type any strong password.	

Verify that all information on the Summary page is accurate, and then click Finish. After the Active Directory Installation Wizard finishes, you are prompted to restart the computer. The installation is not complete until the computer restarts.

> **Note**   Configure all additional domain controllers that you add to your single domain forest as Global Catalog servers.

After you install Windows Server 2003 Active Directory, enable Remote Desktop for Administration, formerly known as Terminal Services in Remote Administration mode, to enable administrators to log on remotely if necessary.

To enable Remote Desktop for Administration

■   In Control Panel, double-click **System**, select the **Remote** tab, and then select **Allow users to connect remotely to this computer**.

If the additional domain controller was also a DHCP server, you will need to authorize the server to allow it to continue to lease IP addresses. For more information about authorizing a DHCP server, see "Authorize the DHCP Service" earlier in this chapter.

Install DNS on Additional Domain Controllers

Install DNS on all Windows Server 2003–based domain controllers that you add to the domain.

To install DNS on additional domain controllers

1.   In **Control Panel**, double-click **Add or Remove Programs**, and then click **Add/Remove Windows Components**.

2.   In **Components**, select the **Networking Services** check box, and then click **Details**.

3.   In **Subcomponents of Networking Services**, select the **Domain Name System (DNS)** check box, click **OK**, and then click **Next**.

4.   If prompted, in **Copy files from**, type the full path to the distribution files and then click **OK**. The required files will be copied to your hard disk.

Reconfigure the DNS Service

After deploying additional domain controllers in a single domain forest, do the following to reconfigure the DNS service:

■   Configure the DNS client settings of the first and subsequent domain controllers.

After you have deployed an additional domain controller, modify the DNS client settings on the first domain controller. Because no other domain controllers were running when you deployed the first domain controller, modify the DNS client settings on the first domain controller to include the additional domain controller. As you deploy more domain controllers, you might also need to modify the Alternate DNS server setting specified on existing domain controllers to ensure that this setting points to the closest DNS server.

■ Update the DNS delegation.

If you have delegated the DNS zone to an existing DNS server, update the DNS delegation for the domain after you install the DNS Server service on new domain controllers.

■ Enable aging and scavenging for DNS on one additional domain controller.

It is best to enable aging and scavenging for DNS on two servers that are running the DNS Server service in your environment. You enabled aging and scavenging on the PDC when you upgraded the PDC to Windows Server 2003 Active Directory. For information about setting aging and scavenging properties for the additional DNS server, see "Enable Aging and Scavenging for DNS" earlier in this chapter.

Add Windows NT 4.0 BDCs to the Windows Server 2003 Domain

If you have applications in your environment that can run only on a Windows NT 4.0–based domain controller, and if you have upgraded all the Windows NT 4.0 BDCs to Windows Server 2003 or if the existing Windows NT 4.0 BDC in your environment becomes unavailable, you might need to add an additional Windows NT 4.0 BDC to your environment. You can do this by installing a new Windows NT 4.0 BDC in the domain. Prior to installing the new Windows NT 4.0 BDC in the domain, you must first add the new computer account to the Windows Server 2003 domain.

> **Note**   You will not be able to install a new Windows NT 4.0–based BDC in your environment if you have SMB packet signing and secure channel signing enabled. If these security policies are enabled in your environment, modify them before installing a new Windows NT 4.0–based BDC. For information about modifying security policies, see "Modify Security Policies" earlier in this chapter.

To add a Windows NT 4.0 BDC to a Windows Server 2003 domain

1. In Active Directory Users and Computers, right-click the **Domain Controllers** folder.

2. Point to **New**, and then click **Computer**.

3. Type the computer name of the BDC.

4. Ensure that the check boxes are selected for **Assign this computer account as a pre-Windows 2000 Computer** and **Assign this computer account as a backup domain controller**.

5. Install the BDC in the domain.

Perform Post-Upgrade Tests

After you upgrade each additional domain controller, verify that the upgrade was successful. Use the same tests and tools that you used to verify that the upgrade of the Windows NT 4.0 PDC was successful. For more information about developing a test plan, see "Planning the Migration" in this book.

Also, verify that DNS recursive name resolution is configured according to your organization's the DNS design for your organization. For more information about verifying recursive name resolution, see "Verify DNS Server Recursive Name Resolution" earlier in this chapter.

Completing Post-Upgrade Tasks

After you upgrade all domain controllers in the domain to Windows Server 2003, complete the following post-upgrade tasks:

- Eliminate anonymous connections to domain controllers.

- Raise domain and forest functional levels.

- Redirect the Users and Computers containers.

- Complete the upgrade.

Eliminate Anonymous Connections to Domain Controllers

After you upgrade all the servers in the domain hosting services that run as Local System and use Anonymous or null credentials when accessing a domain controller, such as Windows NT 4.0 RAS servers, remove the Everyone and Anonymous Logon groups from the Pre-Windows 2000 Compatible Access built-in group. This task increases the security of your domain by preventing anonymous connections to domain controllers.

To remove groups from the Pre-Windows 2000 Compatible Access Group by using the command line

- At the command line, type:

```
net localgroup "Pre-Windows 2000 Compatible Access" GroupName /delete
```

When using the **net localgroup** command to add or delete any group or group member name that includes spaces, such as the Anonymous Logon group, you must enclose the group name in quotation marks.

Raise Domain and Forest Functional Levels

Although the Windows Server 2003 domain functional level provides a number of features and advantages, enable this functional level only when you have upgraded all your Windows NT 4.0 BDCs and you are certain that your environment is ready.

> **Important**   If you raise the domain and forest functional levels to Windows Server 2003, this action cannot be reversed and you cannot add Windows NT 4.0–based or Windows 2000–based domain controllers to the environment. Any existing Windows NT 4.0 or Windows 2000–based domain controllers in the environment will no longer function. Before you raise functional levels to take advantage of advanced Windows Server 2003 features, ensure that you will never need to install domain controllers that run Windows NT 4.0 or Windows 2000 in your environment.

After you determine that your environment is ready, use Active Directory Domains and Trusts to enable the Windows Server 2003 domain functional level.

After you upgrade all domain controllers to Windows Server 2003, raise the forest functional level to Windows Server 2003 to take advantage of all Windows Server 2003 forest-level features.

For more information about enabling functional levels and **the features available at the Windows Server 2003 domain and forest functional levels**, see "Enabling Advanced Windows Server 2003 Active Directory Features" in *Designing and Deploying Directory and Security Services* in the *Microsoft Windows Server 2003 Deployment Kit* (or see "Enabling Advanced Windows Server 2003 Active Directory Features" on the Web at http://www.microsoft.com/reskit).

Complete the Upgrade

Complete the following tasks to finalize the upgrade process:

- Review, update, and document the domain architecture to reflect any changes that you made during the upgrade process.

- Review your operating procedures and administrative tasks to determine whether new Windows Server 2003 features, such as Group Policy objects or distributed administration, affect the operations environment. Be sure to document any changes that you identify.

- After you ensure that your Windows Server 2003 Active Directory environment is operating successfully for a period of time, you can redeploy the rollback server that you reserved for the recovery process. If you do not need the Windows NT 4.0 BDC to achieve the required load balance among your domain controllers, maintain the rollback server for one week. Maintain the backup of the rollback server for a longer period of time for additional security. For information about developing a recovery plan, see "Planning the Migration" in this book.

- Some Windows NT 4.0 applications, such as Microsoft® Systems Management Server (SMS), can have an unpredictable effect on the domain when installed after the domain has been upgraded to Active Directory. Ensure that you are running SMS 2.0 and have installed Service Pack 4. For more information about SMS, see the SMS Downloads link on the Web Resources page at http://www.microsoft.com/windows/reskits/webresources.

After you complete the above tasks successfully, the upgrade process is complete.

Configuring the Site Topology

If your organization includes users and computers in more than one physical location, you can create Active Directory sites. Active Directory uses site configuration information to manage and optimize the process of replication. Designing a site topology involves determining where you need to create subnets, sites, and site links.

A subnet is a segment of a TCP/IP network to which a set of logical IP addresses are assigned. Subnets group computers in a way that identifies their physical proximity on the network. Subnet objects in Active Directory identify the network addresses that are used to map computers to sites. Before you begin to create sites, document the subnets that you created for your routers in your Windows NT 4.0 environment.

Sites are one or more TCP/IP subnets with highly reliable and fast network connections. Sites are represented in Active Directory as site objects. Site objects are a set of subnets, and each domain controller in a forest is associated with an Active Directory site according to its IP address. Sites can host domain controllers from more than one domain, and a domain can be represented in more than one site.

It is recommended that you use legal DNS names when you create new site names; otherwise, your site will only be accessible where a Microsoft DNS server is used. Legal DNS names can contain only the following characters: uppercase letters (A-Z), lowercase letters (a-z), numbers (0-9), and the hyphen (-).

A site link is an object that is stored in Active Directory that represents a set of sites that can communicate at uniform cost through a specified intersite transport. Creating a site link between two or more sites is a way to influence replication topology. By creating a site link, you provide Active Directory with information about what connections are available, which ones are preferred, and how much bandwidth is available. Active Directory uses this information to choose times and connections for replication that provide the best performance.

When you install Active Directory on the first domain controller in the forest, a site object named Default-First-Site-Name is created in the Sites container in Active Directory. The server object for the first domain controller is created in this site.

If no additional sites have been defined in Active Directory, then the server object for all subsequent domain controllers is added to the Default-First-Site-Name site object. However, if additional sites are defined in Active Directory and the IP address of the installation computer matches an existing subnet in a defined site, then the domain controller is added to that site.

> **Note**   Domain controllers are only added to sites based on their IP address at the time of installation. After installation, if the IP address, subnet, or site information of a domain controller changes, an administrator must manually move the domain controller to the new site.

To simplify the placement of the domain controller into the appropriate site, configure your site topology before you install Active Directory on additional domain controllers. After all sites are created, a server object for each additional domain controller is created in the appropriate site according to its IP address.

For more information about configuring your site topology, see "Configure site settings: Active Directory" and "Configure replication between sites: Active Directory" in Help and Support Center for Windows Server 2003.

Creating a site topology involves the following steps:

- Creating Active Directory sites

- Creating and assigning Active Directory subnets

- Creating Active Directory site links

- Moving the domain controller into the new site

To help illustrate the process for creating a site topology, sample data for a fictitious company, Fabrikam, Inc., is provided within the context of the tasks that must be performed. In this example, Fabrikam has users and computers at two physical locations, Seattle and Boston.

Create Active Directory Sites

Create Active Directory sites by using Active Directory Sites and Services.

To create the Active Directory sites

1. Log on to the domain controller by using an account that is a member of the Domain Admins group or the Enterprise Admins group.

2. Open Active Directory Sites and Services.

3. Right-click the **Sites** folder, and then click **New Site**.

4. In the **Name** box, type the name of the new site.

5. Click a site link object, and then click **OK**.

Fabrikam created the Seattle site, as shown in Figure 2.11 and Figure 2.12.

Figure 2.11   Creating a New Site

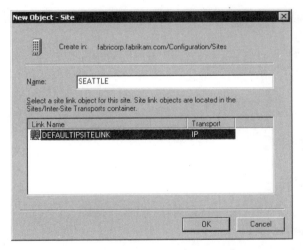

Figure 2.12   New Object - Site Creation Page

Create and Assign Active Directory Subnets

Create and assign Active Directory subnets by using Active Directory Sites and Services.

To create Active Directory subnets and associate them with sites

1. Log on to the domain controller by using an account that is a member of the Domain Admins group or the Enterprise Admins group.

2. Open Active Directory Sites and Services.

3. In the console tree, right-click **Subnets**, and then click **New Subnet**.

4. In the **Address** box, type the subnet address.

5. In the **Mask** box, type the subnet mask that describes the range of addresses included in this subnet.

6. Under **Select a site object for this subnet**, click the site to associate with this subnet, and then click **OK.**

7. To associate a subnet with a site, in the console tree, right-click the subnet with which you want to associate the site, and then click **Properties**.

8. In the **Site** box, click the site with which to associate this subnet.

Fabrikam created the subnet 172.16.12.0/22, as shown in Figure 2.13 and Figure 2.14.

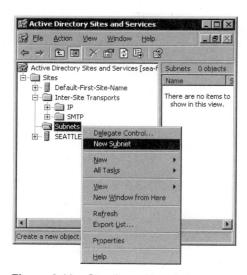

Figure 2.13   Creating a New Subnet

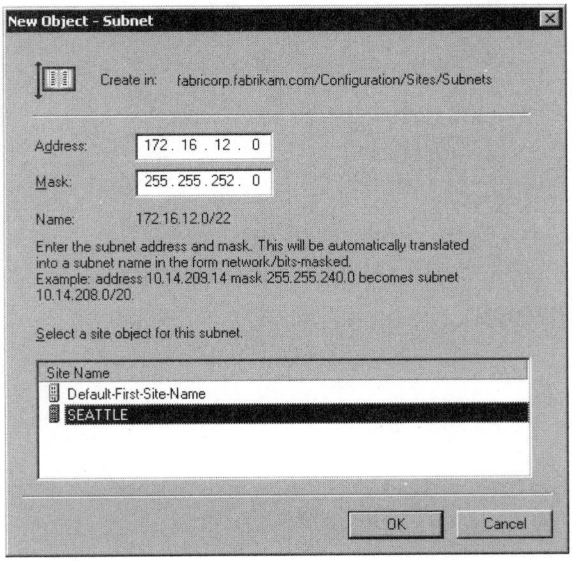

Figure 2.14   New Object - Subnet Creation Page

Fabrikam associated the subnet with the Seattle site, as shown in Figure 2.15

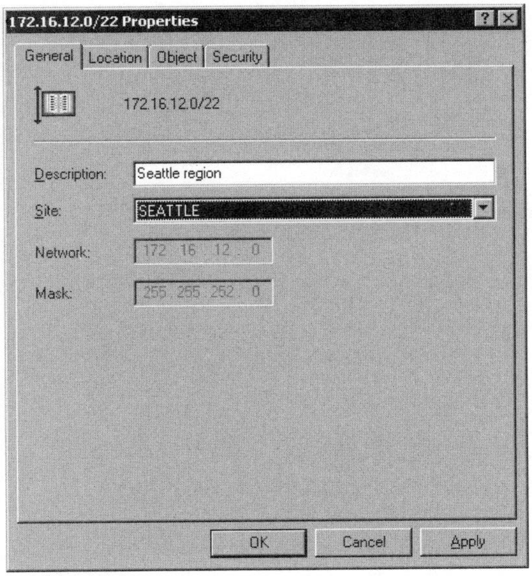

Figure 2.15   Subnet Properties Page

Create Active Directory Site Links

Create Active Directory site links and configure the site link by using Active Directory Sites and Services.

To create Active Directory site links

1. Log on to the domain controller by using an account that is a member of the Domain Admins group or the Enterprise Admins group.

2. Open Active Directory Sites and Services.

3. In the console tree, right-click the intersite transport protocol that you want the site link to use (generally IP), and then click **New Site Link**.

4. In the **Name** box, type the name to be given to the link.

5. Click two or more sites to connect, and then click **Add**.

6. Configure the cost, schedule, and replication frequency for the site link.

Fabrikam first created the Boston site and the subnet 172.16.28.0/22, following the same procedures that they used to create the Seattle site. They then created the site link SEA-BOS, as shown in Figure 2.16 and Figure 2.17.

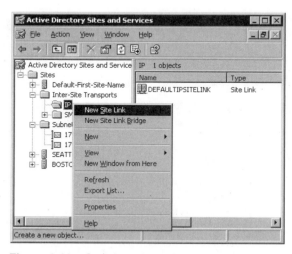

Figure 2.16   Creating a New Site Link

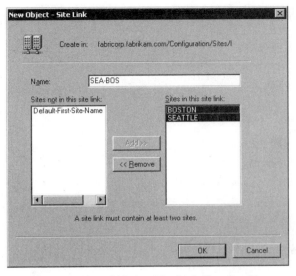

Figure 2.17   New Object - Site Link Creation Page

Move the Domain Controller into the New Site

Move the domain controller from Default-First-Site-Name into the correct site by using Active Directory Sites and Services.

To move the domain controller into a new site

1. Log on to the domain controller by using an account that is a member of the Domain Admins group or the Enterprise Admins group.

2. Open Active Directory Sites and Services.

3. In the console tree, expand Default-First-Site-Name, and then click **Servers**.

4. In the **Servers** pane, right-click the name of the domain controller that you upgraded from Windows NT 4.0, and then click **Move**.

5. In the **Move Server** box, click the site that should contain the server, and then click **OK**.

Fabrikam moved the domain controller SEA-FAB-DC01 into the Seattle site, as shown in Figure 2.18 and Figure 2.19.

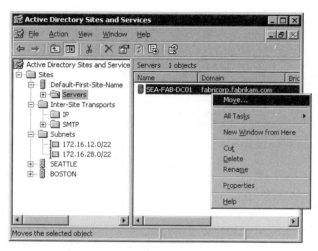

Figure 2.18   Moving a Server

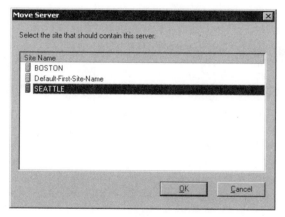

Figure 2.19   Move Server Page

Figure 2.20 shows the site topology for Fabrikam after they created two sites, two subnets, and a site link, and moved the first domain controller into the Seattle site.

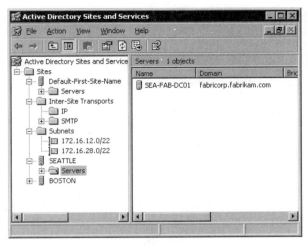

Figure 2.20   Fabrikam Site Topology

Additional Resources

These resources contain additional information and tools related to this chapter.

Related Information

- "Restructuring Windows NT 4.0 Domains to an Active Directory Forest" in *Designing and Deploying Directory and Security Services* in the *Microsoft Windows Server 2003 Deployment Kit* (or see "Restructuring Windows NT 4.0 Domains to an Active Directory Forest" on the Web at http://www.microsoft.com/reskit) for more information about restructuring domains when upgrading from Windows NT 4.0 to Windows Server 2003.

- "Designing the Active Directory Logical Structure" in *Designing and Deploying Directory and Security Services* in the *Microsoft Windows Server 2003 Deployment Kit* (or see "Designing the Active Directory Logical Structure" on the Web at http://www.microsoft.com/reskit) for more information about the Active Directory logical structure.

- "Designing the Site Topology" in *Designing and Deploying Directory and Security Services* in the *Microsoft Windows Server 2003 Deployment Kit* (or see "Designing the Site Topology" on the Web at http://www.microsoft.com/reskit) for more information about Active Directory site topology.

- "Enabling Advanced Windows Server 2003 Active Directory Features" in *Designing and Deploying Directory and Security Services* in the *Microsoft Windows Server 2003 Deployment Kit* (or see "Enabling Advanced Windows Server 2003 Active Directory Features" on the Web at http://www.microsoft.com/reskit) for more information about enabling functional levels.

- "Deploying DNS" in *Deploying Network Services* in the *Microsoft Windows Server 2003 Deployment Kit* (or see "Deploying DNS" on the Web at http://www.microsoft.com/reskit) for more information about deploying DNS.

Related Tools

- Adsiedit.exe

    The ADSI Edit tool (Adsiedit.exe) is a Microsoft Management Console snap-in that you can use to edit objects in the Active Directory database. For more information about Adsiedit.exe, in Help and Support Center for Windows Server 2003, click **Tools,** and then click Windows Support Tools.

- Ldp.exe

    Ldp.exe provides an interface to perform LDAP operations against Active Directory. For more information about Ldp.exe, in Help and Support Center for Windows Server 2003, click **Tools,** and then click Windows Support Tools.

Related Help Topics

For best results in identifying Help topics by title, in Help and Support Center, under the **Search** box, click **Set search options**. Under **Help Topics**, select the **Search in title only** check box.

- "Active Directory" in Help and Support Center for Windows Server 2003.

- "Windows Support Tools" under "Tools" in Help and Support Center for Windows Server 2003.

- "Microsoft network server: Digitally sign communications (always)" in Help and Support Center for Windows Server 2003 for more information about SMB packet signing.

- "Domain member: Digitally encrypt or sign secure channel data (always)" in Help and Support Center for Windows Server 2003 for more information about secure channel signing.

- "Active Directory support tools" in Help and Support Center for Windows Server 2003 for more information about the options that are available for the Active Directory support tools.

- "Security options: Security Setting Descriptions" in Help and Support Center for Windows Server 2003 for more information about security policies.

- "Configure site settings: Active Directory" and "Configure replication between sites: Active Directory" in Help and Support Center for Windows Server 2003 for more information about configuring your site topology.

- "Understanding aging and scavenging: DNS" in Help and Support Center for Windows Server 2003 for more information about how to configure aging and scavenging of stale resource records.

3

Upgrading and Migrating WINS and DHCP Servers to Windows Server 2003

Running the Windows Internet Name Service (WINS) and the Dynamic Host Configuration Protocol (DHCP) service on the Microsoft® Windows Server™ 2003 operating system provides access to several new features and substantially increases the performance and stability of these services over the Microsoft Windows NT® version 4.0 operating system. When planning to upgrade or migrate your existing WINS and DHCP infrastructure, you need to consider the hardware, software, and infrastructure requirements and configuration issues discussed in this chapter. If you are deploying an entirely new WINS and DHCP infrastructure on your network, or if you are completely restructuring your current environment, you can consult the references provided here.

In This Chapter:

71

Related Information

- "Upgrading to Windows Server 2003 Active Directory" in this book.

Overview of WINS and DHCP Migration

The WINS and DHCP services in Windows Server 2003 are significantly enhanced and include many new features not available in Windows NT 4.0. Moving your Windows NT 4.0–based WINS and DHCP servers to Windows Server 2003 allows you to take advantage of the improvements and new features added to these services since Windows NT 4.0. For example, WINS now includes the ability to replicate records owned by an explicitly specified list of servers, and both WINS and DHCP have improved management through Microsoft Management Console (MMC) snap-ins and the Netsh command-line tool. For more information about some of the new features available in Windows Server 2003, see "Feature Comparison: Windows NT, Windows 2000, and the Windows Server 2003 family" in Help and Support Center for Windows Server 2003.

In addition, if DHCP or WINS is running on a domain controller, you can raise the functional level of the Active Directory® directory service and enable new features of Active Directory by upgrading all of the domain controllers on your network to Windows Server 2003. For more information about moving to Active Directory, see "Upgrading to Windows Server 2003 Active Directory" in this book.

If you already have a working WINS and DHCP infrastructure on your network, you can migrate the databases and server configuration from your existing servers to new Windows Server 2003–based servers. Migrating can save you time because you do not need to reconfigure the scope, lease, and option information on the new DHCP servers, and allows retention of your existing WINS database. If your existing infrastructure is efficient for your current and planned IT and business needs, migration can greatly simplify your move to Windows Server 2003. If your infrastructure is currently inefficient, or you anticipate significant growth and change in your organization over the next few years, consider planning a new WINS and DCHP design.

The information in this chapter is for organizations that are moving from Windows NT 4.0 to Windows Server 2003, and are keeping the same WINS and DHCP configuration. If you are redesigning your WINS strategy, or you are adding, removing, or rearranging subnets, see "Deploying WINS" and "Deploying DHCP" in *Deploying Network Services* of the *Microsoft® Windows Server™ 2003 Deployment Kit* (or see "Deploying WINS" and "Deploying DCHP" on the Web at http://www.microsoft.com/reskit) .

> **Tip**   The procedures in this chapter will work whether the WINS and DHCP services are each on their own servers, running together on the same server, running on a server with other services, or running on a domain controller.

Examining Your Current Hardware

The first step in upgrading your servers from Windows NT 4.0 to Windows Server 2003 is to determine whether your current hardware supports Windows Server 2003.

If your current systems support Windows Server 2003 but are close to the end of their expected lifecycle, consider upgrading your hardware and migrating to Windows Server 2003 at the same time.

For information about hardware life expectancy, contact your hardware vendor or refer to any internal metrics that your organization uses.

For a current list of hardware compatible with Windows Server 2003, see the Windows Server Catalog link on the Web Resources page at http://www.microsoft.com/windows/reskits/webresources.

Examining Your Current Infrastructure

Upgrading from Windows NT 4.0 to Windows Server 2003 provides an opportunity to not only determine if you need to upgrade your hardware, but to also determine if you want to continue using your existing WINS and DHCP design. Before upgrading or migrating existing WINS and DHCP servers to Windows Server 2003, make sure your existing infrastructure is appropriate for your current needs.

For example, if you have recently upgraded most client computers in your organization to the Microsoft Windows 2000 or Windows XP operating systems, or if you have recently stopped using an application that relies heavily on WINS, your current WINS structure might be more robust than you need, and might not be structured as efficiently as possible.

Likewise, before you migrate existing DHCP databases, consider if your current DHCP infrastructure best meets your organization's current or planned needs. For example, you might have added new wireless clients and want to organize them into their own subnet, or your subnets might otherwise be inefficiently arranged. In such a case, consider starting your deployment with a design phase, rather than migrating the existing database.

For more information about designing and deploying a WINS infrastructure, see "Deploying WINS" in *Deploying Network Services* of the *Microsoft Windows Server 2003 Deployment Kit* (or see "Deploying WINS" on the Web at http://www.microsoft.com/reskit). For more information about designing and deploying a DHCP infrastructure, see "Deploying DHCP" in *Deploying Network Services* of the *Microsoft Windows Server 2003 Deployment Kit* (or see "Deploying DCHP" on the Web at http://www.microsoft.com/reskit).

Upgrading WINS and DHCP Servers

If your hardware is compatible with Windows Server 2003 and will continue to support the performance you require from your WINS servers, your DHCP servers, or both, you might want to upgrade these servers in place instead of migrating these services to new servers.

Both WINS and DHCP are designed to automatically upgrade their databases when you upgrade from Windows NT 4.0 to Windows Server 2003, so there are no additional steps to take in upgrading these services once you have upgraded the operating system. However, if you have also upgraded to Active Directory, you must authorize your Windows Server 2003-based DHCP servers in Active Directory before they will continue to lease IP addresses. For more information about authorizing DHCP servers in Active Directory, see "Authorizing DHCP Servers in Active Directory" later in this chapter.

Upgrading can take more than 30 minutes each, depending on the number of services and the size of the databases being upgraded. Because status is not reported during the upgrade, a lengthy upgrade might appear to have failed. Therefore, be sure to allow a sufficient amount of time before attempting to restart a service after an upgrade, particularly if you are upgrading a large database, or if you are upgrading multiple services.

> **Note**   If your existing WINS services, DHCP services, or both are on a primary domain controller (PDC) or backup domain controller (BDC) that is upgraded in place, the WINS and DHCP databases are automatically upgraded along when the operating system is upgraded. This might cause the upgrade of the domain controller to take additional time.

After the server operating system is upgraded to Windows Server 2003, you should test the WINS and DHCP services to ensure performance continues at appropriate levels. If performance is not satisfactory, you can migrate the services to a different computer.

To move the WINS service from one Windows Server 2003–based computer to another Windows Server 2003–based computer, follow the procedure in "Migrating the WINS Service" later in this chapter.

To move the DHCP service from one Windows Server 2003–based computer to a different Windows Server 2003–based computer, follow the export procedure in this section and then follow the import procedure in "Importing DHCP Settings" later in this chapter.

To export the DHCP database from Windows Server 2003

1. At the command prompt, type:

```
netsh DHCP server export path all
```

This will export the file to the path you specify. This can take more than 30 minutes to complete, depending on the size of the database, and gives you no indication of progress while exporting the file. Do not assume that the process has failed until you allow sufficient time, which might be longer than 30 minutes, depending on the size of your database. When the export is complete, a message appears that tells you the command has completed successfully.

2. Copy the exported file to a location where you can access it from the new Windows Server 2003–based server.

For more information about the Netsh command-line tool, see "Netsh" in Help and Support Center for Windows Server 2003.

Migrating the WINS Service

You might decide to move your WINS service to a different computer instead of upgrading in place. If so, you can migrate WINS from an existing Windows NT 4.0–based computer by manually copying the WINS database from the existing WINS server to the new WINS server.

> **Important**   Before you begin the migration, create a backup of your working configuration and test the migration procedures in a lab environment.

Complete the following steps to migrate WINS to a new computer:

- Install and configure the WINS service on the new computer.
- Convert the WINS database.
- Access additional files for conversion, if necessary.

To install and configure the WINS service on Windows Server 2003

You can install WINS either during or after installing Windows Server 2003. You can use the Manage Your Server Wizard to install the WINS service on your new Windows Server 2003-based computer, or you can use the following procedure to install WINS:

1. Open the Windows Components Wizard. To open the Windows Components Wizard, click **Start**, click **Control Panel**, double-click **Add or Remove Programs**, and then click **Add/Remove Windows Components**.

2. Under **Components**, scroll to and click **Networking Services**.

3. Click **Details**.

4. Under **Subcomponents of Networking Services**, click **Windows Internet Name Service (WINS)**, click **OK**, and then click **Next**.

    If prompted, type the full path of the Windows Server 2003 distribution files, and then click **Continue**.

5. Ensure that NetBIOS is enabled. You can do this by viewing **WINS** tab of the Transmission Control Protocol/Internet Protocol (TCP/IP) properties of your network adapter.

    To view the TCP/IP properties:

    a. Click **Start**, click **Control Panel**, click **Network Connections**, and then click your network connection.

    b. In the *connection* **Status** dialog box, click **Properties**.

    c. In the *connection* **Properties** dialog box, click **Internet Protocol (TCP/IP),** and then click **Properties**.

    d. Click **Advanced**.

    e. Click the **WINS** tab.

        On the **WINS** tab, you can configure your NetBIOS settings. Figure 3.1 shows the **WINS** tab in the **Advanced TCP/IP Settings** dialog box.

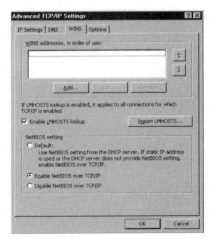

Figure 3.1   The **WINS** Tab in the **Advanced TCP/IP Settings** Dialog Box

If you have more than one WINS server, you can maintain continuity of service by moving the servers one at a time, as long as the servers have recently replicated with each other. If you have only one WINS server, convert the database during non-peak hours to mitigate WINS downtime.

After you have installed and configured the new WINS server, manually convert the database using the following procedure:

To convert the WINS database

1. At the command prompt, type **net stop wins** on both the existing and new servers.

2. Copy the contents of the *systemroot*\System32\Wins folder from the existing server to the new Windows Server 2003–based server.

> **Note**   This is the default location of the WINS database, if the database is in a different location, you should copy it from that location. The path of the WINS folder on the new server must be identical to the path of the WINS folder on the old server.

3. At the command prompt, type **net start wins** on the new Windows Server 2003-based server.

> **Note** This process can take 30 minutes or more to complete depending on the size of the database. Do not stop the process until it is finished. It is normal for Jetconv.exe to require heavy CPU usage during the conversion.

During the conversion process, you might be prompted for additional files from the Windows Server 2003 operating system CD.

To access additional WINS files that might be required for conversion

1. Copy the Edb500.dl_ file from the I386 folder on the CD to the *systemroot*\System32 folder on the server.

2. At the command prompt, type **expand edb500.dl_ edb500.dll** to expand the Edb500.dl_ file on the server.

3. At the command prompt, type **net start wins** to finish the conversion process.

    Figure 3.2 shows an example of using the Expand utility to extract additional files.

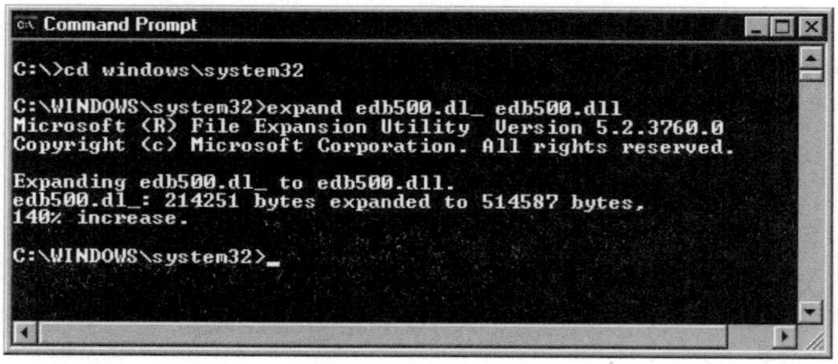

Figure 3.2 Extracting Additional Files

4. Verify that the WINS database is shown in the WINS snap-in on the server.

5. Once the database has been successfully migrated to the new server, test the new server before taking the old server offline.

> **Important**   Ensure that you have migrated all the necessary services from the old server before taking it offline. For example, if WINS is on the same server as DHCP, export the DHCP database and save it in a location that can be reached by the new DHCP server before taking the old server offline.

6.   Disconnect the old WINS server from your network.

7.   Assign the name and IP address of the old WINS server to the new WINS server. By using the IP address of the old WINS server, you will not need to change the WINS setting on any other computers that are pointing to the WINS server.

   If you cannot change the IP address of the new WINS server, and all of your clients are using DHCP, you can instead change DHCP option 44 on your DHCP server to the IP address of the new WINS server. If you choose this option, make the new WINS server the first WINS server in DHCP option 44 and use the old WINS server, if it is still online, as a secondary WINS server until all clients have renewed their DHCP lease and received the new settings. For more information about how to assign options, see "Assigning options" in Help and Support Center for Windows Server 2003.

Migrating the DHCP Service

You can export your database from a Windows NT 4.0–based DHCP server and import the database directly to a Windows Server 2003–based server by using the procedures in this section. This is a good option if your current hardware does not support Windows Server 2003, or does not support the current or projected needs of your organization. The following procedures allow you to migrate lease, scope, and option information, including reservations and exclusions. If you have changed any registry settings from their defaults on the existing server, you must manually make these changes to the registry on the new Windows Server 2003–based server for them to take effect.

> **Caution**   The registry editor bypasses standard safeguards, allowing settings that can damage your system, or even require you to reinstall Windows. If you must edit the registry, back it up first and see the Registry Reference at http://www.microsoft.com/reskit.

If you have multiple DHCP servers on your network, and have split the scopes for each subnet between servers, you can maintain continuity of service by upgrading one server at a time. Alternatively, you can take all DHCP servers offline during the upgrade. If you have a long lease time, there might not be any interruption in DHCP service, even if you take all the DHCP servers offline for several hours. However, it is best to perform the migration during off-peak hours to reduce any possibility of interruption in DHCP service.

Exporting DHCP Settings

When migrating from an existing DHCP server the first step is to export the current DHCP settings. Use the following procedure to export the DHCP database from an existing Windows NT 4.0–based server.

> **Important**   Before you begin the migration, create a backup of your working configuration and test the migration procedures in a lab environment.

To export the DHCP server settings from a Windows NT 4.0–based server

1.   Run DHCPExim.exe. This opens the **DhcpExim** dialog box.
        To download and install DHCPExim.exe, see the Resource Kit Tools link on the Web Resources page at http://www.microsoft.com/windows/reskits/webresources.

> **Tip**   If you get an error when trying to run the DhcpExim setup file, DHCPExim_setup.exe, you might need to first install the Windows Installer software on your Windows NT 4.0–based computer. To download and install Windows Installer, see the Windows Installer 2.0 Redistributable for Windows NT 4.0 and Windows 2000 link on the Web Resources page at http://www.microsoft.com/windows/reskits/webresources.

2.   In the **DhcpExim** dialog box, click **Export configuration of the local service to a file**.
        Figure 3.3 shows this page of the DhcpExim tool.

Figure 3.3   The DHCPEXIM Tool

3.   In the DHCPEXIM Export To File dialog box, type a file name, select a location to save the file, and then click **OK**.

The location that you use to save the file is shown in the **DhcpExim Export To File** dialog box.

Figure 3.4 shows this page of the DhcpExim tool.

Figure 3.4   Export To File Dialog Box

4.   In the **DhcpExim Export** dialog box, select all of the scopes on the list to migrate all settings on the server. Alternatively, if you are not migrating the entire server configuration, you can export specific scopes.

> **Note**   These procedures assume that you are migrating all the scopes from a Windows NT 4.0–based DHCP server to a corresponding Windows Server 2003–based DHCP server. You can modify the procedures to export and import only selected scopes, or to consolidate multiple DHCP servers. These cases, however, are beyond the scope of this chapter. If you choose to redesign your DHCP implementation, ensure that you have considered all the planning, design, and deployment implications of changing your DHCP infrastructure, such as ensuring that you have sufficient routers or DHCP Relay Agents between subnets. For more information about designing and deploying DHCP, see "Deploying DHCP" in *Deploying Network Services* in the *Microsoft Windows Server 2003 Deployment Kit*.

5.   Click to select the **Disable the selected scopes on local machine before export** check box to disable the scopes on this server before exporting, and then click **Export**.

Figure 3.5 shows this page of the DhcpExim tool.

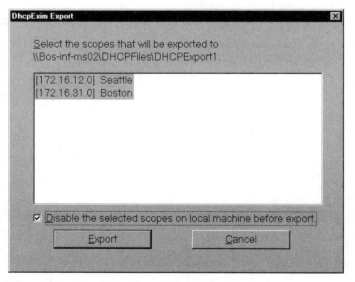

Figure 3.5   DhcpEximExport Dialog Box

> **Tip**   This step might take several minutes to complete, and there is no dialog box to indicate the progress of the export. You can, however, view the process running on the **Processes** tab of the Windows Task Manager.

6. Click **OK** when the message "The operation was completed successfully" appears.

7. Copy the exported file to a location where you can access it from the new Windows Server 2003–based server.

    Once you have finished exporting your DHCP database, you will import the file to configure your new Windows Server 2003-based DHCP server.

Importing DHCP Settings

After exporting the DHCP settings and moving the exported file to a location where you can access it, you are ready to use the Netsh command-line tool to import the DHCP settings to the new DHCP server running Windows Server 2003.

Use the following procedure to import your DHCP server settings to your new Windows Server 2003-based computer.

To import DHCP server settings to a Windows Server 2003–based DHCP server

1. Install DHCP on the Windows Server 2003–based server. DHCP must be installed before you can import the file. To install DHCP, do the following:

    a. Open the Windows Components Wizard. To open the Windows Components Wizard, click **Start**, click **Control Panel**, double-click **Add or Remove Programs**, and then click **Add/Remove Windows Components**.

    b. Under **Components**, scroll to and then click **Networking Services**.

    c. Click **Details**.

    d. Under **Subcomponents of Networking Services**, click **Dynamic Host Configuration Protocol (DHCP)**, and then click **OK**.

e. Click **Next**. If prompted, type the full path of the Windows Server 2003 distribution files, and then click **Next**.

The required files are copied to your hard disk. After you have finished installing DHCP, continue with the rest of the procedure to import the DHCP settings.

> **Important** This procedure assumes that you have installed the DHCP service, but have not configured any scopes. Your scopes will be automatically configured by the import process.

2. Ensure that the user who will perform the import is a member of the Local Admins group.

3. At the command prompt, type:

```
netsh DHCP server import path all
```

This will import the file from the path you specify. This can take more than 30 minutes to complete, depending on the size of the database, and gives you no indication of progress while importing the file. Do not assume that the process has failed until you allow sufficient time, which might be longer than 30 minutes depending on the size of your database. When the import is complete, a message appears that tells you the command has completed successfully.

This imports the configurations of all scopes that you exported from the server running Windows NT 4.0.

4. Once the database has been successfully imported to the new server, test the new server before taking the old server offline.

> **Important** Ensure that you have migrated all the necessary services from the old server before taking it offline. For example, if WINS is on the same server as DHCP, migrate the WINS database before taking the old server offline.

5. Disconnect the old DHCP server from your network.

6. Assign the name and IP address of the old DHCP server to the new DHCP server. By using the IP address of the old DHCP server, you will not need to change the DHCP setting on any other computers that are pointing to the DHCP server.

> **Tip**   Consider configuring conflict detection to prevent conflicts among clients when migrating your scopes to a new computer. However, because server-side conflict detection uses Address Resolution Protocol (ARP) and Internet Control Message Protocol (ICMP) messages to detect conflicts, Internet Connection Firewall (ICF) or other firewalls that are installed on clients on your network might interfere with conflict detection.

Integrating DHCP with Other Services

DHCP interoperates with other services in Windows Server 2003. When planning to upgrade or migrate your DHCP service to Windows Server 2003, you need to take into account how DHCP interacts with other services that might be running on your network. The following sections describe some of these interactions, as well as any steps you need to take to ensure smooth integration following a migration.

Configuring Dynamic Update and Secure Dynamic Update

Windows Server 2003 DHCP supports both DNS dynamic updates and secure DNS dynamic updates. DHCP and DNS work together to perform dynamic updates and work with Active Directory to perform secure DNS dynamic updates. DNS dynamic updates and secure DNS dynamic updates eliminate the need for administrators to update DNS records manually when a client's IP address changes.

Clients running Windows 2000, Windows XP, or Windows Server 2003 can also perform dynamic updates. Clients running versions of Windows earlier than Windows 2000 do not support DNS dynamic update. For these clients, the DHCP server can be configured to update both the PTR and the A resource records.

By itself, dynamic update is not secure; any client can modify DNS records. When secure dynamic update is configured, the authoritative name server accepts updates only from clients and servers that are authorized to make dynamic updates to the appropriate objects in Active Directory. Secure dynamic update is available only on Active Directory–integrated zones.

Secure dynamic update protects zones and resource records from being modified by unauthorized users by enabling you to specify the users and groups that can modify zones and resource records. By default, Windows Server 2003, Windows XP Professional, and Windows 2000 clients attempt unsecured dynamic updates first. If that request fails, they attempt secure updates.

Use the DHCP snap-in to enable dynamic update on behalf of clients.

To configure dynamic update

1. In the DHCP snap-in, right-click the DHCP server you want to configure, and then click **Properties**.

2. In the *server_name* **Properties** dialog box, click the **DNS** tab.

3. On the **DNS** tab, click to select the **Enable DNS dynamic updates according to the settings below** check box.

4. On the **DNS** tab, select the dynamic update method you want: either always updating DNS A and PTR, or only updating the records when requested by the DHCP client.

5. Click to select the **Dynamically update DNS A and PTR records for DHCP clients that do not request updates (for example, clients running Windows NT 4.0** check box, if applicable.

Use the DNS snap-in to enable secure dynamic update by the DHCP server on behalf of the clients.

To configure secure dynamic update

1. In the DNS snap-in, select and right-click the applicable zone, and then click **Properties**.

2. On the **General** tab, verify that the zone type is either **Primary** or **Active Directory–integrated**. To allow secure dynamic updates only, verify that the zone type is **Active Directory–integrated**.

3. To allow dynamic updates and secure dynamic updates, in **Dynamic Updates**, click **Nonsecure and secure**.

4. To allow secure dynamic updates only, in **Dynamic Updates**, click **secure only**.

When using multiple DHCP servers and secure dynamic updates, add each of the DHCP servers as members of the domain global DnsUpdateProxy security group so that any DHCP server can perform a secure dynamic update for any record. Otherwise, when a DHCP server performs a secure dynamic update for a record, the DHCP server that originally created the record is the only computer that can update the record.

Authorizing DHCP Servers in Active Directory

DHCP also works with Active Directory to prevent unauthorized DHCP servers from running on the network. Windows Server 2003-based DHCP servers that are part of an Active Directory domain will not lease IP addresses unless they are authorized in Active Directory. Because of this, you will need to authorize your DHCP servers in Active Directory immediately after upgrading to Active Directory and upgrading or migrating your DHCP servers.

An unauthorized DHCP server on a network can cause a variety of problems, such as the leasing of incorrect IP addresses and options. To protect against this type of problem, when a Windows Server 2003 domain member DHCP server attempts to start on the network, it first queries Active Directory. The DHCP server compares its IP address and server name to the list of authorized DHCP servers. If either the server name or IP address is found on the list of authorized DHCP servers, the server is authorized as a DHCP server. If no match is found, the server is not authorized in Active Directory and does not respond to DHCP traffic. The process of authorizing DHCP servers is useful for only Windows 2000–based or Windows Server 2003–based DHCP servers. This process cannot be used for DHCP servers running Windows NT Server, or servers running non-Windows-based DHCP services. Only a member of the Enterprise Admins group can authorize or unauthorize a DHCP server in Active Directory.

> **Important**   You must be an enterprise administrator to authorize a DHCP server.

To authorize a DHCP server in Active Directory

1. In the DHCP snap-in, right-click **DHCP**.

2. Click **Manage authorized servers**.

3. In the **Manage Authorized Servers** dialog box, click **Authorize**.

4. In the **Authorize DHCP Server** dialog box, type the name or IP address of the DHCP server, and then click **OK**.

Detection of unauthorized DHCP servers requires the deployment of Active Directory and the DHCP service running on Windows 2000 or Windows Server 2003. Other DHCP servers do not attempt to determine whether they are authorized by Active Directory before offering IP address leases.

Additional Resources

These resources contain additional information and tools related to this chapter.

Related Information

- "Deploying WINS" in *Deploying Network Services* of the *Microsoft® Windows Server® 2003 Deployment Kit* (or see "Deploying WINS" on the Web at http://www.microsoft.com/reskit).

- "Deploying DHCP" in *Deploying Network Services* of the *Microsoft® Windows Server® 2003 Deployment Kit* (or see "Deploying DHCP" on the Web at http://www.microsoft.com/reskit).

- The *Networking Guide* of the *Microsoft® Windows Server™ 2003 Resource Kit* (or see "Networking Guide" on the Web at http://www.microsoft.com/reskit) for more technical reference information about WINS and DHCP.

- "Dynamic Host Configuration Protocol" in the *TCP/IP Core Networking Guide* of the *Microsoft® Windows® 2000 Server Resource Kit* (or see "Dynamic Host Configuration Protocol" on the Web at http://www.microsoft.com/reskit).

- RFC 1542: *Clarifications and Extensions for the Bootstrap Protocol.*

- RFC 2131: *Dynamic Host Configuration Protocol.*

- RFC 2132: *DHCP Options and BOOTP Vendor Extensions.*

- RFC 1001: *Protocol Standard for a NetBIOS Service on a TCP/UDP Transport: Concepts and Methods.*

- Article 193887, "Replacing a Local WINS Database from a Replica Server" in the Microsoft Knowledge Base for information about moving a WINS database by using replication partners. To find this article, see the Microsoft Knowledge Base link on the Web Resources page at http://www.microsoft.com/windows/reskits/webresources.

Related Tools

- DHCPExim tool

    For more information about DHCPExim, see the Resource Kit Tools link on the Web Resources page at http://www.microsoft.com/windows/reskits/webresources.

- Netsh

    For more information about Netsh, in Help and Support Center for Windows Server 2003, click **Tools**, and then click **Command-line reference A-Z**.

Related Help Topics

For best results in identifying Help topics by title, in Help and Support Center, under the **Search** box, click **Set search options**. Under **Help Topics**, click to select the **Search in title only** check box.

- "Checklist: Installing a DHCP Server" in Help and Support Center for Windows Server 2003.

- "Checklist: Installing a WINS Server" in Help and Support Center for Windows Server 2003.

- "Configure the DHCP Relay Agent" in Help and Support Center for Windows Server 2003.

- "Netsh," "Netsh Commands for WINS," and "Netsh Commands for DHCP" in Help and Support Center for Windows Server 2003.

- "New Features for WINS" in Help and Support Center for Windows Server 2003.

- "New Features for DHCP" in Help and Support Center for Windows Server 2003.

4

Migrating File and Print Servers to Windows Server 2003

The Microsoft® Windows Server™ 2003 operating system includes significant advancements in file and print server capabilities. Migrating Microsoft® Windows NT® version 4.0 file and print servers to Windows Server 2003 increases reliability, availability, ease of use, and ease of management. New Windows Server 2003 features such as shadow copies of shared folders and disk quotas make it easier to set up, access, and manage a file infrastructure on Windows Server 2003. Print servers are also easier to manage with features such as the ability to manage the print sub-system by using Visual Basic scripts to perform routine print administration tasks.

To successfully migrate your file and print servers you need to examine your server requirements, decide which Windows Server 2003 features to implement, and plan how to efficiently migrate your files and printer configurations.

Overview of Windows Server 2003 File and Print Servers

Information worker productivity begins with data. Protecting information and making it more accessible to users is the most important job for IT departments. Windows Server 2003 optimizes your storage investment by providing intelligent storage and print services to help you manage and share files across your enterprise. It protects end-user data, simplifies complexity, and provides a scalable storage architecture.

Migrating your print servers to new servers running the Microsoft® Windows® Server 2003, Standard Edition or Windows Server 2003, Enterprise Edition operating systems lets your organization's IT staff manage printing resources more efficiently across the network. Windows Server 2003 provides a number of solutions that can benefit your organization.

Using data sharing and collaboration features can significantly improve the productivity of information workers. Windows Server 2003 enables Windows SharePoint Services to deliver enhanced file sharing services for collaborative work processes. Windows SharePoint Services sites provide communities for team collaboration and let users share and collaborate on documents, tasks, contacts, events, and other information. Using Windows SharePoint Services, team and site managers can easily manage site content and user activity. The environment is designed for simple and flexible deployment, administration, and application development.

New file and print server features in Windows Server 2003 that improve performance and ease administration are described in the following sections.

File Server Improvements

The following sections identify some of the new file server features that Windows Server 2003 offers to help reduce support costs and administrative overhead.

Shadow copies of shared folders Users who accidentally delete or overwrite files can recover the files themselves by using shadow copies for shared folders — point-in-time copies of files in shared folders — instead of requesting administrators to restore the files from backup media.

Distributed File Services (DFS) If users need to access files on multiple file servers without having to keep track of all the server names, you can use DFS to logically group physical shared folders located on different servers by transparently connecting them to one or more hierarchical namespaces. DFS also provides fault-tolerance and load-sharing capabilities.

Virtual Disk Services (VDS)   To more easily manage disks and administer storage hardware, VDS implements a single uniform interface. VDS offers a robust set of solutions that provides flexibility for making long-term investment decisions regarding SANs, NAS, and other storage options.

Effective NTFS permissions   To prevent unauthorized users from accessing folders, you can use NTFS file system permissions to specify and check the groups and users whose access you want to restrict or allow and the type of access you want to manage.

For more information about these file server features, see *Planning Server Deployments* of the *Microsoft® Windows Server™ 2003 Deployment Kit* (or see "Planning Server Deployments" on the Web at http://www.microsoft.com/reskit).

Print Server Improvements

The following sections identify some of the print sub-system features that Windows Server 2003 offers to help reduce support costs and administrative overhead.

Cross-platform printing support   Windows Server 2003 supports printing from Microsoft® Windows® 95, Windows® 98, Windows® Millennium Edition, Windows NT 4.0, Windows® 2000, Windows® XP Professional, and UNIX or Linux operating systems.

Point and Print   Windows Server 2003 automatically installs printer drivers with no administrative overhead, reducing both management and complexity while enhance the end user experience.

Driver versioning   To improve stability, Windows Server 2003 restricts the installation of older printer drivers, which can cause the system to become unresponsive. You can override these restrictions if your network has clients that require older printer drivers.

Consolidation tools   If you have too many print servers to manage efficiently in your current printing environment, you can use the Print Migrator tool to help automate printer consolidation. Instead of manually recreating all of the printer objects, you can back up existing printers and restore them to your new print servers.

Rich printer status reporting   If you use the standard port monitor, you can receive status reports when the printer runs out of paper, runs low on toner, or is stopped by a paper jam.

Easy location of nearby printers   If you implement the Active Directory® directory service, your users can easily find printers that are published in Active Directory by searching for attributes that you designate, such as a color laser printer.

Improved security   You can use new local Group Policy settings to control which users have access to the print queue over the network.

Centralized printer management   You can remotely manage and configure printers from any computer running Windows Server 2003.

For more information about these print server features, see *Planning Server Deployments* of the *Microsoft® Windows Server™ 2003 Deployment Kit* (or "Planning Server Deployments" on the Web at http://www.microsoft.com/reskit).

Planning a File Server Migration

When you migrate files to a new server running Windows Server 2003, you need to plan for hardware and software compatibility and for meeting business goals, as well as planning the migration itself. It is highly recommended that you use the migration opportunity to create or update a standard file server configuration. This involves defining a specific server hardware and software combination that works well for your organization and requires minimal maintenance. A specific standard file server configuration varies from business to business, and the needs of your organization might dictate more than one standard configuration.

Planning and carrying out a file server migration involves the following tasks:

1.   Determine whether to create or update a standard file server configuration.

2.   Select to deploy either general purpose or Windows Powered Network Attached Storage servers.

3.   Determine the amount of RAM and CPU performance you require.

4.   Determine your storage requirements.

5.   Plan for securing data stored on your servers.

6.   Plan and carry out the migration of data to new Windows Server 2003–based servers.

These tasks are described in the following sections.

Using a Standard File Server Configuration

To maximize the reliability, availability, and performance of file servers, use one or more standard hardware and software configurations for file servers in your organization. Using a standard configuration for file servers provides a number of benefits:

- You experience less complexity managing and maintaining the hardware. Instead of learning to perform hardware tasks on multiple types of file servers, you need only learn the task once.

- You reduce the amount of testing that must be done when updating drivers or applications on the file server. Instead of testing the fixes on multiple hardware configurations, you can test the updates on one file server and then deploy the updates to the other file servers.

- You can keep fewer spares on-site. For example, if you use the same type of hard disks in all file servers, you need fewer spare disks, reducing the cost and complexity of providing spares.

If your organization already has a standard file server configuration, make sure that it is supported on Windows Server 2003. To determine if your standard file server configuration is supported on Windows Server 2003, or to plan for updating your configuration or creating a new one, carry out the remaining tasks described in the following sections.

Choosing the File Server Type

Two types of servers run Windows Server 2003: general-purpose servers and Windows Powered Network Attached Storage.

General-purpose servers   A general-purpose server can function in a number of roles, including domain controller, print server, Windows Internet Name Service (WINS) server, Dynamic Host Configuration Protocol (DHCP) server, application server, or an e-mail or database server. General-purpose servers provide administrators with the flexibility to configure server software and hardware as they choose. Administrators perform the necessary configuration and optimization that the server requires to perform its role.

Windows Powered Network Attached Storage   Windows Powered Network Attached Storage solutions are dedicated file servers running Windows 2000 Server or Windows Server 2003. With built-in support for UNIX and Apple file protocols, Windows Powered Network Attached Storage solutions offer seamless integration in a heterogeneous environment.

Table 4.1 describes the features and capabilities of each file server type.

Table 4.1   Features and Capabilities of File Server Types

Description	General-Purpose Server	Windows Powered Network Attached Storage
Comes preinstalled with Windows 2000 or Windows Server 2003.	X[*]	X
Offers the file system, security, reliability, and scalability features of Windows 2000 or Windows Server 2003.	X	X
Can provide services for purposes other than file sharing, such as domain controller or print, WINS, or DHCP server.	X	
Can run applications, such as Microsoft® SQL Server 2000 or Exchange 2000 Server.	X	
Comes preconfigured with NFS, File Transfer Protocol (FTP), AppleTalk, HTTP, WebDAV, UNIX and NetWare protocol support.	X	X
Can be deployed in as little as 15 minutes.		X
Can run Windows SharePoint Services	X	

[*] Some general-purpose servers come preinstalled with the appropriate operating system; however, other general-purpose servers require you to configure the volumes and install the operating system

Some hardware vendors offer Windows Powered Network Attached Storage solutions in a cluster configuration. If your organization requires highly available servers, consult your hardware vendor for more information.

Determining RAM and CPU Specifications

As hardware continues to improve, hardware vendors frequently change the RAM and CPU configurations in the servers they offer. Use the information about performance improvements and scaling factors in the sections that follow to choose the hardware that best meets your organization's needs.

Reviewing Windows Server 2003 CPU Specifications

Table 4.2 describes the recommended CPU speed and number of processors supported by Windows Server 2003.

Table 4.2   CPU Requirements for Windows Server 2003

Specification	Windows Server 2003, Standard Edition	Windows Server 2003, Enterprise Edition
Minimum recommended CPU speed	550 MHz	550 MHz
Number of CPUs supported	1–4	1–8

Reviewing Operating System Performance Improvements

Even if you plan to use existing hardware to run Windows Server 2003, you can benefit from performance enhancements available in Windows Server 2003, as well as client and server protocol improvements available when using clients running Windows XP Professional.

Table 4.3 describes performance improvements that can be gained by migrating to new operating systems on identical hardware.

Table 4.3   Operating System Performance Improvements on the Same Hardware

Current Server and Client Operating Systems	New Server and Client Operating Systems	Improvement Factor
Microsoft® Windows NT® Server 4.0 with Windows NT® Workstation 4.0 clients	Windows Server 2003 with Windows XP Professional clients	Up to 2.75X

These figures are based on the following assumptions:

- The server is uniprocessor (UP), 2P, 4P, or 8P.

- For each comparison, the server hardware is the same.

- No memory, disk, or network bottlenecks prevent the processor from performing at full capacity.

Determining RAM Specifications

Using adequate RAM in file servers ensures that Windows Server 2003 can temporarily cache (store) files in memory, reducing the need to retrieve files from disk. Table 4.4 describes the minimum recommended RAM and maximum RAM for Windows Server 2003.

> **Tip**   Increasing the amount of RAM significantly reduces the time required to run Chkdsk.

Table 4.4   Minimum and Maximum RAM for Windows Server 2003

RAM Specification	Windows Server 2003, Standard Edition	Windows Server 2003, Enterprise Edition
Minimum recommended RAM	256 megabytes (MB)	256 MB
Maximum RAM	4 gigabytes (GB)	32 GB

Determining Storage Specifications

It is important to make sure that file servers have adequate, fault-tolerant storage. When determining storage specifications, perform the following tasks:

1.   Estimate the amount of data to be stored.

2.   Plan the amount of storage for each server configuration.

3.   Determine the maximum volume size.

4.   Plan the layout and redundant array of independent disks (RAID) level of volumes.

The following sections describe each of these steps.

Estimating the Amount of Data to Be Stored

When you estimate the amount of data to be stored on a new file server, include the following information:

■   The amount of data currently stored on any file servers that will be migrated onto the new file server.

■   The amount of replicated data that will be stored on the new file server, if the file server will be a replica member.

■   The amount of data that you will need to store on the file server in the future.

A general guideline is to plan for faster growth than you experienced in the past. Investigate whether your organization plans to hire a large number of people and whether any groups in your organization are planning large projects that require extra storage.

You must also take into account the amount of space used by operating system files, applications, RAID redundancy, log files, and other factors. Table 4.5 describes some factors that affect file server capacity.

Table 4.5 Factors That Affect File Server Capacity

Factor	Storage Capacity Required
Operating system files	At least 1.5 GB. To allow space for optional components, future service packs, and other items, allow an additional 3 GB to 5 GB for the operating system volume.
Paging file	1.5 times the amount of RAM, by default.
Memory dump	Depending on the memory dump file option that you choose, the amount of disk space required can be as large as the amount of physical memory, plus 1 MB.
Applications	Varies according to the program, which can include antivirus, backup, and disk quota software; database applications; and optional components, such as Recovery Console, Windows Services for UNIX, and Windows Services for NetWare.
Log files	Varies according to the program that creates the log file. Some applications allow you to configure a maximum log file size. You must make sure that you have adequate free space to store the log files.
RAID solution	Varies. For more information about the RAID solutions, see "Planning the Layout and RAID Level of Volumes" later in this chapter.
Shadow copies	Ten percent of the volume by default, although increasing this size is recommended. For more information about shadow copies, see "Designing and Deploying File Servers" in *Planning Server Deployments* of the *Microsoft Windows Server 2003 Deployment Kit* (or see "Designing and Deploying File Servers" on the Web at http://www.microsoft.com/reskit/).

Planning Storage for Each Server Configuration

The amount of disk space that is supported by a file server can be in the ter-abytes if the server is connected to high-capacity, direct-attached storage arrays or storage area network (SAN)–connected external storage arrays. However, your goal should not be to attach as much storage as possible to a file server. Instead, plan the amount of storage on a file server by examining your current backup solution and answering the following questions:

- How quickly do you need to restore data? In other words, do you need to be able to restore data and get the file server up and running within eight hours? Twenty-four hours? Verify that you can restore data within the required time.

- How much data can your backup solution contain? Your backup solution should have the capacity to back up the entire file server.

- How much time do you have to complete your backup? You must be able to perform a full backup within a period of time that is accept-able to your organization and users. For organizations that use hard-ware-based snapshots and backup software that can back up open files, the backup window might not be an issue.

If your organization provides file services to groups who have different storage requirements, you can design file server configurations with different amounts of storage. For example, a low-end file server might have 100 GB of storage, but a high-end file server might have 400 GB of storage. Because the high-end server will typically support more users, make sure that the RAM and CPU configuration is more robust than for the low-end server.

> **Important**   If you choose file server hardware that supports future storage expansion, answer the previous questions taking the addi-tional storage into account. In other words, if you add more storage to an existing file server but cannot back up or restore the file server in the required time, you must deploy additional file servers or acquire a backup solution that can handle the extra storage.

Backup solutions are becoming faster and more sophisticated. If your cur-rent backup solution is not meeting your organization's needs, investigate new solutions, such as those that provide the following types of benefits:

■   Many backup programs, including the backup program that is available in Windows Server 2003, can back up files that are open, allowing administrators to back up a server without having to disconnect users or shut down processes that might have files open.

■   Some backup programs offer software-based snapshots that take point-in-time images of a volume, creating virtual replicas without physically copying the data. Servers running Windows Server 2003 provide a similar feature, known as *shadow copies*. For more information about shadow copies, see "Designing and Deploying File Servers" in *Planning Server Deployments* of the *Microsoft Windows Server 2003 Deployment Kit* (or see "Designing and Deploying File Servers" on the Web at http://www.microsoft.com/reskit/).

Determining Maximum Volume Size

Volume sizes often vary, but it is important to set a maximum volume size. NTFS supports volumes up to 256 terabytes minus 64 kilobytes (KB) (2^{32} clusters minus 1 cluster), but it is recommended that you take the following factors into account when you determine the size of volumes in your file servers.

Backup and restoration times   Sizing your volumes to be the same size or smaller than your backup solution's capacity is a good guideline but not an absolute rule. For example, some organizations might back up files on a per-folder basis rather than on a per-volume basis. In this case, the organization would make sure that the size of each folder is smaller than the backup solution. This method, however, requires more backups — one for every folder. In the event that you must restore the data, this method also requires more restorations to restore all the folders on the volume, increasing the overall complexity and length of the process. Because emergency restorations are often done in a hurry and under pressure, let restoration time and simplicity be your guide for sizing volumes.

Chkdsk times   Although file system errors are rare on NTFS volumes, you need to consider the time required to run Chkdsk to repair any errors that occur. Chkdsk times are determined by the number of files on the volume and by the number of files in the largest folder. Chkdsk performance has improved significantly since Windows NT 4.0 and Windows 2000. As a result, downtime due to Chkdsk should be minimal. However, it is important to avoid having volumes that contain so many files that Chkdsk requires longer to complete than the amount of downtime your users can tolerate.

To determine how long Chkdsk takes to complete, run Chkdsk on a test server with a similar number of files as those stored on a typical file server volume. Based on these results, you can limit the number of files to be stored on a volume so that Chkdsk can complete within the acceptable time limit.

Note   Windows Server 2003 provides some Chkdsk parameters that shorten the time required to run Chkdsk. However, if the volume contains file system errors, you must consider the volume at risk until you are able to run a full Chkdsk. For more information about running Chkdsk, see "Chkdsk" in Help and Support Center for Windows Server 2003.

If you need to store a large number of files on a file server and are concerned about Chkdsk times, you can distribute the files on separate volumes on the file server. If, however, you need those files to appear as though they are on a single volume, you can use mounted drives. When you create a mounted drive, you mount one local volume at any empty folder on another local NTFS volume. For example, you can create a folder called Data on volume E and then mount volume F to that folder. When you open the Data folder, the contents of volume F appear.

Mounted drives are also useful when you want to add more storage to an existing volume without having to extend the volume. For more information about mounted drives, see "Using NTFS mounted drives" in Help and Support Center for Windows Server 2003.

Planning the Layout and RAID Level of Volumes

When you design a standard hardware configuration, determine what type of data you plan to store on the file server, the RAID type and level that is appropriate for each data type, and how you plan to divide the disk space into volumes.

Evaluating Data Types   Table 4.6 describes the types of data that are typically stored on file servers and the disk I/O characteristics of the data. Knowing the I/O characteristics can help you choose the RAID level that offers the best performance for that particular type of I/O. If you have other types of data stored on the file server, be sure to estimate their I/O characteristics as well.

Table 4.6   Data Types and Their Characteristics

Data Type	Description	Disk I/O Characteristics
Operating system	The operating system, drivers, and any applications installed on the server, such as antivirus, backup, or disk quota software.	Server startup consists mostly of large reads, because the data required for startup is optimized on the disk. After startup completes, the disk I/O is mostly small reads.
Paging space	Space used by the paging file.	If the server memory is sized correctly, the disk I/O consists of small reads and writes. If the server experiences heavy reads and writes, the server needs more memory.
User and shared data	Documents, spreadsheets, graphics, and other data created by users and stored on the file server.	For user and shared data, disk I/O must be measured on a workload-by-workload basis.
Application files	Software that users install or run from the network.	For application files, disk I/O must be measured on a workload-by-workload basis.
Log files	Files used by database, communications, or transaction applications to store a history of operations (for example, the FRS log file).	Small or large writes, depending on the application.

Choosing Between Hardware and Software RAID   Many computer manufacturers provide server-class computers that support hardware-based RAID. With hardware RAID, you use the configuration utility that is provided by the hardware manufacturer to group one or more physical disks into what appears to the operating system as a single disk, sometimes called a *virtual disk* or *logical unit (LUN)* . When you create the virtual disk, you also select a RAID level. Hardware RAID typically provides a choice of RAID-0 (striped), RAID-1 (mirrored), RAID-5 (striped with parity), and in some servers, RAID-0+1 (mirrored stripe). After creating these virtual disks, you use the Disk Management snap-in or the command-line tool DiskPart.exe in Windows Server 2003 to create one or more volumes on each virtual disk.

If your server hardware does not have built-in hardware RAID support, you can use the software RAID provided in Windows Server 2003 to create RAID-0 volumes, RAID-1 volumes, and RAID-5 volumes on dynamic disks. Although software RAID has lower performance than hardware RAID, software

RAID is inexpensive and easy to configure because it has no special hardware requirements other than multiple disks. If cost is more important than performance, software RAID is appropriate. If you plan to use software RAID for write-heavy workloads, use RAID-1, not RAID-5.

> **Note**   Before you can use the software RAID in Windows Server 2003, you must convert basic disks to dynamic disks. In addition, dynamic disks are not supported on cluster storage. For more information about basic disks, dynamic disks, software RAID, and disk management, see the *Server Management Guide* of the *Microsoft® Windows Server™ 2003 Resource Kit* (or see the "Server Management Guide" on the Web at http://www.microsoft.com/reskit).

Choosing the RAID Level   Choosing the RAID level involves a trade-off among the following factors:

- Cost
- Performance
- Availability
- Reliability

You can determine the best RAID level for your file servers by evaluating the read and write loads of the various data types and then deciding how much you are willing to spend to get the performance, reliability, and availability that your organization requires. Table 4.7 describes four common RAID levels; their relative costs, performance, and availability; and their recommended uses. The performance descriptions in Table 4.7 compare RAID performance to the performance of *just a bunch of disks (JBOD)* — a term used to describe an array of disks that is not configured using RAID.

Table 4.7   Comparing RAID Levels

Factors	RAID-0	RAID-1	RAID-5	RAID-0+1
Minimum number of disks	2	2	3	4
Usable storage capacity	100 percent	50 percent	(N-1)/N disks, where N is the number of disks	50 percent

Table 4.7   Comparing RAID Levels

Factors	RAID-0	RAID-1	RAID-5	RAID-0+1
Fault tolerance	None. Losing a single disk causes all data on the volume to be lost.	Can lose multiple disks as long as a mirrored pair is not lost.	Can tolerate the loss of one disk.	Can lose multiple disks as long as a mirrored pair is not lost.
Read performance	Generally improved by increasing concurrency.	Up to twice as good as JBOD (assuming twice the number of disks).	Generally improved by increasing concurrency.	Improved by increasing concurrency and by having multiple sources for each request.
Write performance	Generally improved by increasing concurrency.	Between 20 percent and 40 percent worse than JBOD for most workloads.	Worse unless using full-stripe writes (large requests). Can be as low as 25 percent of JBOD.	Can be worse or better depending on request size.
Best use	■ Temporary data only	■ Operating system ■ Log files	■ Operating system ■ User and shared data[*] ■ Application files[†]	■ Operating system ■ User and shared data ■ Application files ■ Log files

* Place user and shared data on RAID-5 volumes only if cost is the overriding factor.

† Place application files on RAID-5 volumes only if cost is the overriding factor.

When determining the number of disks to compose a virtual disk, keep in mind the following factors:

■ Performance increases as you add disks.

■ Mean time between failure (MTBF) decreases as you add disks to RAID-5 or RAID-0 arrays.

■ RAID-0+1 almost always offers better performance than RAID-1 when you use more than two disks.

■ Usable storage capacity increases as you add disks, but so does cost.

Using Dynamic Disks with Hardware RAID   Using dynamic disks with hardware RAID can be useful in the following situations:

■   You want to extend a volume, but the underlying hardware cannot dynamically increase the size of LUNs.

■   You want to extend a volume, but the hardware has reached its maximum LUN size.

Before converting hardware RAID disks to dynamic disks, review the following restrictions:

■   If you plan to use hardware snapshots of dynamic disks, you cannot import the snapshot again on the same server, although you can move the snapshot to other servers.

For more information about dynamic disks, see "Dynamic disks and volumes" in Help and Support Center for Windows Server 2003. For best practices on using dynamic disks, see article 329707, "Best Practices for Using Dynamic Disks on Windows 2000-Based Computers," in the Microsoft Knowledge Base. To find this article, see the Microsoft Knowledge Base link on the Web Resources page at http://www.microsoft.com/windows/reskits/webresources.

If a server contains multidisk volumes, review the following issues:

■   If you are upgrading from Windows NT Server 4.0 to Windows Server 2003, verify that your backup software and hardware are compatible with both Windows NT Server 4.0 and Windows Server 2003. Next, back up and then delete all multidisk volumes (volume sets, mirror sets, stripe sets, and stripe sets with parity) before you upgrade, because Windows Server 2003 cannot access these volumes. Be sure to verify that your backup was successful before deleting the volumes. After you finish upgrading to Windows Server 2003, create new dynamic volumes, and then restore the data.

■   If you are upgrading from Windows NT Server 4.0 to Windows Server 2003, and the paging file resides on a multidisk volume, you must use System in Control Panel to move the paging file to a primary partition or logical drive before beginning Setup.

■   If you are upgrading from Windows 2000 Server to Windows Server 2003, you must use Disk Management to convert all basic disks that contain multidisk volumes to dynamic disks before beginning Setup. If you do not do this, Setup does not continue.

Configuring the New File Server

This chapter assumes that you are configuring a new server running Windows Server 2003. Windows Server 2003 allows you to configure the server for single or multiple roles within your organization. One of the basic needs of any organization is the need for file servers. File servers provide a central location for files to be stored and make it easier to backup user's files.

The best way to set up your new Windows Server 2003–based file server is to use the Configure Your Server Wizard and choose the **File Server** role from the list of choices. If you are going to combine file and print services on this server, also choose the **Print Server** role.

Planning File Server Security

Planning for file server security is vital for protecting your organization's sensitive or business-critical files. When planning for file server security, you need to protect not only the data but the physical server as well. In addition, if you plan to implement availability strategies, such as DFS or clustering, you need to take additional steps to secure the resources associated with these features.

Ensuring the Physical Security of Each File Server   For file servers that must maintain high availability, restrict physical access to only designated individuals. In addition, consider to what extent you need to restrict physical access to network hardware. The details of how you implement physical security depend on your physical facilities and your organization's structure and policies. You should also implement methods to restrict access to backup media and any instruction sheets that you create, such as the instructions that go in the recovery manual for a file server. If you allow unauthorized people to study documentation or configuration manuals, they can quickly cause harm to the system if they are able to obtain access.

Even if the physical server is in a secure room, the file server might still be accessible through remote administration tools. Therefore, implement methods for restricting access to remote administration of file servers, and ensure that remote administration tools do not weaken your organization's security model. For example, remote administration tools do not always use strong authentication protocols, such as Kerberos V5, to authenticate users across the network. You might be able to implement weaker protocols, such as NTLM, depending on the remote management tool you use and the operating system that is running on the host you are administering. In addition, certain remote administration tools might transmit unencrypted data (plaintext) across the network. This makes your data vulnerable to network sniffers.

For more information about security and remote administration, see the *Server Management Guide* of the *Microsoft Windows Server 2003 Resource Kit* (or see the "Server Management Guide" on the Web at http://www.microsoft.com/reskit).

Planning Baseline Security   The Windows 2000 Server Baseline Security Checklist provides instructions for configuring a baseline level of security on servers running Windows Server 2003. The checklist contains tasks such as using NTFS, using strong passwords, disabling unnecessary services, disabling unnecessary accounts, and more. For more information about the baseline security checklist, see the Windows 2000 Server Baseline Security Checklist link on the Web Resources page at http://www.microsoft.com/windows/reskits/webresources.

Run the Microsoft Baseline Security Analyzer (Mbsa.exe for the graphical user interface version; Mbsacli.exe for the command-line version). For more information about the Microsoft Baseline Security Analyzer, see the MBSA link on the Web Resources page at http://www.microsoft.com/windows/reskits/webresources.

To further enhance security, review the Microsoft Windows Update Web site regularly for patches that fix vulnerabilities and provide security enhancements. For more information about Windows Update, see the Windows Update link on the Web Resources page at http://www.microsoft.com/windows/reskits/webresources.

Planning Virus Protection for File Servers   To protect file servers from viruses, plan to take the following precautions:

- Use Windows Server 2003–compatible antivirus software, and regularly update virus signature files.

- Back up files regularly so that damage is minimized if a virus attack does occur.

Planning Access to Shared Folders   When you plan access to shared folders, determine the type of permissions to use, who needs access to the folders, and the level of access that users require. You can also disable administrative shares and hide shared folders.

Determining the Type of Permissions to Use   Permissions define the type of access granted to a user or group for a file or folder. Windows Server 2003 offers two types of permissions:

- NTFS permissions restrict local and remote access to files and folders on NTFS volumes. When you create a new folder, it inherits permissions from its parent folder. When you create a file in a folder, the file inherits permissions from the parent folder.

■ Share permissions restrict remote access to shared folders, but share permissions do not restrict access to users who log on to the server locally. Share permissions are available on both file allocation table (FAT) and NTFS volumes.

To simplify administering and troubleshooting permissions, use NTFS permissions to control user and group access to file system resources.

Although NTFS is recommended as the primary method for securing folders, you must keep in mind that default share permissions are assigned when you share a folder, and the default share permissions have changed for Windows Server 2003. Windows 2000 and Windows XP grant the Everyone group the Full Control share permission, but Windows Server 2003 grants the Everyone group the Read share permission. This change increases the security of shared folders and helps prevent the spread of viruses.

Because the more restrictive permissions always apply when you use a combination of share and NTFS permissions, you might need to change the default share permissions if you want users to be able to add or change files in the folder. If you do not change the default share permissions, users will have the Read share permission even if you grant users NTFS permissions such as Write or Modify.

Determining Who Needs Access to the Folders   To increase security and prevent users from browsing through shared folders that are not relevant to their jobs, assign permissions only to groups that require access to the shared folders.

To reduce administrative overhead when assigning permissions, do the following:

■ Assign permissions to groups rather than to users.

■ Place users in global groups or universal groups, nest these groups within domain local groups, and then assign the domain local groups permissions to the folder.

You do not need to deny permissions for specific groups. When permission to perform an operation is not explicitly granted, it is implicitly denied. For example, if you allow the Marketing group, and only the Marketing group, permission to access a shared folder, users who are not members of the Marketing group are implicitly denied access. The operating system does not allow users who are not members of the Marketing group to access the folder.

Deny access to folders only in the following scenarios:

■ You want to exclude a subset of a group (for example, an individual user) that has permissions.

■ You want to exclude one or more special permissions when you have already granted Full Control to a user or group.

Determining the Level of Access That Users Require   Assign the most restrictive permissions that still allow users to perform required tasks. The following descriptions explain the permissions that are associated with folders on NTFS volumes.

■ **Write**. Users can copy or paste new files and subfolders in the folder and change folder attributes. However, users cannot open or browse the folder unless you grant the Read permission. Assigning Write permission is useful for folders where users can file confidential reports, such as timesheets, that only the manager or shared folder administrator can read.

■ **Read**. Users can see the names of files and subfolders in a folder and view folder attributes, ownership, and permissions. Users can open and view files, but they cannot change files or add new files. Assign the Read permission if users need only to read information in a folder and they do not need to delete, create, or change files.

■ **List Folder Contents**. Users can see the names of files and subfolders in the folder. However, users cannot open files to view their contents.

■ **Read & Execute**. Users have the same rights as those assigned through the Read permission, as well as the ability to traverse folders. Traverse folders rights allow a user to reach files and folders located in subdirectories, even if the user does not have permission to access portions of the directory path.

■ **Modify**. Users can delete the folder and perform the actions permitted by the Write and Read & Execute permissions. Because Modify gives users the ability to delete the folder, use Modify permission only for administrators or for the group or department owner of the folder.

■ **Full Control**. Users can change permissions, take ownership, delete subfolders and files, and perform the actions granted by all other permissions. Because Full Control gives users the ability to delete the folder, use Full Control permission only for administrators or for the group or department owner of the folder.

For more information about permissions and file servers, see "Permissions on a file server" in Help and Support Center for Windows Server 2003.

Determining Whether to Disable Administrative Shares   Windows Server 2003 creates shared folders, known as *administrative shares*, by default when you start a server or when you stop and then start the Server service. These folders are shared for administrative purposes, and they allow users and applications with the appropriate administrative rights to gain access to the system remotely. For example, some backup software applications use these shares to remotely connect to systems to back up data.

Administrative shares have default share permissions that restrict access to members of only a few security groups. Each share name is appended with a dollar sign ($), which hides the share from users who browse the server. One type of administrative share is the root folder of every volume (C$, D$, and so on).

You can disable these administrative shares temporarily or permanently. For more information about disabling administrative shares and an overview of remote administration, see the *Server Management Guide* of the *Microsoft Windows Server 2003 Resource Kit* (or see the "Server Management Guide" on the Web at http://www.microsoft.com/reskit).

Determining Whether to Hide Shared Folders   You can hide a shared folder by appending a dollar sign ($) to the shared folder name. Hiding shared folders is useful when you want to make a shared folder available over the network while keeping it hidden from people browsing on the network.

Hiding shared folders does not necessarily make them more secure, because anyone who knows the name of the server and the shared folder can connect to it. Therefore, you must set the correct NTFS permissions on the shared folder so that access is granted only to the appropriate groups.

Migrating File Server Data

Once you have planned how to configure and secure your Windows Server 2003–based servers, you are ready to plan for the actual migration of existing applications and data to the new servers. To ensure the success of the migration, create a detailed and well-tested migration plan that does the following:

■ Minimizes the amount of time that data is unavailable to users

■ Minimizes the impact on network bandwidth

■ Minimizes the cost of the migration

■ Ensures that no data loss occurs during the migration

The following sections describe the tasks for creating a migration plan, performing the migration, and enabling Windows Server 2003 features following the migration.

Identifying Data to Migrate

Large organizations rarely have time to take all production data offline before migrating it. Instead, they typically move data gradually, migrating different classes of data in stages. A migration plan should identify which data to move, where to move it, and the order in which it should be moved. File server data can usually be classified in the following classes:

■   Business-critical data

■   Application data

■   Personal data (such as home directories)

■   Profiles or other configuration data

■   Departmental or group data

■   Other data types, such as special projects or temporary data

> **Important**   Be sure to review any legal or copyright issues that might arise when you migrate data. For example, if users are storing MP3 files on the file server, you might violate copyrights by copying those files. If you are copying applications, make sure that doing so does not violate any licensing agreements.

When creating your migration plan, determine whether you want to consolidate different classes of data at different rates, onto different hardware, onto servers with different SLAs, or to different locations. Also, consider the importance of the data when planning your migration. For example, to minimize the impact of any problems during the migration, you might choose to move non-essential data first, followed by business-critical data.

In addition to identifying which data to move, you can also identify data that you do not need to move, such as duplicate, obsolete, or non-business-related files. Eliminating these files from your migration plan decreases the number of files that you need to migrate and increases the amount of available storage on the target server after the migration.

Identifying Migration Risks

The next step is to assess the risks associated with data migration. The best way to identify these risks is to set up a test lab with clients and servers, similar to those in your production environment, and conduct trial migrations. In addition to testing your actual migration method, test any applications that are installed on client computers to determine if the applications are affected by the migration. For example, applications that depend on components stored on a particular file server might not work correctly if the file server or share is renamed after the migration is complete. If you identify problems, update your migration plan so that you prevent or mitigate those problems.

No migration plan is complete until you develop and test *back-out* procedures to follow if the migration fails at any stage in the process. Verify that you can restore data to its previous state and location in the event that you need to roll back the migration.

If you use domain local groups to assign permissions to files and folders, members of those groups will have the same access to the files and folders after they are moved to the new server. However, if you assign permissions to computer local groups, members of those groups cannot access the files after the migration. Either reconfigure permissions to use domain local groups before the migration, or plan to create new computer local groups on the target server and give those groups the appropriate permissions to the files after the migration is complete.

Migrating Your Data

In addition to identifying the data to migrate and planning to mitigate known migration risks, you need to plan to minimize the impact of the migration on the availability of data. To do that, you need to choose a migration method that is appropriate to the needs of your organization and the scope of your migration. Because many migration methods require downtime to move data, migrating data can be challenging in the following situations:

- The data has high uptime requirements as specified by service level agreements (SLAs) in your organization, and the migration method might require more downtime than the SLA allows.

- Users expect to be able to access the data throughout their workday or at all times.

The backup and restore migration method involves making a backup of the source server and restoring the data on a target server. Depending on your backup method and hardware, this method might involve moving tapes from one backup device to another (for direct-attached backup hardware) or restoring data from a tape library. There are both advantages and disadvantages to this migration method.

Advantages are:

■ Large organizations routinely back up and restore data, so you can use existing backups to begin the migration.

■ Backing up and restoring data does not impact network bandwidth when it is performed on the local servers.

Disadvantages are:

■ Both the source server and the target server must support the backup device and its related software.

■ If users are accessing files during the backup, you must make arrangements to migrate files that change while the backup occurs.

■ Backup programs do not migrate shared folder information to the destination server. As a result, folders that are shared on the source server are not shared when you restore them on the destination server. You must share the destination folders manually or by using scripts, and then use Permcopy.exe, which is available on the *Windows Server 2003 Deployment Kit* companion CD, to migrate any share permissions. The Permcopy.exe tool is included in Resource Kit Tools for Windows Server 2003, available on the *Microsoft Windows Server 2003 Deployment Kit* companion CD, or on the Web at http://www.microsoft.com/reskit.

To migrate share permissions for migrated folders, first download and install Permcopy.exe, then use the following procedure.

To migrate share permissions by using Permcopy.exe

1. Create identical file shares on the new Windows Server 2003 file server that matches your current Windows NT 4.0 file server structure.

2. Backup the Windows NT 4.0 file server shares and restore the data to the newly created file shares.

3. At the command prompt run Permcopy.exe using the following syntax:

```
permcopy \\SourceServer SourceShare \\DestinationServer Destination-
Share
```

SourceServer and SourceShare are the server and share names on the source Windows NT 4.0 file server, and DestinationServer and DestinationShare are the names of the destination Windows Server 2003 file server.

4. Repeat step three for all file shares on the server.

> **Note**   PermCopy does not follow the Universal Naming Convention (UNC) standard, in which you specify the server name and share name together: *ServerName\ShareName*. Instead, PermCopy requires that you type a space character between the server name and the share name. If you do not type the space character, then PermCopy displays a syntax summary and does not copy share permissions.

Completing the Migration

After you migrate the data, verify that users can access it on the new servers by completing the following tasks:

- Verify that NTFS and share permissions are migrated correctly.

- If logon scripts map drives to the old file servers, update the scripts so that they point to the new file servers.

> **Tip**   You should check the Download Center on www.microsoft.com for tool and documentation updates to help with your migration.

Enabling New Windows Server 2003 File Server Features

After the migration is complete, you might want to enable some new Windows Server 2003 features that make managing your file servers easier. The following sections explain some of these features.

DFS   DFS can be deployed throughout your organization progressively. You do not need to deploy DFS all at once; you can choose to add as much or as little of your physical storage as you need to the DFS namespace, at a pace that works with your overall migration schedule.

A DFS namespace is a virtual view of shared folders on different servers. A DFS namespace consists of a single root and many links and targets. The namespace starts with a root that maps to one or more root targets. Below the root are links that map to their own targets.

Organizations of any size, with any number of file servers, can benefit from implementing DFS. DFS is especially beneficial for organizations in which any of the following conditions exist:

- The organization plans to deploy additional file servers or consolidate existing file servers.

■ The organization has data that is stored in multiple file servers.

■ The organization wants to replace physical servers or shared folders without affecting how users access the data.

■ Most users require access to multiple file servers.

■ Users experience delays when accessing file servers during peak usage periods.

■ Users require uninterrupted access to file servers.

For more information about DFS, see "Planning Server Deployments" in the *Microsoft Windows Server 2003 Deployment Kit*.

Shadow Copies for Shared Folders   Shadow copies are point-in-time copies of files that are located on shared resources, such as a file server. You can use shadow copies to recover files that were accidentally deleted or overwritten, as well as to compare different versions of files.

When you enable shadow copies on a volume, you can specify the maximum amount of volume space to be used for the shadow copies. The default limit is 10 percent of the source volume (the volume being copied). Increase the limit for volumes where users frequently change files. Also, setting the limit too small causes the oldest shadow copies to be deleted frequently, which defeats the purpose of shadow copies and which will likely frustrate users. In fact, if the amount of changes is greater than the amount of space allocated to storing shadow copies, no shadow copy is created. Therefore, carefully consider the amount of disk space that you want to set aside for shadow copies, while keeping in mind user expectations for how many versions they want to be available. Your users might expect only a single shadow copy to be available, or they might expect three days' or three weeks' worth of shadow copies. The more shadow copies the users expect, the more storage you need to allocate for storing them.

To enable Shadow Copies for Shared Folders

1. Open Computer Management.

2. In the console tree, right-click **Shared Folders**, select **All Tasks**, and then click **Configure Shadow Copies**.

3. Click the volume on which you want to enable Shadow Copies of Shared Folders, and then click **Enable**.

> **Note**   It is recommended that you select a separate volume on another disk where shadow copies are not enabled as the storage area for shadow copies. Using a separate volume provides better performance and reduces the possibility of high I/O loads that can cause shadow copies to be prematurely deleted.

To access shadow copies from previous versions of Windows, including Windows 2000 and Windows XP Professional, you can download and install the Shadow Copy Client. For more information and to download the Shadow Copy Client, see the Shadow Copy Client Download link on the Web Resources page at http://www.microsoft.com/windows/reskits/webresources.

> **Note**   The Previous Versions Client and the Shadow Copy Client provide the same functionality, but the Shadow Copy Client can be installed on multiple operating systems, such as Windows 2000 and Windows XP Professional, whereas the Previous Versions Client can only be installed on Windows XP Professional.

Although the shadow copy client installs correctly on computers running Windows 98, this configuration is not supported.

For more information about shadow copies for shared folders, see "Shadow Copies for Shared Folders overview" in Help and Support Center for Windows Server 2003.

Disk Quotas   When you enable disk quotas, you can set two values: the disk quota limit and the disk quota warning level. For example, you can set a user's disk quota limit to 500 MB, and the disk quota warning level to 450 MB. In this case, the user can store no more than 500 MB of files on the volume. If the user stores more than 450 MB of files on the volume, you can configure the disk quota system to log a system event.

To enable disk quotas

1. Open My Computer

2. Right-click the volume for which you want to assign default disk quota values, and then click **Properties**.

3.   In the **Properties** dialog box, click the **Quota** tab.

4.   On the **Quota** tab, click to select the **Enable quota management** check box, and then select the **Limit disk space to** option.

5.   Type numeric values for the disk space limit and warning levels, select the appropriate units from the drop-down lists, and then click **OK**.

Note   If the volume is not formatted with the NTFS file system, or if you are not a member of the Administrators group, the **Quota** tab does not appear in the **Properties** dialog box for the volume.

For more information about disk quotas, see "Disk quotas overview" in Help and Support Center for Windows Server 2003.

Planning a Print Server Deployment

When you deploy Windows Server 2003–based print servers, you should begin by examining your current, Windows NT 4.0–based printing environment. You can then plan whether to perform clean installations of Windows Server 2003 or upgrade existing servers, and whether to *migrate* existing print servers (move existing printers to new print servers) or *create* new ones (add printers to new print servers). You also need to plan for network connectivity and security for your print servers. Once you install Windows Server 2003 on your new print servers, you can implement your plans to complete your new printing infrastructure.

The easiest way to migrate print servers from Windows NT 4.0 is to perform a clean installation of Windows Server 2003 on a new server and then migrate print server settings, drivers, and queues to the new server. The new Print Migrator 3.1 tool can help you accomplish the migration with minimal disruption of your printing services.

Inventorying the Current Printing Environment

The first phase in migrating from a Windows NT 4.0 — based printing environment to a Windows Server 2003–based printing environment is gathering information about your current environment. Document the port types, printer names, share names, IP address, driver models and driver versions of each printer that you plan to migrate. This information helps you plan the details of the migration process and gives you a way to rebuild the print server if it fails.

To inventory your Windows NT 4.0 environment, you can use the PrnAdmin utility. (By contrast, you can inventory a Windows Server 2003–based printing environment by using supplied scripts written in the Microsoft®Visual Basic® Scripting Language.) PrnAdmin enumerates ports, drivers, printers, or forms on local or remote printers. The Visual Basic script for the PrnAdmin utility is named Prnmgr.vbs.

The PrnAdmin utility is included in Resource Kit Tools for Windows Server 2003, available on the *Microsoft Windows Server 2003 Deployment Kit* companion CD, or on the Web at http://www.microsoft.com/reskit. To install PrnAdmin, type the following command:

```
regsvr32 C:\Path\PrnAdmin.dll
```

PrnAdmin syntax   The command-line syntax for PrnAdmin is as follows:

```
cscript prnmgr.vbs [-adx[c]] [1] [-c server] [-b printer] [-m driver model]
[-p driver path] [-r port] [-f file]
```

PrnAdmin example   The following example command lists all printers on the print server \\adminserver:

```
cscript prnmgr.vbs -1 -c \\adminserver
```

Choosing the Print Server Installation Method

Print server installation includes installing or upgrading to the Windows Server 2003 operating system on the print server and creating or migrating printers. The type of installation that you choose depends on your existing printing environment. For new servers with no operating system installed, you must perform a clean installation of the Windows Server 2003 operating system. If you have existing servers, you can perform a clean installation or, if the server is running Windows 2000 or Windows NT 4.0, you can upgrade.

Certain third-party kernel-mode printer drivers might cause the system to stop responding. Windows Server 2003 gives you the ability to control the installation of printer drivers. By default, all editions of Windows Server 2003 block the installation of kernel-mode drivers, but you can allow their installation by disabling the **Disallow installation of printers using Kernel Mode drivers** Group Policy setting. This setting only affects the installation of new kernel-mode drivers. If you are upgrading your system, existing kernel-mode drivers remain unaffected. If you choose to migrate your existing printers from a server running Windows NT 4.0, to a new server running Windows Server 2003, you should disable this policy before restoring the printer configurations.

Other considerations might also play a part in your decision. For example, some organizations have software standards that prohibit upgrading the operating system on servers. These organizations choose to perform only clean installations. With a clean installation, you can install the latest printer drivers from the independent hardware vendor (IHV), thus eliminating older, potentially problematic drivers.

Consider the following points when choosing between a clean installation and an upgrade.

Choosing to Upgrade

■   Configuration is simpler when you upgrade. You retain your existing print queues, drivers, and ports, minimizing the impact on users.

■   When you upgrade, however, you might encounter interoperability issues with your existing printer drivers.

Choosing a Clean Installation

■   In a clean installation, you must create all new printers or migrate existing printers.

■   If you want to practice good print queue management (for example, by bringing a non-complying environment into conformance with the company's print queue naming conventions), you might want to perform a clean installation instead of upgrading a server.

If you decide that a clean installation of Windows Server 2003 is best for your organization, you must also decide if moving some of your existing printers from other print servers makes sense. If you intend to add new print servers to your existing environment, consider migrating some of your existing print servers to these new, typically more powerful servers to take full advantage of your improved hardware resources.

Automated Print Server Migration with Print Migrator

Microsoft has developed a printer migration utility called Print Migrator that can back up and restore print server configurations with minimal user intervention. Print Migrator handles the migration of print queues, drivers, and printer ports. You can also use Print Migrator to consolidate print servers.

Print Migrator does not change printer driver versions when moving printers. For example, Print Migrator copies any Version 2 drivers used on a Windows NT 4.0 print server and recreates them on a new Windows Server 2003 print server. Using this process (instead of installing the printers with newer drivers) provides a much higher level of interoperability with any Windows NT 4.0 clients that might still be using print services from that server. To download Print Migrator, see the Print Services link on the Web Resources page at http://www.microsoft.com/windows/reskits/webresources.

> **Note**   Print Migrator ships with documentation about its operation and use. Review the material carefully for more details about this tool's capabilities and limitations.

Version Support Across Operating Systems

Differences in the way that Version 3 and Version 2 drivers work present interoperability issues when you migrate printers across versions of the Windows operating system. Cross-version support in Print Migrator 3.1 ensures successful migration from Windows NT 4.0 to Windows 2000 or Windows Server 2003.

Determining the Print Server Network Connection Method

You also need to plan how to connect Windows Server 2003–based print servers to the network. You can choose one of the following three methods:

- Whenever possible, use the standard Transmission Control Protocol/Internet Protocol (TCP/IP) port, which is also known as the *standard port*. The standard port is the preferred printer port in Windows Server 2003.

- For older devices that do not function correctly with the standard port, use the Line Printer Remote (LPR) port.

- To connect to printers over the Internet or an intranet, use the Internet Printing Protocol (IPP).

When creating printer ports, Windows Server 2003 installs the associated port monitor for that port type.

Connecting Through the Standard TCP/IP Port

The standard port is designed for Windows Server 2003–based print servers that use TCP/IP to communicate with printing devices, including network-ready printers, network adapters such as Hewlett-Packard JetDirect, and external print servers such as Intel NetPort. The standard port uses the standard TCP/IP port monitor (TCPMon.dll), also known as the *standard port monitor*. The standard port monitor can support many printers on one server. It is faster and easier to configure than the LPR Port Monitor (Lprmon), and it provides rich status information and error condition reporting that eases administration of your print servers.

The standard port monitor uses Simple Network Management Protocol (SNMP) and the standard printer message information base as defined in RFC 1759, "Printer MIB." As a result, the standard port monitor provides much more detailed status information than does LPR when, for example, the printer generates an error indicating a paper jam or low toner, or a print job is not responding and must be purged.

Although Windows Server 2003 requires TCP/IP on the print server to communicate with the printer, clients do not need TCP/IP. Because clients communicate with the print server rather than with the printer, they can do so using any common network protocol.

For example, a Novell NetWare client might use the Internetwork Packet Exchange (IPX) protocol to send documents to a Windows Server 2003 print server. The server then passes the document to the printer using the TCP/IP protocol. Status and error information is relayed from the printer to the print server using TCP/IP, and from the print server to the client using IPX.

Planning for Print Server Security

Planning for print server security is vital to protect your organization's resources. As with any production server, you need to protect the physical print server and safeguard access to data stored on the server. Consequently, your printing security plan must address three areas:

- Physical location
- Group Policy settings
- Printer permissions

Ensuring the Physical Security of Each Print Server

Locate your print servers in a physically secure location that only designated individuals can access. Allowing unauthorized access to your print servers risks harm to the system. In addition, consider to what extent you also need to restrict physical access to network hardware. The details of implementing these security measures depend on your physical facilities as well as your organization's structure and policies.

Securing the Print Environment

Windows Server 2003 adds new Group Policy settings that affect how clients connect to print servers on the network. Two of these policy settings are particularly useful for security.

Allow print spooler to accept client connections   This Group Policy setting, which is configured on the server, determines how clients access the print server over the network. If an individual with administrative credentials creates shared printers for use by managed clients, the spooler automatically allows connections upon creation of the first shared printer. To administer print services on a server running Windows Server 2003, log on to the server locally, or log on remotely through a Remote Desktop session.

Point and Print restrictions   This Group Policy setting, which is configured on client computers, determines the print servers to which the client can connect. To provide a higher level of security for managed workstations, this policy setting controls a client computer's ability to connect to and install a printer driver from specified print servers. By default, managed clients can use Point and Print only with servers that are within their forest. An administrator can use this policy to add additional servers to the list of trusted print servers. Alternatively, administrators can disable this policy to enable managed clients to connect to any accessible print server and install a printer driver from it.

Using Printer Permissions to Control Access to Shared Printers

Even if the physical server is in a secure room, the print server might still be accessible through remote administration tools. Therefore, you need to implement methods for restricting access to remote administration of print servers. You can restrict access to a print server by setting printer permissions.

You might also want to restrict access to a particular network printer. For example, the graphics department in your organization might use a high-speed color printer regularly. The cost of supplies for a color printer is substantially higher than for a black-and-white printer, so you might want to deny access to anyone outside the graphics department. The best way to restrict access is to establish a new security group. To do this, you can establish a group named Graphics Department and grant access only to members of this group.

For a procedure describing how to restrict access to printers by using printer permissions, see "Restricting Access to Printers" later in this chapter.

Installing Windows Server 2003 on Print Servers

The details of the print server deployment process vary depending on whether you have decided to perform a clean installation or upgrade an existing print server. If you are upgrading existing print servers, the upgrade process also differs depending on the version of the Windows operating system installed on your existing print servers.

Deploying Print Servers with Clean Installations

If you deploy print servers with clean installations of Windows Server 2003, you can decide whether to create new printers or migrate existing printers to the new servers. If you create new printers, you can enforce any standard printer naming conventions your organization mandates. If you have existing printers, it is recommended that you migrate them by using Print Migrator 3.1.

Deploying a New Print Server   The first step in deploying a new print server is to install and configure Windows Server 2003. Identify each operating system that the print server must support to determine any special selections that you must make while setting up your server. For example, if you support computers running Windows NT 4.0, you must install additional printer drivers during the upgrade process. After installing Windows Server 2003, you can begin adding printers. For more information about adding printers, see "Adding Printers" later in this chapter.

Migrating Printers by Using Print Migrator 3.1   Instead of adding new printers to your new print server, you can migrate printers and settings from your existing print servers. By using Print Migrator 3.1, you can back up your current print server configuration and restore the settings on a new print server, eliminating the need to manually recreate print queues and printer ports, install drivers, and assign IP addresses. Having to manually perform these tasks is a significant obstacle for most organizations. Using Print Migrator greatly reduces the manual intervention required when migrating your print servers from previous versions of Windows.

To ensure that your printer migration goes smoothly, read the documentation provided with Print Migrator 3.1.

Deploying Print Servers with Upgrade Installations

Deploying an upgraded installation of Windows Server 2003 can be a simple process depending on the printer drivers installed on your servers. One of the biggest challenges of upgrading is resolving any printer driver problems. Before upgrading your servers, use the command-line utility Fixprnsv.exe, provided with Windows Server 2003, to help you identify any printer driver problems. If you are upgrading from Windows NT 4.0 or Windows 2000, consider the issues presented in the following sections.

> **Important**   As with any major software installation, it is recommended that you back up the hard disk before beginning an upgrade.

Using Fixprnsv.exe to Resolve Driver Issues   To manage driver-related issues, use the command-line utility Fixprnsv.exe. Fixprnsv.exe automatically replaces incompatible printer drivers or those with known problems. It locates existing printer drivers that can replace unsuitable drivers. In many cases, IHVs provide new printer drivers for this purpose. If replacement drivers are available, Fixprnsv.exe replaces problem drivers with Microsoft-provided drivers. If Fixprnsv.exe does not find a suitable replacement driver, it displays a message advising you to check the printer manufacturer's Web site for a newer version of the driver. Fixprnsv.exe installs drivers only for printers that are already configured on the print server.

The Fixprnsv.exe utility is located on the Windows Server 2003 installation CD in the \Windows\Printers\ folder. For a list of commands for use with Fixprnsv.exe, use the following procedure.

To list the commands for Fixprnsv.exe

1. Insert the Windows Server 2003 installation CD in the CD-ROM drive.

2. At the command prompt, change to the CD-ROM drive that contains the CD, and then type:

```
fixprnsv.exe /?
```

Upgrading from Windows NT 4.0   When upgrading from Windows NT 4.0 to Windows Server 2003, one or more of the following situations might occur:

- Windows NT 4.0 drivers that shipped with the operating system are upgraded to the new version of these drivers in Windows 2000, Windows XP, or Windows Server 2003. The Windows NT 4.0 driver remains as an additional driver.

- If the name of an IHV driver matches the name of a driver that ships with Windows 2000, Windows XP, or Windows Server 2003, the installation might upgrade the driver to the a Version 3 inbox driver (a driver that ships with Windows Server 2003). This upgrade occurs with no user intervention.

- Unstable drivers are blocked and are not carried through the upgrade. Printers that use these drivers are removed during the upgrade process. If the printer is connected directly to the computer and has a recognized Plug and Play ID, Windows searches for a suitable driver. If a suitable driver is found, the printer is installed during the upgrade as a new printer.

- Drivers that are not blocked and do not have name matches are carried through the upgrade unchanged.

Windows NT 4.0 inbox drivers   All Windows NT 4.0 Printer Control Language (PCL) drivers and Raster Device Drivers (RASDD) are upgraded to the latest Unidrv drivers as part of the upgrade process. The latest Unidrv drivers include UNIDRV5 for Windows 2000 and UNIDRV5.1 for Windows XP or Windows Server 2003. PostScript drivers that were shipped with Windows NT 4.0 are automatically upgraded to PostScript 5.0 in Windows 2000 or PostScript 5.2 in Windows XP or Windows Server 2003.

> **Note** Drivers that you have installed as additional drivers for Point and Print on clients running Windows 95, Windows 98, or Windows Millennium Edition are not preserved during an upgrade from Windows NT 4.0 to Windows 2000 or Windows Server 2003. After you configure the print server, you must reinstall these additional drivers.

IHV drivers with matching names   IHV Windows NT 4.0 drivers are upgraded to Windows 2000, Windows XP, or Windows Server 2003 drivers with no user intervention if the driver name matches the existing Windows NT 4.0 driver name or if a newer version of the driver is available. In this situation, the IHV driver is treated exactly the same as the Microsoft driver.

Because of interaction problems between Windows 2000 drivers and Windows NT 4.0 drivers in Point and Print environments, many IHVs recommend that you reinstall their Windows NT 4.0 driver following the upgrade. This applies to users who plan to use Point and Print between Windows NT and Windows 2000, Windows XP, or Windows Server 2003.

Blocked IHV drivers   Microsoft designed the upgrade path from Windows NT 4.0 so that the new operating system replaces an old driver if a newer driver is available. Windows preserves a driver during an upgrade if the installation utility does not find a newer version and does not identify a driver as causing problems in Windows 2000, Windows XP, or Windows Server 2003. A driver is blocked for one of two reasons:

- Microsoft determines, through testing, that the driver causes substantial instability of the operating system.

- The IHV requests that the driver be blocked based on the IHV's own testing and available updates.

The system file Printupg.inf contains a list of known bad drivers. Drivers in this list might have an alternative inbox driver. If an alternative driver does not exist, the driver is not upgraded during the operating system installation. Instead, you need to install a newer version of the driver from the IHV. The information found in Printupg.inf can be helpful in identifying whether or not a new version from an IHV is blocked. The upgrade report also contains information about all drivers slated for removal during the upgrade.

In addition, the Fixprnsv.exe tool automatically replaces known bad drivers if inbox substitutes are available. If a compatible driver cannot be located, Fixprnsv.exe reports that fact and refers the user to the IHV's Web site. By running Fixprnsv.exe prior to upgrading, you can identify printers that are slated for deletion during the upgrade ahead of time. Otherwise, you might discover after the upgrade that some printers are unexpectedly missing.

Non-blocked IHV drivers   Certain Windows NT 4.0 drivers are not blocked and do not match the driver name of an inbox driver. These drivers continue through the upgrade process without being altered or replaced. Use Fixprnsv.exe to identify drivers that must be replaced. For drivers that are not blocked (either because they are not in the Printupg.inf file or because they have a later date than the date of similar drivers listed in Printupg.inf), Fixprnsv.exe takes no action.

Adding Printers

After installing Windows Server 2003 on the print server, unless you are migrating an existing print server, you must add the printers to the server. Depending on the print server deployment decisions you made and your network infrastructure, adding printers can involve the following steps:

- Installing printer ports
- Adding additional printer drivers
- Publishing printers in Active Directory
- Connecting clients to printers
- Restricting access to printers

Installing Printer Ports

If your users print over a network, you must create printer ports to enable connections between print servers and printers. You can install printer ports from the Printers and Faxes folder on the print server. The printer port can be one of two port types:

- Standard TCP/IP port
- LPR port

Standard TCP/IP Port The standard port is the preferred printer port in Windows Server 2003. The standard port uses the standard TCP/IP port monitor (standard port monitor) and is designed for Windows Server 2003–based print servers that communicate with printers by using TCP/IP. For more information about the advantages of using the standard port and the prerequisites for installing a standard port, see "Determining the Print Server Network Connection Method" earlier in this chapter.

To install a standard port

1. In Control Panel, open the **Printers and Faxes** folder, right-click the printer that you want to configure, and then click **Properties**.

2. On the **Ports** tab, click **Add Port**.

3. In the **Printer Ports** dialog box, select **Standard TCP/IP port**, and then click **New Port** to start the Add Standard TCP/IP Printer Port Wizard.

4. Complete the Add Standard TCP/IP Printer Port Wizard by using the information provided in Table 4.8.

Table 4.8   Using the Add Standard TCP/IP Printer Port Wizard

Wizard Page	Action
Printer Name or IP Address	To identify the printer that will be connected to the port, type its name in the **Printer Name or its IP address in the IP Address** box.
Port Name	In the **Port Name** box, type a port name, which can be any character string, or use the default name that the wizard supplies.
Additional Port Information Required	To configure a standard port, click **Standard**, and then select one of the listed devices. If you do not know the details of the port, try using the **Generic Network Card**.
	To create a custom configuration, click **Custom**, and then configure the port by using the **Configure Standard TCP/IP Port Monitor** screen that appears.

If the wizard cannot determine the appropriate protocol for the port, it prompts you for the information. Follow the vendor's instructions for selecting either the RAW or LPR option.

If you are not prompted for more information, continue to step 5.

5.   Review the port information, and then click **Finish**.

The new port is listed on the **Ports** tab of the **Properties** property sheet.

> **Note**   With Windows Server 2003, administrators can remotely configure and manage ports from any server running Windows Server 2003. This feature applies to local ports, the standard TCP/IP port, and LPR ports. You must configure AppleTalk ports locally on the server.

You can reconfigure the standard port monitor by adjust the settings in the property sheet for the print server.

> **Caution**   The **Configure Port** dialog box does not validate the settings created in the following procedure. If they are incorrect, the port no longer works.

To reconfigure the standard TCP/IP port

1.   In Control Panel, open the **Printers and Faxes** folder, right-click the appropriate printer, and then click **Properties**.

2.   On the **Ports** tab, click the **Configure Port** button.

3.   In the **Configure Standard TCP/IP Port Monitor** dialog box, click either the RAW or LPR protocol.

4.   To configure the protocol, take one of the following actions:

❑   For **RAW Settings**, type the port number that the printer vendor specified (usually 9100).

❑   For **LPR Settings**, type the LPR queue name that the printer vendor specified.

5.   If the printer supports SNMP and RFC 1759, click to select the **SNMP Status Enabled** check box.

If the **SNMP Status Enabled** check box is selected, you can change both the SNMP community name and the host device index:

■   The community name is usually "Public," but you can enter another community name if you want to limit access to the printer.

■   The device index is used mainly for multiport devices that support several printers; each port on a multiport device has a different device index, specified by the device vendor.

Pooling printers   Printer pooling is especially useful in high-volume printing environments. Pooled printers appear to clients as a single printer, but printing throughput is increased because the load is distributed among the printers in the pool.

Before you set up a printer pool, consider the following issues:

■   Two or more printers are required; Windows Server 2003 does not limit the number of printers in a pool.

■   The printers in the pool must be of the same model, and they must use the same printer driver.

■   Printer ports can be of the same type or mixed (such as parallel, serial, and network).

■   If you want to ensure that documents are first sent to the faster printers, add the faster printers to the pool first and the slower printers last. Print jobs are routed in the order in which you create the ports.

■   Because users do not know which printer prints their documents, it is a good idea to locate all of the pooled printers in the same physical location. Otherwise, users might not be able to find their printed documents.

To create a printer pool

1.   In Control Panel, open the **Printers and Faxes** folder, right-click the appropriate printer, and then click **Properties**.

2.   On the **Ports** tab, click to select the **Enable printer pooling** check box.

3.   In the list of ports, click to select the check boxes for the ports that are connected to the printers that you want to pool.

4.   Repeat steps 2 and 3 for each additional printer to be included in the printer pool.

Adding Additional Printer Drivers

By adding additional drivers to your print server, you can support clients that are running various versions of the Windows operating systems. It is preferable to use Version 3 drivers rather than Version 2 drivers as your primary drivers because Version 2 drivers can cause the system to become unstable or stop responding. However, you might need to use Version 2 drivers as additional drivers if you support clients running Windows NT 4.0. If your server has known bad drivers when it is upgraded, those drivers are deleted during the upgrade process. Any additional drivers that are added must have the same name as the primary driver unless they are Windows 95, Windows 98, or Windows Millennium Edition drivers.

Publishing Printers in Active Directory

Publishing your shared printers in Active Directory can make locating printers across a network more efficient for your users. In Windows Server 2003, the print subsystem is tightly integrated with Active Directory, making it possible to search across a domain for printers at different locations. By using the standard printer object that Windows Server 2003 provides, you enable users to search for printer-based attributes such as printing capabilities (including PostScript, color, and paper size) and printer locations (allowing users to find printers located near them).

If you plan to publish printers to Active Directory, follow the naming standard that the print services design team created when you fill out the location fields on the printer properties pages across your network. This enables users to enter a standard string to search for printers by location. If you use subnets to define the sites within your organization, Active Directory can find nearby printers—a process that has formerly been difficult for both administrators and users.

For example, if you are in Los Angeles and want to find all the Los Angeles printers in your deployment, search for a network printer by using the Add Printer Wizard and type **US/LAX** in the **Location** dialog box. If US/LAX matches the printer location syntax in Active Directory, your search might return the following results:

- US/LAX/1/101

- US/LAX/2/103

These results indicate that two printers are available in Los Angeles, located in buildings 1 and 2, in rooms 101 and 103.

Printer publishing is controlled by the **List in the Directory** check box on the **Sharing** tab of the **Properties** sheet for each printer. Printers that are added by using the Add Printer Wizard are published by default, and the wizard does not let you change this setting. If you do not want to publish a printer in Active Directory, after adding the printer, open the printer property sheet and click to clear the **List in the directory** check box on the **Sharing** tab.

The printer is placed in the computer object in Active Directory on the print server. After publishing the printer in Active Directory, you can move or rename the object by using the Users and Computers snap-in in Active Directory.

To publish a printer in Active Directory

1.   In Control Panel, open the **Printers and Faxes** folder.

2.   Right-click the icon for the printer that you want to publish in Active Directory, and then click **Properties**.

3.   On the **Sharing** tab, click to select the **List in the directory** check box.

Connecting Clients to Printers

Generally, clients can establish a connection to a shared network printer hosted on a Windows Server 2003 print server in one of three ways:

- **Entering the Universal Naming Convention (UNC) path**. In the **Run** dialog box, type the UNC path for the printer (for example, \\PrintServer\Printer), and then click **OK**.

- **Using the Add Printer Wizard**. From the **Printer and Faxes** folder, select **Add a Printer**. When the Add Printer Wizard opens, click **Next**, and then select the network printer option. Type, or browse to, the path for the shared printer.

- **Dragging the printer icon**. In the **Run** dialog box, open the shared printers folder on the remote print server. Then drag the desired printer icon into the Printers and Faxes folder on the local workstation.

Restricting Access to Printers

If your design calls for restricting access to certain printers, you can do so by using printer permissions. To do this, it is recommended that you create a user group and then limit access to a printer to members of the group.

To create a local group

1.   Right-click **My Computer**, and then click **Manage**.

2. In the console tree, double-click **Local Users and Groups**.

3. To add the group, right-click **Groups**, and then click **New Group**.

4. In the **Group name** box, type the name of the new local group.

5. To add users to the group, click **Add**, and then type the user names in the **Enter the object names to select** box.

To restrict access to a specific printer

1. In Control Panel, open the **Printers and Faxes** folder.

2. Right-click the icon for the printer to which you want to restrict access, and then click **Properties**.

3. To remove extraneous group members, on the **Security** tab, remove all entries in the **Groups or user names** list box except **Administrator** and **Creator Owner**.

4. To grant access to the printer, click **Add**, and then enter the names of the groups and users who you want to have access to this printer.

Migrating Printers

If you choose to migrate existing print servers to your new Windows Server 2003–based print servers, instead of adding printers you can use Print Migrator. Print Migrator version 3.1 helps automate the process of migrating printers from a Windows NT 4.0 print server to a print server running Windows Server 2003.

Using Print Migrator 3.1

Print Migrator allows you to back up and restore print server settings from one server to another. Having the ability to back up and restore print server settings allows you to easily migrate existing printers to a new print server running Windows Server 2003.

Backing up Print Server Settings   When backing up the printer configuration from a target server, Print Migrator stores the backup in a .cab file. You can type a name for the .cab file and choose a location for the file in the **Printer Configuration Backup** dialog box, as shown in Figure 4.1.

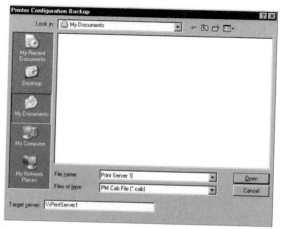

Figure 4.1 Printer Configuration Backup Dialog Box

To back up a printer configuration

1. In Print Migrator, on the **Actions** menu, click **Backup**.

2. In the **Target server** box, type the name of the server that you want to back up, or leave the **Target server** box empty to back up the local system on which Print Migrator is being run.

3. In the **File name** box, type the path and file name of the .cab file to be created, or click **Look in**, browse to the desired location, and then type a file name.

4. Click **Save,** and then click **OK** to begin the backup.

As the backup proceeds, a progress report appears in the lower pane of the Print Migrator 3.1 window. The contents of this report are saved in the file pm.log, which is located in *systemroot*\System32\Spool\Pm.

Once the backup is completed, the cab file contains the required printer registry data and driver files.

You can also back up printer configurations by running Print Migrator from the command line. To back up printer configurations from the command line, run <name of executable file> using the **/b** option followed by the fully qualified path of the .cab file, and optionally specify the target server name as the last parameter on the command line in the form *servername*.

Restoring print server settings To restore printer configurations you can use the Print Migrator graphical user interface (GUI) or the command line interface. When using the Print Migrator GUI, you choose restore options in the **Printer Configuration Restore** dialog box, as shown in Figure 4.2.

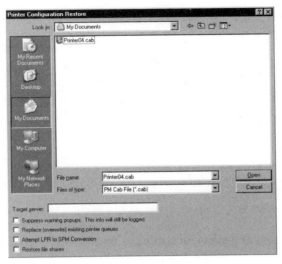

Figure 4.2   Printer Configuration Restore Dialog Box

To restore a printer configuration

1. In Print Migrator, on the **Actions** menu, click **Restore**.

2. Browse to the folder where the .cab file that you want to restore is located.

3. Click the name of the .cab file to use, or type the name of the file in the **File name** box.

4. In the **Target server** box, type the name of the target server in the form *servername*, or leave the Target server box empty to perform the restore on the local system on which Print Migrator is being run.

5. Select any options that you want to use (Suppress warning popups, **Replace (overwrite) existing printer shares**, Attempt LPR to SPM Conversion, and Restore file shares).

    When restoring a printer configuration to another server, by default Print Migrator 3.1, merges the configuration from the .cab file with the existing configuration on the target server. Note that this is different from Print Migrator 1.0, which overwrites the existing configuration on the target with the configuration from the .cab file. To overwrite the existing configuration when using Print Migrator 3.1, select the **Replace (overwrite) existing print shares** check box in **the Printer Configuration Restore** dialog box, or use the **/o** option on the command line.

> **Caution**   When restoring printers that use Windows NT 4.0 printer drivers (Kernel Mode, Version 2 drivers) to a server running Windows 2000, Windows XP or Windows Server 2003, selecting the **Replace (overwrite) existing printer queues** check box has no effect. Instead, you must manually delete the printers from the Printers folder on the target system before performing the restore.

6. Click Open (or press ENTER) to begin the restore.

As the Restore command runs, a progress report appears in the lower pane of the Print Migrator window. This output is also saved to the Pm.log log file, which is located in the *systemroot*\System32\Spool\Pm folder.

> **Note**   Print Migrator 3.1 temporarily stops the Spooler service, Print Services for Macintosh, and TCP/IP Print Services on the destination computer to restore print queue information.

You can also restore printer configurations by running Print Migrator from the command line. To restore printer configurations from the command line, run <name of executable file> using the **/r** option followed by the name of the .cab file, and optionally specify the target server name as the last parameter on the command line in the form *servername*.

Before running the Restore command on a print server, make sure that the following requirements are met:

- The backup computer and the destination computer must be running an x86-compatible CPU.

- Print monitor information must be consistent with the backup computer. If a monitor is missing, Print Migrator displays a warning, and you must install the correct monitor or service and perform the Restore again.

- The current user must have administrative rights on the destination computer.

- If the backup source is a computer running Windows NT 4.0, you must run Fixprnsv.exe to upgrade known-bad kernel mode printer drivers.

For more information about using Fixprnsv.exe, see article 247196, "Overview of Fixprnsv.exe," in the Microsoft Knowledge Base. To find this article, see the Microsoft Knowledge Base link on the Web Resources page at http://www.microsoft.com/windows/reskits/webresources.

Additional Resources

These resources contain additional information and tools related to this chapter.

Related Information

- The Microsoft SharePoint® Products™ and Technologies link on the Web Resources page at http://www.microsoft.com/windows/reskits/webresources for information about sharing information within organizations and over the Internet.

- The *Server Management Guide* of the *Microsoft Windows Server 2003 Resource Kit* (or see the "Server Management Guide" on the Web at http://www.microsoft.com/reskit).

- The Windows Deployment and Resource Kits Web site at http://www.microsoft.com/reskit, or see the MSDN Scripting Clinic link on the Web Resources page at http://www.microsoft.com/windows/reskits/webresources, for more information about scripting.

- RFC 1759: *Printer MIB* for more information about Printer Message Information Base.

- RFC 1179: *Line Printer Daemon Protocol* for more information about using an LPR port that uses the Line Printer Daemon Protocol.

Related Help topics

For best results in identifying Help topics by title, in Help and Support Center, under the **Search** box, click **Set search options**. Under **Help Topics**, click to select the **Search in title only** check box.

- "Dynamic disks and volumes" in Help and Support Center for Windows Server 2003 for more information about dynamic disks.

- "Managing printing from the command line" in Help and Support Center for Windows Server 2003 for more information about managing printers from the command line.

Related Tools

- Permcopy.exe

    Use Permcopy.exe to copy shared folder permissions from one shared folder to another. For more information about Permcopy.exe, click **Tools** in Help and Support Center for Windows Server 2003, and then click **Windows Resource Kit Tools**.

- Print Migrator 3.1 (Printmig.exe)

    Use Printmig.exe to help automate printer consolidation on Windows Server 2003. Instead of recreating all of the printer objects manually, you can back up existing printers and restore them to your new print servers. To download Print Migrator, see the Print Services link on the Web Resources page at http://www.microsoft.com/windows/reskits/webresources.

- Fixprnsv.exe

    Use Fixprnsv.exe to help resolve printer driver compatibility issues between Windows NT 4.0, Windows 2000 and Windows Server 2003. Fixprnsv.exe is located on the Windows Server 2003 installation CD. The executable file is located in Windows\Printers directory. To view a list of commands used with this utility, use the command **fixprnsv.exe /?** from that directory.

- PrnAdmin

    Use PrnAdmin to help migrate from Windows NT 4.0 to Windows Server 2003. You can use Prnadmin.dll to inventory your current environment. PrnAdmin enumerates ports, drivers, printers, or forms on local or remote printers. The Visual Basic script for the PrnAdmin utility is named Prnmgr.vbs. The PrnAdmin tool is included in Resource Kit Tools for Windows Server 2003, available on the *Microsoft Windows Server 2003 Deployment Kit* companion CD, or on the Web at http://www.microsoft.com/reskit. To install PrnAdmin, type the following command:

```
regsvr32 C:\Path\PrnAdmin.dll
```

5

Migrating to Dial-up and VPN Remote Access Servers Running Windows Server 2003

This chapter helps you evaluate your options for upgrading or migrating your remote access solution from servers that are running Microsoft® Windows NT® Server version 4.0 to servers that are running a product in the Microsoft® Windows Server™ 2003 family. This chapter describes the differences between Remote Access Service (RAS) or Routing and Remote Access Service (RRAS) in Windows NT Server 4.0 and Routing and Remote Access in Windows Server 2003 and the benefits of upgrading or migrating. It also describes how to reuse your settings from RAS or RRAS and the requirements for upgrading a server that is running RRAS from Windows NT Server 4.0 to Windows Server 2003.

In This Chapter:

Overview of Remote Access Migration

Although there are similarities between RAS or RRAS running on Windows NT Server 4.0 and Routing and Remote Access running on the Windows Server 2003 family, there have been major changes and improvements since Windows NT Server 4.0 was released. This section discusses some of those changes and improvements, and later sections explain how you can reuse settings from RAS or RRAS to facilitate your Routing and Remote Access deployment.

Before you begin to migrate from RAS or RRAS to Routing and Remote Access, or upgrade from RRAS to Routing and Remote Access, you should understand the functional differences between these components and the differences in how you perform tasks that involve these components. You should also consider in what ways your existing remote access solution does and does not meet your needs and which of your existing settings to migrate to your new remote access solution.

Feature Enhancements from RAS to RRAS

Both RAS and RRAS are available for Windows NT Server 4.0. RAS supports both dial-up connections and virtual private networks (VPNs) that use Point-to-Point Tunneling Protocol (PPTP). After the release of Windows NT Server 4.0, RRAS was made available as a free released-to-Web offering. RRAS enhances RAS by creating a unified routing and remote access service.

RRAS for Windows NT Server 4.0 improved upon RAS by supporting:

■ Routing Information Protocol (RIP) version 2 routing protocol for IP.

■ Open Shortest Path First (OSPF) routing protocol for IP.

■ Demand-dial routing, the routing over on-demand or persistent WAN links such as those over analog phone or ISDN connections that use PPTP.

■ Internet Control Message Protocol (ICMP) Router Discovery.

■ Remote Authentication Dial-In User Service (RADIUS) client.

■ IP and Internetwork Packet Exchange (IPX) packet filtering.

■ PPTP support for site-to-site (also known as router-to-router) VPN connections.

■ A graphical user interface administrative program called Routing and RAS Admin and a command-line utility called Routemon.

Changes in Features from RRAS to Routing and Remote Access

Routing and Remote Access for the Microsoft® Windows® 2000 Server family continued the evolution of multiprotocol routing and remote access services. The Routing and Remote Access features introduced in the Windows 2000 Server family include:

- Internet Group Management Protocol (IGMP) and support for multicast boundaries.

- Network address translation with addressing and name resolution components that simplify making the connection between a small office/home office (SOHO) network and the Internet.

- Integrated AppleTalk routing.

- Layer Two Tunneling Protocol with Internet Protocol Security (L2TP/IPSec) support for remote access and site-to-site VPN connections.

- Improved administration and management tools. The graphical user interface program is Routing and Remote Access in MMC. The command-line utility is Netsh.

Additional enhancements to Routing and Remote Access have been made in the Windows Server 2003 family. Two of the enhancements are specifically designed for small businesses.

Enhancements for Small Businesses

The following enhancements are specifically designed for small businesses.

Broadcast Name Resolution   Broadcast name resolution is a NetBIOS over TCP/IP (NetBT) name resolution proxy that is built into Routing and Remote Access. This proxy allows remote access clients connecting to a network consisting of one or more subnets with a single router (the remote access server running a member of the Windows Server 2003 family) to resolve names without having to query a Domain Name System (DNS) or Windows Internet Name Service (WINS) server.

This feature allows a small business to configure a remote access or VPN server so that employees can work offsite. With broadcast name resolution enabled, clients connecting remotely can resolve the names of computers on the small business network without requiring the deployment of a DNS or WINS server.

PPPoE for Demand-Dial Connections   With this feature, organizations can use Point-to-Point Protocol over Ethernet (PPPoE) for demand-dial connections (also known as dial-on-demand connections). Demand-dial connections are used by Routing and Remote Access to make point-to-point connections between LANs over which packets are routed. You can access this feature by clicking **Connect using PPP over Ethernet (PPPoE)** on the **Connection Type** page of the Demand-Dial Interface Wizard.

By allowing PPPoE as a connection type for demand-dial connections, a small business can use the NAT/Basic Firewall component of Routing and Remote Access and its broadband Internet connection to connect an office network to the Internet.

Other Enhancements

The following enhancements are not specifically designed for small businesses; however, some of them (such as network address translation and Basic Firewall) can be used in a small business environment.

NAT and Basic Firewall   The network address translation and Basic Firewall components of Routing and Remote Access have been enhanced to support a basic firewall. These components allow you to protect a computer that is running a product in the Windows Server 2003 family and to enable your server to act as a network address translator (NAT) to allow access to the Internet. The computers on the private network are protected because the NAT does not forward traffic from the Internet unless a private network client requests it. However, the NAT itself can be vulnerable to attack. If Basic Firewall is enabled on the public interface of the NAT, all packets that are received on that interface and that do not correspond to traffic requested by the NAT (either for itself or for private intranet clients) are discarded.

You can enable this functionality from the **NAT/Basic Firewall** tab in the **Properties** dialog box of an interface that is configured to use the NAT/Basic Firewall IP routing protocol component of Routing and Remote Access.

Snap-in and Setup Wizard Enhancements   The Routing and Remote Access Server Setup Wizard has been modified to make it easier to initially configure Routing and Remote Access. Routing and Remote Access has been modified to make it easier to configure server settings after the initial configuration has been completed.

Improved Configuration for EAP-TLS Properties   The **Smart Card or other Certificate Properties** dialog box has been improved to allow the configuration of multiple RADIUS servers and multiple root certification authorities for local and remote connections. You can access the **Smart Card or other Certificate Properties** dialog box from the **Properties** dialog box of each connection in the Network Connections folder.

Network Access Quarantine Control   Network Access Quarantine Control is a feature of both Routing and Remote Access and Internet Authentication Service. It delays normal remote access to a private network until the configuration of the remote access computer has been examined and validated by an administrator-provided script. Network Access Quarantine Control is designed to prevent computers with unsupported configurations from accessing resources on a private network.

When a remote access computer initiates a connection to a remote access server, the user is authenticated and the remote access computer is assigned an IP address. However, the connection is placed in quarantine mode, in which network access is limited. The administrator-provided script is run on the remote access computer. If the script notifies the remote access server that it has successfully run and that the remote access computer complies with current network policies, quarantine mode is removed, and the remote access computer is granted normal remote access.

Network Access Quarantine Control in Routing and Remote Access supports new RADIUS vendor-specific attributes for quarantine restrictions and a new *MprAdminConnectionRemoveQuarantine()* application programming interface (API) to remove the quarantine restrictions from the remote access connection.

For more information, see the Network Access Quarantine Control link on the Web Resources page at http://www.microsoft.com/windows/reskits/webresources.

Manage Your Server and Routing and Remote Access Integration   This feature provides an integrated method for configuring the initial setup of Routing and Remote Access. With this feature, an IT administrator can configure multiple features in the Windows Server 2003 family from the same initial interface.

Ability to Enable the Routing and Remote Access Internal Interface as a Network Address Translation Private Interface   On a computer that is running Windows 2000 Server, providing remote access to a private intranet, and acting as a NAT to provide access from the intranet to the Internet, there is no way to provide Internet access to connected remote access clients. On computers that are running Windows Server 2003, you can add the Internal interface as a private interface to the NAT/Basic Firewall component of Routing and Remote Access. This allows connected remote access clients to access the Internet.

Improvements in Default Behavior for Internal and Internet Interfaces   To prevent potential problems with resolving the name of the VPN server and accessing services that are running on the VPN server, Routing and Remote Access by default disables DNS dynamic update registration for the Internal interface and disables both dynamic DNS and broadcast name resolution for the interface identified in the Routing and Remote Access Server Setup Wizard as the Internet interface.

L2TP/IPSec Connections and IPSec NAT Traversal   In Windows 2000, Internet Key Exchange (IKE) and Encapsulating Security Payload (ESP) traffic cannot traverse a NAT because if the NAT translates the IP addresses or ports of the packet, it invalidates the security of the packets. This means that you cannot create an L2TP/IPSec connection from behind a NAT and that you must use PPTP for VPN connections.

The Windows Server 2003 family supports User Datagram Protocol (UDP) encapsulation of IPSec packets to allow IKE and ESP traffic to pass through a NAT. This feature allows L2TP/IPSec connections to be created between client computers and servers that are running products in the Windows Server 2003 family and that are located behind one or more NATs.

To create such connections from client computers that are running Microsoft® Windows® 98, Windows® Millennium Edition, or Windows NT® Workstation 4.0, users must install the Microsoft L2TP/IPSec VPN Client. For more information, see the Microsoft L2TP/IPSec VPN Client link on the Web Resources page at http://www.microsoft.com/windows/reskits/webresources.

The Internet Drafts titled "UDP Encapsulation of IPSec Packets" (draft-ietf-ipsec-udp-encaps-02.txt) and "Negotiation of NAT-Traversal in the IKE" (draft-ietf-ipsec-nat-t-ike-02.txt) describe support in the Windows Server 2003 family for IPSec traffic traversing NATs.

NLB Support for L2TP/IPSec Traffic   In Windows 2000, Network Load Balancing (NLB) could not manage IPSec security associations (SAs) among multiple servers. If a server in the cluster became unavailable, the SAs managed by that cluster were orphaned and eventually timed out. This meant that you could not cluster L2TP/IPSec VPN servers. You could use DNS round-robin for load distribution across multiple L2TP/IPSec VPN servers, but there was no fault tolerance.

In the Windows Server 2003 family, NLB has been enhanced to provide clustering support for IPSec SAs. You can create a cluster of L2TP/IPSec VPN servers, and NLB will provide both load balancing and fault tolerance for L2TP/IPSec traffic.

This feature is provided only with Windows Server 2003, Enterprise Edition, and Windows Server 2003, Datacenter Edition.

Preshared Key Configuration for L2TP/IPSec Connections   Windows Server 2003 supports both computer certificates and a preshared key as authentication methods to establish IPSec SAs for L2TP connections. A preshared key is a string of text that is configured on both the VPN client and the VPN server. Preshared key authentication is a relatively weak authentication method; therefore, it is recommended that you use preshared key authentication only while your public key infrastructure (PKI) is being deployed or when VPN clients require the use of preshared key authentication. You can enable the use of preshared key authentication and specify a preshared key for L2TP connections from Routing and Remote Access by opening the **Properties** dialog box of a remote access server and clicking the **Security** tab.

VPN clients in Microsoft® Windows® XP and the Windows Server 2003 family also support preshared key authentication. You can enable preshared key authentication and specify a preshared key for L2TP connections from Network Connections by opening the **Properties** dialog box of a VPN connection, clicking the **Security** tab, and changing the **IPSec settings** or by configuring a Connection Manager Administration Kit (CMAK) profile for your users. For more information about configuring a CMAK profile, see "Deploying Remote Access Clients Using Connection Manager" in *Deploying Network Services* of the *Microsoft® Windows Server™ 2003 Deployment Kit* (or see "Deploying Remote Access Clients Using Connection Manager" on the Web at http://www.microsoft.com/reskit).

Preshared key authentication is also supported for site-to-site VPN connections between computers that are running products in the Windows Server 2003 family. You can enable preshared key authentication and configure a preshared key for demand-dial interfaces from Routing and Remote Access by opening the **Properties** dialog box of a demand-dial interface, clicking the **Security** tab, and changing the **IPSec settings**.

Feature Limitations

VPN Connection Limit for Windows Server 2003, Web Edition   Windows Server 2003, Web Edition, supports only one VPN connection at a time, whether the connection is based on PPTP or L2TP. This limitation also exists for Windows XP. To support more than one VPN connection, you must use Windows Server 2003, Standard Edition; Windows Server 2003, Enterprise Edition; or Windows Server 2003, Datacenter Edition.

IPX Routing Support Removed   Routing and Remote Access in the Windows Server 2003 family does not support IPX routing, which includes the following:

- The forwarding of IPX traffic
- The use of Routing Information Protocol (RIP) for IPX
- The use of Service Advertising Protocol (SAP) as a router
- The forwarding of NetBIOS over IPX broadcasts

Accessing RAS, RRAS, and Routing and Remote Access

Understanding how you access Routing and Remote Access in the Windows Server 2003 family compared to how you access RAS and RRAS in Windows NT Server 4.0 will assist you during the migration or upgrade process. Table 5.1 shows how to perform common tasks using RAS or RRAS in Windows NT Server 4.0 and Routing and Remote Access in Windows Server 2003.

Table 5.1   Performing Common Tasks with RAS or RRAS (Windows NT Server 4.0) and in Routing and Remote Access (Windows Server 2003)

To:	In Windows NT Server 4.0, use:	In Windows Server 2003, use:
Enable and configure remote access	In Control Panel, in Network, the **Services** tab	Routing and Remote Access found in the Administrative Tools folder
Configure authentication and encryption options	In Control Panel, in Network, the **Services** tab	Routing and Remote Access
Manage remote access servers and clients	Remote Access Admin or Routing and RAS Admin	Routing and Remote Access
Grant remote access permission to user accounts	Remote Access Admin or User Manager for Domains	Active Directory Users and Computers or Computer Management, Local Users and Groups (if the remote access server is not part of a domain)

Upgrading from RRAS to Routing and Remote Access

Because of the many enhancements and differences between RRAS and Routing and Remote Access, it is recommended that instead of upgrading your server, you reuse the settings from RRAS to configure Routing and Remote Access on a new server running a product in the Windows Server 2003 family. Moving from Windows NT Server 4.0 to the Windows Server 2003 family also provides an opportunity to determine whether you want to continue using your existing remote access settings or update your settings to reflect any changes in your organization.

Before attempting to upgrade, check Windows Catalog to verify whether the Windows Server 2003 family supports all of the hardware and devices on the computer that you want to upgrade. For example, if Windows NT Server 4.0 recognizes and supports the network adapter but the Windows Server 2003 family does not, then pre-configured networking information, including the protocols installed for RRAS, will not be upgraded. For more information, see the Windows Catalog link on the Web Resources page at http://www.microsoft.com/windows/reskits/webresources.

To upgrade from RRAS on Windows NT Server 4.0 to Routing and Remote Access on a product in the Windows Server 2003 family, you must have installed Service Pack 5 and the optional download component for RRAS on the computer that you want to upgrade. For more information on the download component, see the Routing and Remote Access Service Download link on the Web Resources page at http://www.microsoft.com/windows/reskits/webresources.

Migrating to Routing and Remote Access

Because there is no direct migration from RAS or RRAS to Routing and Remote Access, it is recommended that you document the configuration parameters of the computer that you intend to keep in your new Routing and Remote Access environment.

By documenting your current configuration, you will be able to more easily reuse the settings to configure Routing and Remote Access on a computer that is running Windows Server 2003. Even if you do not reuse all the settings that you document from your computer that is running Windows NT Server 4.0, documenting these settings will give you a record of your previous settings that you can refer to.

Tables 5.2 and 5.3 list the settings you might want to document and reuse in Routing and Remote Access on the Windows Server 2003 family. The exact settings that you document depend on which features of RAS or RRAS you use. Refer to Table 5.1 for more information about performing common remote access tasks in the Windows Server 2003 family.

You can record your information in this book or print out copies of these pages by downloading the online version of this chapter. To download this chapter from the Web, see the "Migrating from Microsoft Windows NT Server 4.0 to Windows Server 2003" link on the Windows Deployment and Resource Kits Web site at http://www.microsoft.com/reskit/. You might need to attach additional sheets or create your own table if you need more space.

Table 5.2 Worksheet to Record Routing Settings

Description of settings to record	Your existing settings
Open Shortest Path First (OSPF): Is this routing protocol enabled in your RRAS solution?	
Routing Information Protocol (RIP): Is this routing protocol enabled in your RRAS solution?	
Internet Control Message Protocol (ICMP) Router Discovery: Is this enabled in your RRAS solution?	
DHCP relay agent: Is RRAS acting as a DHCP relay agent? If so, list appropriate DHCP server IP addresses and global settings.	
If you migrate the DHCP server to a computer that is running Windows Server 2003 with a new IP address, also list the IP address for the replacement DHCP server. For more information about migrating DHCP servers, see "Upgrading and Migrating WINS and DHCP Servers to Windows Server 2003" in this book.	
Demand-dial interfaces: List the interface name, IP address of the router to which you are connecting, user name credentials, and configuration details.	
IP packet filtering: List the source and destination IP address and subnet mask for input and output filters on each interface.	
List logging and route preference levels.	
Static routes: For each static route, list the interface destination, subnet mask, gateway, and metric.	
List routemon scripts to convert to Netsh scripts.	

Table 5.3   **Worksheet to Record Remote Access Settings**

Description of settings to record	Your existing settings
Multilink: Is this enabled in your RAS or RRAS solution?	
List authentication methods to migrate to Routing and Remote Access and remote access policy settings.	
List the encryption level to migrate to remote access policy.	
Authentication provider settings. List RADIUS server connection information, if applicable, including server name, IP address, and configuration details.	
List remote access server TCP/IP settings, including IP address, subnet mask, and default gateway.	
List remote access service settings, including IP address ranges and other settings.	
List the name and IP address of the VPN server. If you do not reuse these settings, ensure that all users that connect to this VPN server receive the new VPN connection information.	

Before you begin to configure Routing and Remote Access on a computer running Windows Server 2003, you might want to read "Deploying Dial-up and VPN Remote Access Servers" in *Deploying Network Services* of the *Microsoft Windows Server 2003 Deployment Kit* (or see "Deploying Dial-up and VPN Remote Access Servers" on the Web at http://www.microsoft.com/reskit). Also, if you plan to use a dial-up or VPN connection for a site-to-site connectivity solution, then you might want to review "Connecting Remote Sites" in *Deploying Network Services* of the *Microsoft Windows Server 2003 Deployment Kit* (or see "Connecting Remote Sites" on the Web at http://www.microsoft.com/reskit).

For information about setting up VPN-based remote access in a test lab, see "Step-by-Step Guide for Setting Up VPN-based Remote Access in a Test Lab." To find this guide, see the Web Resources page at http://www.microsoft.com/windows/reskits/webresources, click the Virtual Private Networks link, and search for "Step-by-Step Guide for Setting Up VPN-based Remote Access in a Test Lab."

Configuring a VPN Remote Access Server

The configuration of a VPN remote access server involves the following tasks:

■ Configure TCP/IP on the server.

■ Configure the server as a VPN remote access server.

■ Configure name resolution on the server.

■ Configure packet filters for the server.

Configuring TCP/IP on the VPN Server

Before you configure the server as a remote access server, configure the TCP/IP settings for the Internet or perimeter network interface and for the intranet interface.

> **Note**   Because of routing issues related to configuring TCP/IP automatically, it is recommended that you not configure a VPN server as a DHCP client. Instead, manually configure TCP/IP on the intranet interfaces of a VPN server. For a full discussion of the routing options for a VPN server, see "Configuring Routing on a VPN Server" later in this chapter.

Manually configure the Internet or perimeter network interface of the VPN server with a default gateway. Configure the TCP/IP settings with a public IP address, a subnet mask, and the default gateway of either the firewall (if the VPN server is connected to a perimeter network) or an Internet service provider (ISP) router (if the VPN server is connected directly to the Internet).

To configure TCP/IP for the Internet or perimeter network interface

1. In **Control Panel**, double-click **Network Connections**, and then double-click the network adapter for the Internet or perimeter network interface.

2. In the network adapter status dialog box (for example, **Local Area Connection Status**), click **Properties**.

3. Click **Internet Protocol (TCP/IP)**, and then click **Properties**.

4. On the **General** tab, configure the IP address, subnet mask, and default gateway.

The IP address must be a public address assigned by an ISP. You can configure the VPN server with a private IP address but assign it a published static IP address by which it is known on the Internet. When packets are sent to and from the VPN server, a NAT that is positioned between the Internet and the VPN server translates the published IP address to the private IP address.

When you configure a VPN connection, give your VPN servers names that can be resolved to IP addresses using DNS.

5.   Click **Advanced** to display the **Advanced TCP/IP Settings** dialog box.

To configure TCP/IP for the intranet interface

1.   In **Control Panel**, double-click **Network Connections**, and then double-click the network adapter for intranet interface.

2.   In the network adapter status dialog box (for example, **Local Area Connection 2 Status**), click **Properties**.

3.   Click **Internet Protocol (TCP/IP)**, and then click **Properties**.

4.   On the **General** tab, configure the IP address, subnet mask, and the addresses of internal DNS servers.

   To prevent default route conflicts with the default route pointing to the Internet, do not configure the default gateway on the intranet connection.

5.   Click **Advanced** to display the **Advanced TCP/IP Settings** dialog box.

6.   On the **WINS** tab, specify the IP addresses of your WINS servers.

Configuring the Server as a VPN Remote Access Server

To configure the server as a VPN remote access server, use the Configure Your Server Wizard and click **Remote access/VPN server** as the server role, or use the Routing and Remote Access snap-in. You can use the information that you recorded in Tables 5.2 and 5.3 earlier in this chapter to assist you in configuring your VPN server. For instructions on using the wizard, see "Remote access/VPN server role: Configuring a remote access/VPN server" in Help and Support Center for Windows Server 2003.

Note   If you are configuring your server as both a VPN and dial-up remote access server, specify both VPN and dial-up in the Routing and Remote Access Server Setup Wizard.

Configuring Name Resolution on a VPN Server

If you use Domain Name System (DNS) to resolve intranet host names or Windows Internet Name Service (WINS) to resolve intranet NetBIOS names, manually configure the VPN server with the IP addresses of the appropriate DNS and WINS servers.

During the PPP connection setup process, VPN clients receive the IP addresses of DNS and WINS servers. By default, the VPN clients inherit the DNS and WINS server IP addresses configured on the VPN server. However, VPN clients that are capable of sending a DHCPINFORM message (computers running Windows 2000, Windows XP, or Windows Server 2003) can also get their DNS and WINS server IP addresses from a DHCP server, provided the DHCP Relay Agent component is correctly configured.

Configuring Packet Filters for a VPN Server

Firewalls are configured with rules to filter the packets that a VPN server sends and receives and to control intranet traffic to and from VPN clients, based on your network security policies. Packet filtering is based on the fields of inbound and outbound packets.

The Routing and Remote Access Server Setup Wizard for Windows Server 2003 automatically configures the appropriate packet filters for VPN traffic. Alternatively, you can use the Routing and Remote Access snap-in to configure the packet filters.

For more information, see "Deploying Dial-up and VPN Remote Access Servers" in *Deploying Network Services* of the *Microsoft Windows Server 2003 Deployment Kit* (or see "Deploying Dial-up and VPN Remote Access Servers" on the Web at http://www.microsoft.com/reskit).

For procedures explaining how to configure packet filters, see "VPN servers and firewall configuration" in Help and Support Center for Windows Server 2003.

Configuring Routing on a VPN Server

To enable a VPN server to correctly forward traffic to locations on your intranet, perform one of two routing configurations:

- Configure the server with static routes that summarize all possible IP addresses on the intranet.

- Configure the server with routing protocols that enable it to act as a dynamic router, automatically adding routes for intranet subnets to its routing table.

In a small, stable networking environment, static routing might be an appropriate choice for a VPN solution. However, in most corporate networking environments, the increased administrative overhead required to maintain static routes is prohibitive. If applicable, you can use the information you recorded in Table 5.2 to assist you in configuring this information.

Configuring Static Routes on the Server   If you manually configure IP address ranges for a static address pool on any of your VPN servers, and if any of the ranges is an off-subnet range, your intranet routing infrastructure must include routes representing the off-subnet address ranges. To provide the best summary of address ranges for routes, choose your address ranges so that they can be expressed using a single prefix and subnet mask.

To ensure this, add static routes representing the off-subnet address ranges to the routers neighboring the VPN servers, and then use the routing protocol of your intranet to propagate the off-subnet routes to other routers. When you add the static routes to the neighboring routers, specify that the gateway or the next hop address is the intranet interface of the VPN server.

For information about adding static routes, see "Configuring the branch office network" in Help and Support Center for Windows Server 2003.

Configuring the Server as a Dynamic Router   If you are using RIP or OSPF, you can configure any VPN server that is using off-subnet address ranges as a RIP or OSPF router.

For OSPF, you must also configure the VPN server as an autonomous system boundary router (ASBR). For more information, see "OSPF design considerations" in Help and Support Center for Windows Server 2003.

If you use a routing protocol other than RIP or OSPF, such as Interior Gateway Routing Protocol (IGRP), on the VPN server's neighboring intranet router, configure the interface connected to the subnet to which the VPN server is assigned for RIP or OSPF, configure all other interfaces for IGRP, and then configure the router for route redistribution between protocols. See your router documentation for details on how to configure route redistribution.

For information about:

■   Configuring the VPN server as a RIP router, see "Configure RIP for IP" in Help and Support Center for Windows Server 2003.

■   Configuring the VPN server as an OSPF router, see "OSPF design considerations" and "Configure OSPF" in Help and Support Center for Windows Server 2003.

Configuring a Dial-up Remote Access Server

To provide dial-up access to your organization's intranet, configure a computer running Windows Server 2003 as a dial-up remote access server.

Use the Routing and Remote Access Server Setup Wizard to configure the server as a dial-up remote access server and enable the Routing and Remote Access service, which is installed automatically with the Windows Server 2003 family. For instructions on using the wizard, see "Remote access/VPN server role: Configuring a remote access/VPN server" in Help and Support Center for Windows Server 2003.

With Routing and Remote Access enabled, configure the properties of a dial-up remote access server by using the Routing and Remote Access snap-in. If applicable, you can use the information that you recorded in Table 5.3 to assist you in configuring your dial-up remote access server.

To configure a server for dial-up remote access

1. Open the Routing and Remote Access snap-in.

2. In the console tree, right-click the server name, and then click **Properties**.

3. On the **General** tab of the properties dialog box for the server, verify that the **Remote access server** check box is selected.

4. On the **Security** tab, set up authentication for dial-up remote access clients:

   a. Click **Authentication Methods**, and in the **Authentication Methods** dialog box, select the check boxes for the authentication methods that the server will accept for dial-up connections.

> **Note** The server is configured by default to accept certain authentication methods. To allow additional authentication methods, you must configure Routing and Remote Access. You can use remote access policies to control which authentication methods to accept for specific types of connections. For more information about using Windows Server 2003 remote access policies, see "Introduction to remote access policies" in Help and Support Center for Windows Server 2003.

   b. Under **Authentication Provider** on the **Security** tab, specify the authentication provider to use for dial-up remote access clients.

    c.   Under **Accounting Provider**, specify and configure the accounting provider to use for recording dial-up connection accounting information.

5.   On the **IP** tab, set up routing for dial-up remote access clients:

    a.   Verify that the **Enable IP routing** and **Allow IP-based remote access and demand-dial connections** check boxes are selected.

    b.   If you are using DHCP to obtain IP addresses for dial-up remote access clients, click **Dynamic Host Configuration Protocol (DHCP)**.

          –or–

          Select **Static address pool**, and then configure ranges of IP addresses that are dynamically assigned to dial-up remote access clients.

          If the static IP address pool consists of ranges of IP addresses for a separate subnet, either enable an IP routing protocol on the remote access server or add static IP routes for each range to your IP routing infrastructure. If the routes are not added, dial-up remote access clients cannot receive traffic from resources on the intranet.

Configuring a Connection to the Intranet

A network adapter provides the connection from a dial-up remote access server to the intranet. To enable this connection, you must configure TCP/IP on the network adapter and, on the dial-up remote access server, configure the modem ports for remote access.

Configuring TCP/IP on the Network Adapter   Configure the following TCP/IP settings on the network adapter that provides the connection from the dial-up remote access server to the intranet:

■   The IP address and subnet mask assigned by a network administrator.

■   The default gateway of a local router.

■   The IP addresses of DNS and WINS servers.

Configuring a Connection to Dial-up Remote Access Clients   To enable multiple dial-up clients to connect to the intranet simultaneously, the dial-up solution must have a modem bank connected to a telecommunications provider. The modem bank adapter includes drivers that you install on the dial-up remote access server.

Configuring Dial-in Ports for Remote Access   With the modem bank adapter drivers installed, the modem bank appears as a device with multiple modem ports. Use the Routing and Remote Access snap-in to configure all of the active modem bank ports on the server for remote access.

To configure the ports of a device for remote access

1.   Open the **Routing and Remote Access** snap-in.

2.   In the console tree, right-click **Ports**, and then click **Properties**.

3.   In the **Ports Properties** dialog box, specify the device that you want to configure, and then click **Configure**.

4.   In the **Configure** Device dialog box, specify the appropriate connection options.

Configuring Encryption for a Dial-up Solution

In the remote access policy that governs connections to the dial-up remote access server, use Routing and Remote Access to set the appropriate encryption level. For a procedure for setting an encryption level in a remote access policy, see "Configuring authentication and data encryption" in Help and Support Center for Windows Server 2003.

In the remote access policy for dial-up connections on the dial-up remote access server, choose one of the following encryption levels:

■   To use MPPE with a 40-bit encryption key, select the **Basic** check box.

■   To use MPPE with a 56-bit encryption key, select the **Strong** check box.

■   To use MPPE with a 128-bit encryption key, select the **Strongest** check box.

If applicable, you can use the information that you recorded in Table 5.3 to assist you in configuring encryption for your dial-up solution.

For more information about using Windows Server 2003 remote access policies, see "Introduction to remote access policies" in Help and Support Center for Windows Server 2003.

Additional Resources

These resources contain additional information and tools related to this chapter.

Related Information

- The *Microsoft Windows Server 2003 Deployment Kit* (or see the Windows Server 2003 Deployment Kit on the Web at http://www.microsoft.com/reskit).

- The Active Directory link on the Web Resources page at http://www.microsoft.com/windows/reskits/webresources.

- The Virtual Private Networks link on the Web Resources page at http://www.microsoft.com/windows/reskits/webresources.

- The Windows Server 2003 link on the Web Resources page at http://www.microsoft.com/windows/reskits/webresources.

Related Help Topics   You can find related Help topics in Help and Support Center for Windows Server 2003. For best results in identifying Help topics by title, in Help and Support Center, under the **Search** box, click **Set search options**. Under **Help Topics**, select the **Search in title only** check box.

- "Remote access/VPN server role: Configuring a remote access/VPN server" for information about configuring a remote access/VPN server

- "Configure RIP for IP" for information about configuring the VPN server as a RIP router

- "OSPF design considerations" and "Configure OSPF" for information about configuring a VPN server as an OSPF router

- "Introduction to remote access policies" for information about remote access policies

- "Configuring authentication and data encryption" for a procedure for setting an encryption level in a remote access policy

- "VPN servers and firewall configuration" for procedures explaining how to configure packet filters on the firewall and the VPN server

- "Configuring the branch office network" for information about configuring demand-dial connections between sites

6

Migrating Web Sites from IIS 4.0 to IIS 6.0

Migrating is installing the Microsoft® Windows Server™ 2003 operating system and Internet Information Services (IIS) 6.0 on a new server and then moving existing Web sites that are hosted on a computer running the Microsoft Windows NT® Server version 4.0 operating system and Internet Information Server (IIS) 4.0 to that server. This process involves minimal outage of service to users who access the Web sites, and it retains the majority of the original configuration settings and fully preserves the content of the Web sites.

In This Chapter:

Related Information

■   For information about migrating a file or print server, see "Migrating File and Print Servers to Windows Server 2003" in this book.

■   For information about installing IIS 6.0 on an existing computer running Windows NT Server 4.0 and IIS 4.0, see "Upgrading an IIS Server to IIS 6.0" in *Deploying Internet Information Services (IIS) 6.0* of the *Microsoft® Windows Server™ 2003 Deployment Kit* (or see "Upgrading an IIS Server to IIS 6.0" on the Web at http://www.microsoft.com/reskit).

Overview of Migrating Web Sites from IIS 4.0 to IIS 6.0

You start the migration process by determining whether the Web site that you want to migrate is compatible with Internet Information Services (IIS) 6.0 and the Microsoft® Windows Server™ 2003, Standard Edition; and the Windows Server™ 2003, Web Edition operating system. Next, you install Windows Server 2003 and IIS 6.0 on the *target server*, which is the server that will host your Web site after migration. Then, you use the IIS 6.0 Migration Tool to help migrate the Web site content and configuration settings from the *source server*, which is a server running the Microsoft Windows NT® Server 4.0 operating system, to the target server.

After the migration of your Web site content, you customize the configuration of IIS 6.0 to meet your needs. Finally, after you have completed the customization of IIS 6.0, you back up the target server, enable client access to the Web site on the target server, and decommission the source server.

> **Tip**   To migrate multiple Web sites, use the process described in this chapter to migrate each of your existing Web sites from the source server to the target server. Then, after moving all of your Web sites to the target server and enabling client access to those sites, decommission the source server.

The migration process focuses on transferring the Web site content and configuration settings only. If your Web site contains only static content, you can most likely complete the migration process in a few steps. However, if your IIS Web site contains dynamic content, such as Active Server Pages (ASP), you might need to modify the code in the dynamic content. For more information about possible code modifications, see "Migrating IIS Web Sites to IIS 6.0" in

Deploying Internet Information Services (IIS) 6.0 of the *Microsoft Windows Server 2003 Deployment Kit* (or see "Migrating IIS Web Sites to IIS 6.0" on the Web at http://www.microsoft.com/reskit).

Upon completing the process outlined in this chapter, you will have a Web server running IIS 6.0 and hosting a single Web site. This server will fulfill your security requirements, but you can further enhance security after migration. Also, to maintain the security of your server, you need to implement continuing security practices such as security monitoring, detection, and response. For more information about enhancing and maintaining Web server security, see "Enhancing and Maintaining Web Site Security After Migration" later in this chapter.

Process for Migrating a Web Site from IIS 4.0 to IIS 6.0

The process for migrating a Web site hosted on IIS 4.0 consists of preparing for and performing the migration. During the preparation phase, you gather information about your existing server running Windows NT Server 4.0 and about the Web site that you are going to migrate to IIS 6.0. This information will be used as input when you run the IIS 6.0 Migration Tool. Then, you perform the migration with the IIS 6.0 Migration tool. After the migration is complete, you must change several settings in the IIS metabase. You can also enhance security by further configuring your server after migration.

The procedure for migrating one of your existing Web sites from IIS 4.0 to IIS 6.0, as described in this chapter, is based on the following assumptions:

■ Your existing server is a *dedicated Web server*. A dedicated Web server is a server that is being used only as a Web server and not for other purposes, such as a file server configured to run the File Transfer Protocol (FTP), a mail server configured to run the Simple Mail Transfer Protocol (SMTP), or a database server running Microsoft SQL Server™.

> **Note** In many small and medium-sized organizations, a single server supports multiple roles. For example, combining a Web server with a file or print server is a common scenario. If your Web server will also function as a file or print server, you should still be able to migrate your IIS 4.0 Web site by using the process described in this chapter. For more information about migrating a file or print server, see "Migrating File and Print Servers to Windows Server 2003" in this book.

- The Web site that you want to migrate to IIS 6.0 is a public Internet site that is configured for Anonymous authentication only, using the IUSR_*computername* account.

- The Web site that you want to migrate to IIS 6.0 runs correctly on IIS 4.0.

- The Web site that you want to migrate to IIS 6.0 contains mostly static content (or files that have .htm or .html file name extensions), with some dynamic content, which can include ASP.

- The Web site that you want to migrate to IIS 6.0 uses FrontPage® Server Extensions from Microsoft.

- The content of the Web site that you want to migrate to IIS 6.0 is stored in one of two locations:

  ❑ The home directory and subdirectories of the Web site

  ❑ A virtual directory

- The Web site that you want to migrate to IIS 6.0 does not contain any third-party or custom applications, such as an e-commerce application.

- If the Web site uses Secure Sockets Layer (SSL), one certificate is assigned to the Web site.

If your Web server and site do not meet these requirements, you cannot perform the Web site migration process as described in this chapter. For more information about migrating Web sites to IIS 6.0, see "Migrating IIS Web Sites to IIS 6.0" in *Deploying Internet Information Services (IIS) 6.0* of the *Microsoft Windows Server 2003 Deployment Kit* (or see "Chapter 6: Migrating IIS Web Sites to IIS 6.0" on the http://www.microsoft.com/reskit).

The following quick-start guide shows the steps of the Web site migration process. You can use this guide to identify the steps for which you need to gather additional information to complete, and then you can skip the information with which you are already familiar.

Prepare for Migration

1. Determine hardware compatibility with Windows Server 2003.

2. Gather the following information about your server and Web site:

   ❑ The name of the source server

   ❑ The friendly name of the Web site

❑   Whether the Web site is compatible with worker process isolation mode

❑   Whether the Web site content requires Inetinfo.exe

❑   Whether ASP pages use relative parent paths

3.   Before running the IIS 6.0 Migration Tool, identify the following:

❑   Tasks that are automated by the migration tool

❑   Subsequent tasks that must be performed manually

Deploy the Target Sever

1.   Install and configure Windows Server 2003.

2.   Install and configure IIS 6.0.

3.   Verify connectivity between the source server and the target server.

Migrate the Web Site with the IIS 6.0 Migration Tool

1.   Install the IIS 6.0 Migration Tool.

2.   Verify that clients are not accessing the Web site.

3.   Run the migration tool.

4.   Verify that the migration tool ran successfully.

5.   Modify IIS 6.0 metabase properties that refer to the location where Windows is installed.

Configure IIS 6.0 Properties

1.   Enable ASP and FrontPage Server Extensions.

2.   If applicable for the Web site, migrate server certificates for SSL.

3.   Migrate Microsoft FrontPage® users and roles.

Complete the Migration

1.   Verify that the Web site migrated successfully.

2.   Back up the target server.

3.   Enable client access.

Enhance and Maintain Web Site Security After Migration

1. Further reduce the attack surface of the Web server by configuring Windows Server 2003 security settings:

   ❑ Disable and rename the Administrator account.

   ❑ Convert all disk volumes to the NTFS file system.

   ❑ Remove NTFS permissions that are granted to the Everyone group on the root folder of all disk volumes.

   ❑ Remove any compilers or development environments.

   ❑ Disable NetBIOS over TCP/IP.

2. Prevent unauthorized access to the Web site by doing the following:

   ❑ Store Web site content on a dedicated disk volume that does not contain the operating system.

   ❑ Set IIS Web site permissions.

   ❑ Set NTFS file system permissions.

3. Maintain Web site security by doing the following:

   ❑ Obtain and apply current security patches.

   ❑ Enable Windows Server 2003 security logs.

   ❑ Enable file access auditing for Web site content.

   ❑ Configure IIS logs.

   ❑ Enable IIS logging.

4. Review security policies, processes, and procedures.

Completing the Step-by-Step Procedures

All of the step-by-step procedures that are required to complete the Web site migration process are documented in this chapter. Each procedure has been carefully developed and tested to help you complete the Web site migration process as quickly and simply as possible.

Important   You must be a member of the Administrators group on both the source server and the target server to perform the procedures in this chapter.

IIS Manager

IIS Manager is a Microsoft Management Console (MMC) snap-in. This graphical interface serves as a portal for configuring and managing IIS 6.0. With IIS Manager, you can configure IIS security, performance, and reliability features. Some of the specific tasks that you can complete from IIS Manager include adding or deleting Web sites; starting, stopping, and pausing Web sites; backing up and restoring server configurations; and creating virtual directories for better content management. In IIS 4.0, this tool was called the Internet Service Manager.

To start IIS Manager

■   From the **Start** menu, point to **Administrative Tools**, and then click **Internet Information Services (IIS) Manager**.

To start IIS Manager from the Run dialog box

1.   From the **Start** menu, click **Run**.

2.   In the **Open** dialog box, type **inetmgr**, and then click **OK**.

Security Recommendation

As a security best practice, log on to your computer using an account that is not in the Administrators group, and then use the **Run as** command to run IIS Manager as an administrator. At the command prompt, type the following: **runas** */user:administrative_accountname* **"mmc %systemroot%\ system32\inetsrv\iis.msc"**.

Preparing for Migration

Before migrating your existing IIS 4.0 Web site, ensure that the Web site and its components are compatible with Windows Server 2003 and IIS 6.0. Follow these steps to prepare for migration:

1.   Determine whether your existing system hardware is compatible with Windows Server 2003.

2.   Gather information about your existing server running Windows NT Server 4.0 and about the Web site that you are going to migrate.

3.   Identify the steps of the migration process that you must perform manually after you run the IIS 6.0 Migration Tool.

If you currently use setup programs or provisioning scripts on the source server and you intend to continue using them after migration, ensure that the setup programs and provisioning scripts are compatible with Windows Server 2003 and IIS 6.0.

In some cases, the configuration of a Web site might require you to migrate the Web site to IIS 6.0 running in IIS 5.0 isolation mode. In that case, you cannot follow the steps in this chapter to perform the migration. For more information about migrating Web sites to IIS 6.0 running in IIS 5.0 isolation mode, see "Migrating IIS Web Sites to IIS 6.0" in *Deploying Internet Information Services (IIS) 6.0* of the *Microsoft Windows Server 2003 Deployment Kit* (or see "Migrating IIS Web Sites to IIS 6.0" on the Web at http://www.microsoft.com /reskit).

Determining Hardware Compatibility with Windows Server 2003

At a minimum, your existing system hardware must be compatible with Windows Server 2003 before you migrate the Web site to IIS 6.0. Therefore, you must identify any hardware devices that are incompatible with Windows Server 2003.

When you select the computer that will be the target server, ensure that the computer is compatible with Windows Server 2003. The most common hardware incompatibility is a device driver that is no longer supported or is not yet supported in Windows Server 2003. When a device is no longer supported, remove the existing device and then install an equivalent device that is supported by Windows Server 2003. When a device is not supported, look for updated drivers on the device manufacturer's Web site. It is also important that you have the latest BIOS version that is available from your computer manufacturer.

For example, the target server might have a network adapter that is not included with Windows Server 2003. You can review the manufacturer's Web site to obtain a driver that is compatible with Windows Server 2003.

For more information about the hardware devices supported by the Windows Server 2003 operating systems, see the *Hardware Compatibility List* on the product CD-ROM or see the Hardware Compatibility List link on the Web Resources page at http://www.microsoft.com/windows/reskits/webresources.

Gathering Information About Your Server and Web Site

Before you migrate your Web site content, you must know the following information about the server and Web site:

- The name of the source server
- The friendly name of your Web site
- Whether your Web site will run correctly in IIS 6.0 worker process isolation mode

- Whether any applications on your Web site require Inetinfo.exe

- Whether ASP pages on your Web site use relative parent paths in their #include statements

Determining the Name of the Source Server

When you run the IIS 6.0 Migration Tool, you must provide the name of the source server.

To determine the name of the source server

1. Open Administrative Tools, and then click **Server Manager**.

2. On the **Server Manager** dialog box, note the server name displayed in the **Computer** column.

Determining the Friendly Name of Your Web Site

When you run the IIS 6.0 Migration Tool, you must provide the friendly name of your Web site so the site and its contents migrate correctly.

To determine the friendly name of your Web server on IIS 4.0

1. Open Administrative Tools, and then click **Windows NT 4.0 Option Pack**.

2. Click **Microsoft Internet Information Server**, and then click **Internet Service Manager**.

3. In the console tree, double-click **Internet Information Server**. The friendly name of the Web site appears as a node under the Internet Information Server node.

Determining Web Site Compatibility with Worker Process Isolation Mode

Application isolation separates Web sites and applications so that a failure in one Web site or application does not affect other Web sites and applications running on the same Web server. IIS 6.0 can run in one of the following application isolation modes:

- **Worker process isolation mode.** This mode uses the redesigned architecture for IIS 6.0 to run all application code in an isolated environment. This mode is compatible with most existing Web sites. In this mode, applications run under the Network Service account, which has a lower level of privileges than the Local System account that is used by applications on IIS 4.0. The Local System account enables access to and the ability to alter the resources on the system.

Whenever possible, configure IIS 6.0 to run in worker process isolation mode to benefit from the enhanced performance and security in IIS 6.0.

- **IIS 5.0 isolation mode.** This mode provides compatibility for applications that depend on the architecture of earlier versions of IIS. Run IIS in this mode only when a Web site cannot run in worker process isolation mode (that is, the application must run under the Local System account) and run it only until the compatibility issues are resolved.

> **Important**   IIS 6.0 cannot run both application isolation modes simultaneously on the same server. Therefore, on a single server running IIS 6.0, you cannot run some Web applications in worker process isolation mode and others in IIS 5.0 isolation mode. If you have applications that require separate modes, you must run them on separate servers.

For more information about modifying configuring IIS 6.0 to run in IIS 5.0 isolation mode, see "Migrating IIS Web Sites to IIS 6.0" in *Deploying Internet Information Services (IIS) 6.0* of the *Microsoft Windows Server 2003 Deployment Kit* (or see "Migrating IIS Web Sites to IIS 6.0" on the Web at http://www.microsoft.com/reskit).

Determining Whether Your Web Site Content Requires Inetinfo.exe

Many applications that run on Windows NT Server 4.0 and IIS 4.0 run in-process with Inetinfo.exe. If this is true of some of your Web site content, you must either migrate that content to IIS 6.0 running in IIS 5.0 isolation mode; or you must rewrite the content so that Inetinfo.exe is not required, and then migrate the content to IIS 6.0 running in worker process isolation mode.

Determining Whether ASP Pages Use Relative Parent Paths

If your Web site contains ASP pages, you must ensure that the #include statements in those pages do not use relative parent paths to refer to files that must be included in the .asp page. Relative parent paths present a security risk because they can allow unauthorized users to access content in directories to which they do not have access. By default, IIS 6.0 does not permit the use of relative parent paths. Instead, #include statements must use absolute virtual paths that trace the path from the root directory of the Web site to the file that contains the #include statement.

The following code shows the format of a relative parent path that would be rejected by IIS in its default configuration, and an example:

```
<!--#include file="../<filename.ext>"-->
```

```
<!--#include file="../myAspPage.asp>"-->
```

The following code shows the format of an absolute virtual path and an example:

```
<!--#include virtual="/<virtual path>/<filename.ext>"-->
```

```
<!--#include virtual="/C:\myWebSite/myWebSiteFolder/myAspPage.asp"-->
```

Identifying the Role of the IIS 6.0 Migration Tool

The IIS 6.0 Migration Tool is a command-line utility that automates some of the steps in the process for migrating Web sites from IIS 4.0 to IIS 6.0. The migration tool does not provide an end-to-end migration solution, but it automates some of the time-consuming, repetitive migration tasks.

Migration Tasks That Are Automated by the IIS 6.0 Migration Tool

The IIS 6.0 Migration Tool automates the following steps in the IIS migration process:

- **Transferring the Web site content.** All of the files and folders located in the home directory of the Web site are copied from the source server to the target server. Virtual directories, which can be located outside of the home directory of the Web site, are also copied if the target server uses the same disk volume letter (for example, C:\) that the source server uses as the location of the virtual directory. The NTFS file system permissions assigned to the files and directories that make up the Web site content on the source server are granted to the corresponding files and directories on the target server. You must manually migrate any content that does not meet these requirements.

- **Transferring the Web site configuration in the IIS metabase.** The configuration for each Web site and application, which is stored in the IIS metabase properties on the source server, is translated and then the corresponding IIS 6.0 metabase properties are appropriately configured on the target server.

■   **Backing up the IIS metabase configuration to the target server.** The IIS metabase configuration is backed up on the target server before migration. You can use this backup to restore the target server to a known state in the event that the migration process is not successful.

Migration Tasks That Must Be Completed Manually

You must complete the following steps in the Web site migration process after you run the IIS 6.0 Migration Tool.

Migrating Additional Web Site Content   Some Web sites have content that is not located in the home directory of the Web site or in subdirectories that are inside the home directory. The IIS 6.0 Migration Tool migrates all of the content that is located in the home directory of the Web site and in any subdirectories contained in that home directory. The tool also migrates content in virtual directories, if the disk volume letter (for example, C:\) on which the virtual directory is located is the same on both the source server and the target server. However, if the virtual directory is located on C:\ on the source server, and you decide to configure the target server so that the virtual directory will be located on D:\, for example, you must migrate the virtual directory content manually.

> **Important**   The procedure described in this chapter assumes that you have set up the Web site and virtual directory locations on the target server exactly as they exist on the source server. For more information about migrating content that is stored in folders outside of the home directory of the Web site or the virtual directories beneath the home directory, see the "Migrating Additional Web Site Content" topic in "Migrating IIS Web Sites to IIS 6.0" in *Deploying Internet Information Services (IIS) 6.0* of the *Microsoft Windows Server 2003 Deployment Kit* (or see "Migrating IIS Web Sites to IIS 6.0" on the Web at http://www.microsoft.com/reskit).

Configuring Additional Web Site Properties   After running the IIS 6.0 Migration Tool, the Web site configuration is similar to its configuration on the source server. However, depending on the configuration of the Web site on the source server, you might need to configure additional Web site properties, by completing the following steps:

■   **Change the IIS metabase settings to reflect where Windows is installed.** If the Windows Server 2003 *systemroot* path, which is the location where Windows is installed, does not match the Windows systemroot path on the source server, you must modify the metabase settings on the migrated Web sites to reference the correct folder on the target server. For example, if Windows was installed on C:\WINNT on the source server, the IIS metabase entries for **ScriptMaps** and **HTTPErrors** properties might still reference these paths, and therefore need to be updated on the target server.

■   **Configure IIS properties that reference local user accounts.** There are a number of Web site configuration properties on the source server that you can configure to utilize user accounts that are local to the source server. The IIS 6.0 Migration Tool does not migrate local user and group accounts from the source server to the target server. As a result, the migrated Web site references user accounts that do not exist on the target server. If you have an Active Directory domain, you can work around this situation by creating a domain account for IUSR_*computername* and storing the account information in the IIS metabase. Then, add IIS 6.0 as a member of that domain. Otherwise, you must configure the Web site to utilize user accounts that are domain-based or local to the target server, and then re-create the file system permissions on migrated content.

For example, if NTFS permissions are granted to local user accounts on the source server, you must create new user accounts, or designate existing user accounts, for use on the target server and then grant the corresponding NTFS permissions to the user accounts on the target server.

■   **Configure SSL certificates.** If you use SSL to secure your Web site, you must export the SSL sever certificate from the source server, and then install the certificate on the target server after the migration process is complete.

■   **Configure FrontPage Server Extensions users and roles.** If FrontPage Server Extensions is configured to use a local user account on the source server as the FrontPage administrator, you must create a new user account, or designate an existing user account, for use on the target server. In addition, you must assign the user the same FrontPage role as the corresponding user had on the source server.

For more information about using the IIS 6.0 Migration Tool to perform your migration, see "Migrating a Web Site with the IIS 6.0 Migration Tool" later in this chapter.

Deploying the Target Server

Before you begin the migration process, you must deploy the target server by following these steps:

1. Install Windows Server 2003 on the target server. To follow the process described in this chapter, install Windows Server 2003 with the default options.

2. Install and configure IIS 6.0 on the target server. To follow the process described in this chapter, install IIS 6.0 with the default options.

    By default, IIS 6.0 is configured to run in worker process isolation mode. If you determined that your Web site can run in worker process isolation mode, you can continue to follow the migration process described in this chapter.

    However, if you determined that your Web site cannot run in worker process isolation mode, you must modify the code or configure IIS 6.0 to run in IIS 5.0 isolation mode. For more information about migrating Web sites to IIS 6.0 running in IIS 5.0 isolation mode, see "Migrating IIS Web Sites to IIS 6.0" in *Deploying Internet Information Services (IIS) 6.0* of the *Microsoft Windows Server 2003 Deployment Kit* (or see "Migrating IIS Web Sites to IIS 6.0" on the Web at http://www.microsoft.com/reskit).

3. Verify connectivity between the source server and the target server.

    If you have already installed Windows Server 2003 on the target server, installed and configured IIS 6.0 on the target server, and verified connectivity between the source and target servers, you can proceed to "Migrating Web Sites with the IIS 6.0 Migration Tool" later in this chapter.

Installing and Configuring Windows Server 2003

The primary concern when installing Windows Server 2003 is to ensure that the security of the target server is maintained. When you install Windows Server 2003 as a dedicated Web server, the default components and services are configured to provide the smallest possible attack surface. You can further reduce the attack surface of the target server by enabling only the essential Windows Server 2003 components and services.

Install the Windows Server 2003 operating system on your target server with the default options. If you use other methods for installing and configuring Windows Server 2003, such as unattended setup, your configuration settings might be different.

To start Setup for a new installation using the CD

1. Insert the CD in the CD-ROM drive, and then restart the computer.

2. Follow the instructions for your operating system to boot the computer from the CD.

3. Wait for Setup to display a dialog box, and then follow the Setup instructions.

> **Note**   When you complete the installation of Windows Server 2003, Manage Your Server automatically starts. The migration process described in this chapter assumes that you quit Manage Your Server and then further configure the Web server in **Add or Remove Programs** in Control Panel.

Configuring Windows Server 2003 Services

To enable and disable services, change the startup type of the service. You can configure the startup type of the service to one of the following:

- ■   The service starts automatically when the operating system starts.

- ■   The service can be started by an administrator, a related operating system service, a system device driver, or an action in the user interface that is dependent on the manual service.

- ■   The service cannot be started automatically or manually; to start a disabled service, you must change the startup type to   or   .

Table 6.1 lists the Windows Server 2003 services, as well as the default startup type, the recommended startup type, and comments about the services. For each of the Windows Server 2003 services that are listed in Table 6.1, complete the following steps:

1. Review the recommended startup type to determine whether you need to change the default startup type.

2. Determine, based on the information provided in the comments, if the recommendation applies to your Web server.

3. Configure the startup type for the service based on the decisions made in the previous steps.

Table 6.1   Recommended Service Startup Types on a Dedicated Web Server

Service Name	Default Startup Type	Recommended Startup Type	Comment
Application Management	Manual	See comment	Provides software installation services for applications that are deployed in **Add or Remove Programs** in Control Panel.
			On a dedicated Web server, this service can be disabled to prevent unauthorized installation of software.
Automatic Updates	Automatic	See comment	Provides the download and installation of critical Windows updates, such as security patches and hotfixes.
			This service can be disabled when automatic updates are not performed on the Web server.
Background Intelligent Transfer Service	Manual	See comment	Provides a background file-transfer mechanism and queue management, and it is used by Automatic Update to automatically download programs (such as security patches).
			This service can be disabled when automatic updates are not performed on the Web server.
Distributed File System	Automatic	Disable	Manages logical volumes that are distributed across a local area network (LAN) or wide area network (WAN).
			On a dedicated Web server, disable Distributed File System.

Table 6.1   Recommended Service Startup Types on a Dedicated Web Server

Service Name	Default Startup Type	Recommended Startup Type	Comment
Distributed Link Tracking Client	Automatic	Disabled	Maintains links between NTFS V5 file system files within the Web server and other servers in the domain.
			On a dedicated Web server, disable Distributed Link Tracking.
Distributed Link Tracking Server	Manual	Disabled	Tracks information about files that are moved between NTFS V5 volumes throughout a domain.
			On a dedicated Web server, disable Distributed Link Tracking.
Error Reporting Service	Automatic	See comment	Collects, stores, and reports unexpected application crashes to Microsoft. If this service is stopped, then Error Reporting will occur only for kernel faults.
			On a dedicated Web server, disable Error Reporting Service.
Fax Service	Manual	Disabled	Provides the ability to send and receive faxes through fax resources that are available on the Web server and network.
			On a dedicated Web server, this service can be disabled because sending and receiving faxes is not a typical function of a Web Server.
Indexing Service	Manual	See comment	Indexes content and properties of files on the Web server to provide rapid access to the file through a flexible query language.
			On a dedicated Web server, disable this service unless Web sites or applications specifically leverage the Indexing Service for searching site content.
NetMeeting Remote Desktop Sharing	Manual	Disabled	Eliminates potential security threats by allowing domain-controller remote administration through NetMeeting.

Table 6.1 Recommended Service Startup Types on a Dedicated Web Server

Service Name	Default Startup Type	Recommended Startup Type	Comment
Performance Logs and Alerts	Manual	See comment	Collects performance data for the domain controller, writes the data to a log, or generates alerts.
			This service can be set to automatic when you want to log performance data or generate alerts without an administrator being logged on.
Print Spooler	Automatic	See comment	Manages all local and network print queues and controls all print jobs.
			On a dedicated Web server, this service can be disabled when no printing is required.
Remote Access Auto Connection Manager	Manual	See comment	Detects unsuccessful attempts to connect to a remote network or computer and provides alternative methods for connection.
			On a dedicated Web server, this service can be disabled when no VPN or dial-up connections are initiated.
Remote Access Connection Manager	Manual	See comment	Manages VPN and dial-up connection from the Web server to the Internet or other remote networks.
			On a dedicated Web server, this service can be disabled when no VPN or dial-up connections are initiated.
Remote Desktop Help Sessions Manager	Manual	Disabled	Manages and controls Remote Assistance.
			On a dedicated Web server, this service can be disabled. Use Terminal Services instead.
Remote Procedure Call (RPC) Locater	Manual	See comment	Enables RPC clients using the RpcNs* family of application programming interfaces (APIs) to locate RPC servers and manage the RPC name service database.
			This service can be disabled if no applications use the RpcNs* APIs.

Table 6.1   Recommended Service Startup Types on a Dedicated Web Server

Service Name	Default Startup Type	Recommended Startup Type	Comment
Removable Storage	Manual	See comment	Manages and catalogs removable media, and operates automated removable media devices, such as tape auto loaders or CD jukeboxes.
			This service can be disabled when removable media devices are directly connected to the Web server.
Telephony	Manual	See comment	Provides Telephony API (TAPI) support of client programs that control telephony devices and IP-based voice connections.
			On a dedicated Web server, this service can be disabled when TAPI is not used by applications.
Telnet	Manual	Disabled	Enables a remote user to log on and run applications from a command line on the Web server.
			To reduce the attack surface, disable Telnet unless it is used for remote administration of branch offices or of Web servers that have no keyboard or monitor directly attached (also known as *headless* Web servers). Because Telnet traffic is plaintext, Terminal Services is the preferred method for remote administration.
Terminal Services	Manual	See comment	Allows multiple remote users to be connected interactively to the Web server, and provides display of desktops and run applications.
			To reduce the attack surface, disable Terminal Services unless it is used for remote administration of branch offices or headless Web servers.

Table 6.1   Recommended Service Startup Types on a Dedicated Web Server

Service Name	Default Startup Type	Recommended Startup Type	Comment
Upload Managers	Manual	See comment	Manages the synchronous and asynchronous file transfers between clients and servers on the network. Driver data is anonymously uploaded from these transfers and then used by Microsoft to help users find the drivers they need. The Driver Feedback Server asks for the permission of the client to upload the hardware profile of the Web server and then search the Internet for information about how to obtain the appropriate drivers or how to get support.
			To reduce the attack surface, disable this service on dedicated Web servers.
WinHTTP Web Proxy Auto-Discovery Service	Manual	See comment	Implements the Web Proxy Auto-Discovery (WPAD) protocol for Windows HTTP services (WinHTTP) and enables an HTTP client to automatically discover a proxy configuration.
			On dedicated Web servers, this service can be disabled
Wireless Configuration	Automatic	See comment	Enables automatic configuration for IEEE 802.11 adapters.
			On dedicated Web servers without wireless network adapters, this service can be disabled.
WMI Performance Adapter	Manual	See comment	Provides performance library information from WMI providers to clients on the network.
			On dedicated Web servers that do not use WMI to provide performance library information, this service can be disabled.

After determining which Windows Server 2003 services need to have a different default startup type on your Web server, complete the steps in the following procedure to modify the startup type.

To configure the startup type for Windows Server 2003 services

1.   Open Administrative Tools, and then click **Services**.

2.   In the details pane, right-click the Windows Server 2003 service that you want to change, and then click **Properties**.

3.   On the **General** tab, in the **Startup type** list box, click one of the following:

   ❑   **Automatic.** The service starts automatically when the Web server is restarted.

   ❑   **Manual.** The service can be started manually by an administrator or by another service.

   ❑   **Disabled.** The service cannot be started by an administrator or by another service unless the startup type is changed to **Automatic** or **Manual**.

4.   Click **OK** to save the changes.

Installing and Configuring IIS 6.0

For security reasons, IIS 6.0 is not installed during the default installation of Windows Server 2003. Thus, the next step in deploying the target server is to install and configure IIS 6.0.

As with installing Windows Server 2003, your primary concern when installing and configuring IIS 6.0 is to ensure that the security of the target server is maintained. Enabling unnecessary components and services increases the attack surface of the target server. You can help ensure that the target server is secure by enabling only the IIS 6.0 components and services that you need to use on your Web server.

> **Note**   The migration process presented here assumes that you install IIS 6.0 with the default options in **Add or Remove Programs** in Control Panel. If you use other methods for installing IIS 6.0, the default configuration settings might be different.

Install and configure IIS 6.0 by completing the following steps:

1. Install IIS 6.0 with the default options in **Add or Remove Programs** in Control Panel.

2. If the Web site on the source server uses FrontPage Server Extensions, install FrontPage 2002 Server Extensions from Microsoft on the target server.

3. Configure IIS 6.0 components and services, making sure that you only enable the components and services that your Web site needs to run correctly.

To install IIS 6.0 from Control Panel

1. In Control Panel, double-click **Add or Remove Programs**.

2. Click **Add/Remove Windows Components**.

3. In the **Components** box, click **Application Server**, and then click **Details**.

4. In the **Subcomponents of Application Server** box, click **Internet Information Services (IIS)**, and then click **OK**.

5. Click **Next** to start the installation.

To install FrontPage 2002 Server Extensions from Control Panel

1. In Control Panel, double-click **Add or Remove Programs**.

2. Click **Add/Remove Windows Components**.

3. In the **Components** list box, click **Application Server,** and then click **Details**.

4. In the **Subcomponents of Application Server** box, click **Internet Information Services (IIS)**, and then click **Details**.

5. Click **FrontPage 2002 Server Extensions**, click **OK** twice, and then click **Next** to start the installation.

Enable only the essential IIS 6.0 components and services that are required by your Web sites. Enabling unnecessary components and services increases the attack surface of the Web server.

For each of the subcomponents that are listed in Table 6.2 and Table 6.3, complete the following steps:

1. Review the recommended settings to determine whether you need to make changes to the default settings.

2. Determine, based on the information provided in the comments, whether the recommendation applies to your server.

3. Enable or disable the component based on the decisions made in the previous steps.

Table 6.2   Subcomponents of Internet Information Services (IIS)

Subcomponent	Default Setting	Recommended Setting	Comment
Background Intelligent Transfer Service (BITS) server extension	Disabled	See comment	BITS is a background file transfer mechanism used by applications such as Windows Updates and Automatic Updates.
			Enable this component when you have software that depends on it, such as Windows Updates or Automatic Updates to automatically apply service packs, hot fixes, or install other software on the Web server.
			For more information, see "Obtaining and Applying Current Security Patches" later in this chapter.
FrontPage 2002 Server Extensions	Disabled	See comment	Provides FrontPage support for administer-ing and publishing Web sites.
			On a dedicated Web server, disable when no Web sites are using FrontPage Server Ex-tensions.
World Wide Web Service		Enabled (See Table 6.3 for sub-components)	No change

Table 6.3   Subcomponents of the World Wide Web Service

Subcomponent	Default Setting	Recommended Setting	Comment
Active Server Pages	Disabled	See comment	Provides support for Active Server Pages (ASP).
			Disable this component when none of the Web sites or applications on the Web server uses ASP. You can disable this component in Add or Remove Windows Components, which is accessible from Add or Remove Programs in Control Panel, or in the Web Service Extensions node in IIS Manager.
			For more information, see "Enabling ASP and FrontPage Server Extensions" later in this chapter.
Server-Side Includes	Disabled	See comment	Provides support for .shtm, .shtml, and .stm files.
			Disable this component when none of the Web sites or applications on the Web server includes files with these extensions.
World Wide Web Service	Enabled	No change	Provides Internet services, such as static and dynamic content, to clients.
			This component is required on a dedicated Web server.

Verifying Connectivity Between the Source Server and the Target Server

Before you run the IIS 6.0 Migration Tool, you must ensure that the target server can establish a connection to the source server, and you must verify that the IISAdmin service is started on the source computer.

The IIS 6.0 Migration Tool requires only read access to the Web site content and configuration settings on the source server. Therefore, the source server can remain online in your production environment. However, you might need to remove the source server from your production network and move it to a private network segment that has direct network connectivity to the target server under the following circumstances:

■ Firewalls that exist between the source and target servers prevent the migration tool from performing the migration. This often occurs because the migration tool uses DCOM ports that are blocked by the firewalls for communicating with the source and target servers.

Security-related configuration settings on the source server need to be modified to allow the migration tool to work.

Examples of these security-related configuration settings that can prevent the migration tool from working include the following:

■ Remote access to disk volumes through administrative shares is prohibited.

The IIS 6.0 Migration Tool requires access to the disk volume that contains the Web site content to perform the migration. For example, if the Web site content is stored in D:\Inetpub\Wwwroot, the migration tool must access the administrative share (D$) of the disk volume. The administrative shares are often removed to help prevent unauthorized access to the Web server. In order to use the migration tool, you must re-create the appropriate administrative shares.

■ Remote access to the source server must be allowed for members of the local Administrators group on the source server.

For security reasons, many organizations restrict the members of the local Administrators group so that they can only log on locally, not over the network. However, the migration tool must be able to remotely access the source server over the network, as a member of the local Administrators group.

To verify connectivity between the source server and the target server

1. On the target server, open IIS Manager, click **Action**, and then click **Connect**.

2. Type the name of the source server in **Computer name:** or click **Browse** to navigate to the source server, and then click **OK**.

Migrating a Web Site with the IIS 6.0 Migration Tool

Install the IIS 6.0 Migration Tool by completing the following steps:

1. Download the IIS 6.0 Migration Tool and user guide from the Microsoft Download Center (or see the Microsoft Download Center link on the Web Resources page at http://www.microsoft.com/windows/reskits/webresources).

2. Verify that the migration tool operates correctly by typing **iismt** at the command prompt.

    This command starts the migration tool and displays Help for the tool only. The migration process does not actually begin.

Verifying That Clients Are Not Accessing the Web Site

Verify that clients are no longer accessing the Web site on the source server by completing the following steps:

1. Prevent new clients from accessing the site by pausing the site.

    To ensure that service to clients is not interrupted, pause the Web site on the source server before taking the server offline. Pausing a site prevents the site from accepting new connections, but does not affect requests that are already being processed.

2. Monitor the active Web connections to determine when clients are no longer accessing the source server.

    To ensure that service to clients is not interrupted, monitor the Web server for any active Web connections before taking the Web server offline. Both IIS 4.0 and IIS 6.0 include performance monitor counters that can be used to monitor the active Web connections. Monitor the active Web connections to ensure that one of the following is true:

    ❑ The number of active Web connections is zero.

    ❑ All active Web sessions can be accounted for and can be terminated.

3. When the number of active Web counters is zero, stop the WWW service. Ensure that the IIS Admin service is running because the migration tool requires the IIS Admin service.

    The following procedures explain how to verify that clients are not accessing the Web site.

To pause a Web site by using Internet Service Manager in IIS 4.0

1. From the **Start** menu, point to **Programs**, click **Windows NT 4.0 Option Pack**, click **Microsoft Internet Information Server**, and then click **Internet Service Manager**.

2. In Internet Service Manager, right-click the Web site that you want to pause, and then click **Pause**.

> **Note** If a Web site stops unexpectedly, Internet Service Manager might not correctly indicate the state of the site. In IIS, right-click the **Web Sites** folder and then click **Refresh** to see the current state of the Web site.

To monitor active Web connections in IIS 4.0

1. Open Administrative Tools, and then click **Performance Monitor**.

2. Click **Edit**, and then click **Add to Chart**.

3. The local computer is listed in the **Computers** dialog box. To monitor any other computer on which the monitoring console is run, click the **Browse** button, select a computer from the **Select Computer** list, and then click **OK**.

4. **In Performance object**, **click Web Service** to monitor active Web connections.

5. In **Counters**, click **Current Connections**.

> **Note** The performance counters are not installed when IIS 4.0 is installed on Windows NT Server 4.0. In this case, if the performance counters have not been manually enabled, they do not appear in the Counters list. For more information about enabling the performance counters, see article 226512, "How To: Reinstall IIS 4.0 Performance Monitor Counters," in the Microsoft Knowledge Base. To find this article, see the Microsoft Knowledge Base link on the Web Resources page at http://www.microsoft.com/windows/reskits/webresources.

6. In **Instances**, click **_Total**.

7. Click **Add**, and then click **Done**.

To stop the Web Service in IIS 4.0

1. Open Control Panel, and then double-click **Services**.

2. On the Services page, click World Wide Web Publishing Service, click the **Stop** button, and then click **Close**.

Running the IIS 6.0 Migration Tool

Up to this stage in the migration process, you have completed the initial preparation, deployed the target server, and installed the IIS 6.0 Migration Tool. You should now be ready to run the tool.

The scenario described in this chapter assumes that the following conditions apply:

■ You are logged on with an account that is a member of the Administrators group on both the source server and the target server.

■ You know the name of the source server.

■ You know the friendly name of the Web site on the source server.

■ You want to reapply FrontPage Server Extensions to the migrated site on the target server.

■ You want to display the progress of the migration tool on the screen.

If your situation is different, you might need to run the migration tool with different parameters. For more information about each of the parameters of the IIS 6.0 Migration Tool, see the "IIS 6.0 Migration Tool User Guide" that accompanies the tool.

The following example shows the format of the IIS 6.0 Migration Tool command for the scenario and assumptions described in this chapter:

```
iismt SourceServer WebSite /fpse /verbose
```

Using the sample server name and the friendly name of the Web site in this scenario, the command looks like this:

```
iismt SEA-FAB-MS01 "Fabrikam Sales Site" /fpse /verbose
```

To run the IIS 6.0 Migration tool, replace the sample server name and friendly name with the IP address of your source server and the friendly name of your Web site.

Table 6.4 describes the IIS 6.0 Migration Tool parameters used in this scenario.

Table 6.4   IIS 6.0 Migration Tool Command-Line Parameters Used In This Scenario

Parameter	Required or Optional	Description
SourceServer	Required	Identifies the source server by providing the server name.
WebSite	Required	Identifies the site to be migrated by providing the Web site description (friendly name), for example, "Default Web Site."
/fpse	Optional	Re-applies FrontPage Server Extensions to the migrated site on the target server.
/verbose	Optional	Displays metabase path copy and file copy operations to the screen during the migration process.

Verifying That the IIS 6.0 Migration Tool Ran Successfully

Before continuing with the Web site migration, verify that the IIS 6.0 Migration Tool migrated the Web site content and configuration information successfully. Because you specified the /**verbose** parameter, the migration tool displays output that indicates the success or failure of the migration. If the output indicates that errors occurred, you can use the IIS 6.0 Migration Tool log file to resolve any errors.

Verify that the IIS 6.0 Migration Tool ran successfully by completing the following steps:

1. Open *systemroot*\System32\LogFiles\IISMT\iismt_*date_time*.log in a text editor and determine whether any errors occurred (where *date* is the date when the tool ran and *time* is the time the tool started running).

2. Review the log file and resolve any problems that occurred during migration before proceeding to the next step in the process.

Modifying IIS 6.0 Metabase Properties

The IIS metabase stores most IIS configuration values, which are known as *metabase properties*. For example, the IIS metabase stores a metabase property that references the location of the systemroot, which is the path and folder name where the Windows system files are installed.

The IIS 6.0 Migration Tool migrates metabase properties that reference the systemroot folder on the source server, but does not update the references to point to the systemroot folder on the target server. If the location of the systemroot folder on the target server does not match the location of the systemroot folder on the source server, you will not be able to view your Web site on the target server. You must modify the metabase settings on the migrated Web site to reference the correct systemroot folder on the target server. Because the default systemroot folder name changed from WINNT to Windows in Windows 2000 Server and later versions, you might need to manually modify the metabase properties that reference the systemroot folder on the target server. To implement changes to some metabase properties, you might need to restart the server.

Metabase properties that reference the location of the systemroot folder can include the following:

■ **HttpErrors.** The **HttpErrors** metabase property specifies the custom error string sent to clients in response to HTTP 1.1 errors. If you migrate the Default Web Site on Windows NT 4.0, you must reset the **HttpErrors** metabase property to contain the systemroot folder for Windows Server 2003, even if the systemroot folder exists on the same drive on both the source and target computer.

■ **ScriptMaps.** The **ScriptMaps** metabase property specifies the file name extensions of applications that are used for script processor mappings. This property contains references to paths with default ISAPIs, such as C:\Windows\system32\inetsrv\asp.dll.

Compensate for the differences in the location of the systemroot folder on the target server by completing the following steps:

1. Enable the IIS 6.0 metabase edit-while-running feature.

2. Open the MetaBase.xml file in Microsoft Notepad.

3. Search for any references to the path of the systemroot folder on the source server and replace these references with the path of the systemroot folder on the target server.

    For example, if the source server was installed in C:\WINNT and the target server is installed to C:\Windows, you should replace any occurrences of "C:\WINNT" with "C:\Windows".

4. Save the MetaBase.xml file.

5. Disable the metabase edit-while-running feature.

For more information about the edit-while-running feature, see "Metabase Edit-While-Running Feature" in IIS 6.0 Help, which is accessible from IIS Manager.

The following procedures explain how to modify IIS 6.0 metabase properties.

To enable the edit-while running feature of the metabase by using IIS Manager

1. In IIS Manager, right-click the local computer, and then click **Properties**.

2. Select the **Enable Direct Metabase Edit** check box, and then click **OK**.

To modify the IIS metabase

1. Open the Metabase.xml file in a text editor. The default path to this file is *systemroot*\system32\inetserv\metabase.xml.

2. Modify the metabase properties that you want to change in the Metabase.xml file.

3. Save the changes to the file, and close the text editor.

Most changes to metabase properties are automatically recognized by IIS; in some cases, you must restart IIS for the metabase property changes to go into effect.

To disable the Edit-while running feature of the metabase by using IIS Manager

1. In IIS Manager, right-click the local computer, and then click **Properties**.

2. Clear the **Enable Direct Metabase Edit** check box, and then click **OK**.

Configuring IIS 6.0 Properties

Up to this point in the migration process, you have migrated the Web site content and configuration settings from the source server with the IIS 6.0 Migration Tool. However, you might need to further configure the IIS 6.0 properties on the target server so that the Web site runs as it did before it was migrated. For example, you must enable the appropriate Web server extensions, import the server certificate from the source server, and migrate FrontPage users and roles to the target server. In addition, you should configure your target server even further to utilize the enhanced security and availability capabilities of IIS 6.0.

> **Important** Before you proceed with additional configuration tasks, verify that your migrated Web site serves static content correctly by attempting to open one or more of the site's .htm pages.

Enabling ASP and FrontPage Server Extensions

Many Web sites hosted on IIS 6.0 generate dynamic content, which *extends* the site so that it is able to serve content beyond static Web pages. Specific types of code are required to provide dynamic content and other enhanced capabilities. ASP is one of the *Web service extensions* that provide the necessary code.

If you installed IIS 6.0 as described earlier in this chapter, all Web service extensions are disabled by default, so that IIS serves only static content. If you used another method to install IIS 6.0, such as using Manage Your Server, the configuration of IIS might be different.

For security reasons, you can enable or disable individual Web service extensions in IIS 6.0. However, enabling all of the Web service extensions creates a security risk because it increases the attack surface of IIS by enabling functionality that might be unnecessary for your server.

To configure the Web service extensions for your Web server, enable the predefined Web service extensions that you need based on the information in Table 6.5.

Table 6.5 Predefined Web Service Extensions

Web Service Extension	Description
Active Server Pages	Enable this extension when one or more of the Web sites contains ASP content.
FrontPage Server Extensions 2002	Enable this extension when one or more of the Web sites are FrontPage extended.
Server-Side Includes	Enable this extension when one or more of the Web sites uses server-side include (SSI) directives to instruct the Web server to insert various types of content into a Web page.

The following procedures explain how to configure Web service extensions.

To enable and disable a Web service extension

1. In IIS Manager, double-click the local computer, and then click **Web Service Extensions**.

2. In the details pane, click the Web service extension that you want to enable or disable. Figure 6.1 shows the list of Web service extensions.

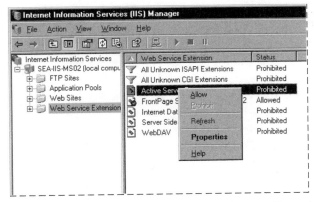

Figure 6.1   Enabling and Disabling Web Service Extensions

3. To enable a disabled Web service extension, click **Allow**.

4. To disable an enabled Web service extension, click **Prohibit**.
    A message box displays a list of applications that will be prevented from running on the IIS Web server.

5. Click **OK** to disable the Web service extension.

6. After enabling the appropriate Web service extensions, use a Web browser on a client computer to verify that the Web sites function correctly on the server.

Migrating Server Certificates for SSL

If you use Secure Sockets Layer (SSL) to encrypt confidential information exchanged between the Web server and the client, you must migrate the server certificate from the source server to the target server, install the certificate on the target server, and then configure the Web site to use the certificate.

> **Note**   Server certificates are installed on the Web server and typically require no additional configuration on client servers. Server certificates allow clients to verify the identity of the server. Alternatively, some Web sites might require client certificates. Client certificates are installed on the client servers and allow the server to authenticate the clients. For more information about configuring client certificates, see "About Certificates" in IIS 6.0 Help, which is accessible from IIS Manager.

Migrate the server certificate for SSL by completing the following:

1.   Export the server certificate for the Web site from the source server.

Web server certificates contain information about the server that allows the client to positively identify the server over a network before sharing sensitive information, in a process called *authentication*. SSL uses these certificates for authentication, and uses encryption for message integrity and confidentiality. SSL is a public key–based security protocol that is used by Internet services and clients to authenticate each other and to establish message integrity and confidentiality.

If you use SSL to protect confidential information exchanged between the Web server and the client, you must migrate or export the certificates and the associated private keys from the source server to the target server.

2.   Install the server certificate to be used by the Web site on the target server.

Web server certificates contain information about the server that allows the client to positively identify the server over a network before sharing sensitive information. This process is called *authentication*. If you use SSL to help protect confidential information exchanged between the Web server and the client and you have exported the certificates from the source server to the target server, the server certificate needs to be installed on the Web server before you can assign the server certificate to Web sites for use with SSL.

3.   Assign the server certificate to the Web site.

Server certificates contain information about the server that allows the client to positively identify the server before sharing sensitive information. After you obtain a server certificate from a trusted certification authority and install the server certificate on the Web server, you need to assign the server certificate to the Web site.

The following procedures explain how to migrate server certificates for SSL.

To export a server certificate from Windows NT Server 4.0

1. From the **Start** menu, point to **Programs**, click **Windows NT 4.0 Option Pack**, point to **Microsoft Internet Information Server**, and then click **Internet Service Manager**.

2. Double-click **Internet Information Server**, and then double-click the name of the computer hosting the Web site that contains the server certificate.

3. Right-click the Web site that contains the server certificate, and then click **Properties**.

4. On the Directory Security tab under **Secure Communications**, click **Edit**.

5. Under **Secure Communications**, click **Key Manager**.

6. In the **Key Manager window**, double-click **WWW**, and then click the key that you want to export.

7. On the **Key Manager** menu, click **Key**, click **Export Key**, and then click **Backup File**.

8. Read the warning, and then click **OK**.

9. Select a secure location on the target server to save the key, and then click **Save**.

To add the Certificates snap-in to MMC on the target server

1. In the **Run** dialog box, type **mmc**, and then click **OK**.
   The Microsoft Management Console appears.

2. On the **File** menu, click **Add/Remove Snap-in**.

3. On the **Standalone** tab, click **Add**.

4. In the **Add Standalone Snap-in** list box, click **Certificates**, and then click **Add**.

5. Click the **Computer account** option, and then click **Next**.

6. Click the **Local computer (the computer this console is running on)** option, and then click **Finish**.

7. Click **Close**, and then click **OK**.

To import a server certificate from the source server

1. In MMC, open the **Certificates** snap-in.

2. In the console tree, click the logical store where you want to import the certificate.

    The default location of the logical store for certificates is on the Console Root in the **Certificates (Local Computer)/ Personal/Certificates** folder.

3. On the **Action** menu, point to **All Tasks**, and then click **Import** to start the Certificate Import Wizard.

Important   You should import certificates obtained only from trusted sources. Importing an altered or unreliable certificate could compromise the security of any system component that uses the imported certificate.

---

4. Click **Next**.

5. Type the name of the file that contains the certificate to be imported, or click **Browse** and navigate to the file.

    Certificates can be stored in several different file formats. The most secure format is Public-Key Cryptography Standard (PKCS) #12, an encryption format that requires a password to encrypt the private key. It is recommended that you send certificates using this format for optimum security.

    If the certificate file is in a format other than PKCS #12, skip to step 8.

    Figure 6.2 shows a certificate that uses the default format, X.509v3.

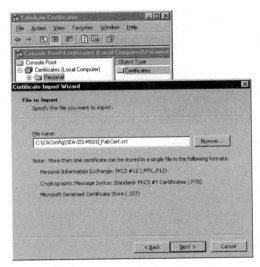

Figure 6.2   Importing an SSL Certificate to the Target Web Server

If the certificate file is in the PKCS #12 format, do the following:

❑   In the **Password** box, type the password used to encrypt the private key. You must have access to the password that was originally used to secure the file.

❑   (Optional) If you want to be able to use strong private key protection, select the **Enable strong private key protection** check box, if available.

❑   (Optional) If you want to back up or transport your keys at a later time, select the **Mark key as exportable** check box.

6.   Click **Next**.

7.   In the **Certificate Store** dialog box, do one of the following:

❑   If the certificate should be automatically placed in a certificate store based on the type of certificate, select **Automatically select the certificate store based on the type of certificate**.

❑   If you want to specify where the certificate is stored, select **Place all certificates in the following store**, click **Browse**, and select the certificate store to use.

8.   Click **Next**, and then click **Finish**.

The file from which you import certificates remains intact after you have completed importing the certificates. You can use Windows Explorer to delete the file if it is no longer needed.

To assign a server certificate to a Web site

1. In IIS Manager, double-click the local computer, and then double-click the **Web Sites** folder.

2. Right-click the Web site or file that you want, and then click **Properties**.

3. Depending on whether you are configuring a Web site or a file, select either the **Directory Security or File Security** tab, and under **Secure communications**, click **Server Certificate**.

    Figure 6.3 shows the Certificate Wizard, which enables you to assign a server certificate to a Web site.

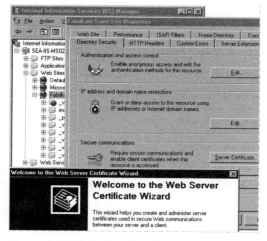

Figure 6.3   Using the Certificate Wizard to Assign a Server Certificate to a Web Site

4. In the Web Server Certificate Wizard, click **Assign an existing certificate**.

5. Follow the steps in the Web Server Certificate Wizard, which guides you through the process of installing a server certificate.

You can view the information about the certificate by clicking the **View Certificate** button on the **Directory Security** or **File Security** tab of the Web site's **Properties** page.

Migrating FrontPage Users and Roles

Accounts stored locally on the Web server are known as *local user accounts*. Local user accounts are valid only on the Web server where they exist, not on other Web servers. When you migrate your Web site to another server, these local user accounts must be re-created on the target server. Once the user accounts have been created, the roles that were assigned to the user accounts on the source server must be assigned to the user accounts on the target server.

You can manage roles from the **Site Administration** page for your Web site. On this page you can view a list of roles, change the rights that are included in a role, add a new role, and delete a role.

When the source server has Web sites that are FrontPage extended and FrontPage roles have been assigned to the Web site users, you need to migrate the FrontPage roles to the target server. FrontPage roles control the types of access that users have on FrontPage extended Web sites. FrontPage 2002 Server Extensions are administered through the Microsoft SharePoint™ Team Services HTML administration tool, which is installed with FrontPage 2002 Server Extensions.

The predefined FrontPage roles include the following:

- **Administrator.** Users assigned this role can view, add, and change all server content; and manage server settings and accounts.

- **Advanced author.** Users assigned this role can view, add, and change pages, documents, themes, and borders; and recalculate hyperlinks.

- **Author.** Users assigned this role can view, add, and change pages and documents.

- **Contributor.** Users assigned this role can view pages and documents, and view and contribute to discussions.

- **Browser.** Users assigned this role can view pages and documents.

In addition to the predefined FrontPage roles, custom FrontPage roles might be defined on the source server.

Migrate FrontPage users and roles by completing the following steps:

1. Identify the FrontPage roles on the source server and compare them to the FrontPage roles on the target server.

2. Create any FrontPage roles on the target server that exist on the source server but do not exist on the target server.

3. For each FrontPage user on the source server that is local to the source server, create a corresponding user on the target server, and then assign that user the same FrontPage roles that are assigned to the corresponding user on the source server.

4. For each FrontPage user on the source server that is in Active Directory, assign the user the same FrontPage roles on the target server.

The configuration of IIS and the Web sites on the source server might reference user accounts that are stored in the local account database on the source server.

The following procedures explain how to migrate FrontPage users and roles.

To add a user account and assign FrontPage server roles to it

1. Open **Administrative Tools**, and click **Microsoft SharePoint Administration**.

2. On the **Server Administration** page, click the name of the extended Web site for which you want to assign user roles.

3. On the **Site Administration** page for the Web site, click **Manage users**.

4. On the **Manage Users** page, click **Add a user**.

5. On the **Add a User** page, in the **User** section, click **Add user or group name (For example, DOMAIN\name)**, and enter a user name in the format *LocalComputerName\UserAccountName*.

6. In the **User Role** section, select the check boxes for all roles that apply to this user account, and then click **Add User**.

To assign FrontPage server roles to an existing user account

1. Open **Administrative Tools**, and click **Microsoft SharePoint Administration**.

2. On the **Server Administration** page, click the name of the extended Web site for which you want to assign user roles.

3. On the **Site Administration** page for the Web site, click **Manage users**.

4. On the **Manage Users** page, click the name of the user for which you need to change the roles.

5. On the **Edit User Role Membership** page, next to **User Role**, select the check box for every role that applies to this user, and then click **Submit**.

For more information about administering FrontPage 2002 Server Extensions, see the SharePoint Team Services Administrator's Guide link on the Web Resources page at http://www.microsoft.com/windows/reskits/webresources.

Completing the Migration

At this point in the process, you have migrated your Web site to the target server and configured the IIS 6.0 properties to match settings on the source server. Now you need to verify that the migration completed successfully, capture the current configuration of the target server, and enable client access to the target server. After you perform these last steps, your migration is complete.

Verifying That the Web Site Migrated Successfully

Before deploying the target server to a production environment, verify that the Web site content and configuration information migrated successfully by completing the following steps:

1. Review the system log in Windows Server 2003 on the target server to determine whether the Web site did not start.

   IIS 6.0 creates entries in the system log when a Web site fails to start for any reason. Search the System log on the target server for to determine if any errors occurred. For more information about how to troubleshoot Web sites that fail to start, see "Troubleshooting" in IIS 6.0 Help, which is accessible from IIS Manager.

2. Verify that the Web site content migrated to the target server.

   Compare the files and folders for the Web site on the target server with the original files and folders on the source server to determine whether the Web site content has been migrated correctly. Ensure that the number and size of the files and folders on the target server approximates the number and size of the same files on the source server.

3. Verify that the Web site configuration migrated to the target server.

   View the configuration information for the Web site that was migrated. Compare the Web site configuration on the target server with the corresponding Web site configuration on the source server. Ensure that the configuration has been migrated correctly.

4. Perform functional testing of the migrated Web sites to ensure that the Web site behaves as expected.

   You can find possible causes of application failure by reviewing the Windows Server 2003 and IIS 6.0 Migration Tool logs and application configuration, but the only way to accurately assess whether your Web site migrated successfully is to perform functional testing. Functional testing is designed to ensure that Web sites are functioning correctly in the most common usage scenarios (for example, URLs and inputs).

   Procedures for performing functional testing of Web sites are beyond the scope of this chapter. For more complete information about general testing, see the MSDN Online link on the Web Resources page at http://www.microsoft.com/windows/reskits /webresources, and then search for "testing".

Backing Up the Target Server

Before you enable client access to the target server, perform a complete image backup of the target server. Performing this image backup provides you with a point-in-time snapshot of the Web server. If you need to restore the target server in the event of a failure, you can use this backup to restore the Web server to a known configuration.

> **Important** Do not proceed further unless you have a successful backup of the entire target server. Otherwise, you can lose Web sites, applications, or data that you migrated to the target server.

You should back up a Web server before upgrading it or making configuration changes to it. A complete Web server backup includes all Web sites, applications, and data stored on the Web server. For example, before an upgrade, or before you enable client access to a target Web server, perform a complete image backup before you change any of the configuration settings on the existing Web server. The image backup provides a point-in-time snapshot of the Web server. If unforeseen problems occur during the upgrade or configuration process, you can use this backup to restore the Web server to a known configuration

A backup file can be saved to a hard disk, a floppy disk, or to any other nonremovable or removable media on which you can save a file. Backup files usually have the file name extension .bkf, but you can change it to any extension you prefer.

You should back up all boot and system volumes, including the System State, when you back up the Web server.

The following procedures explain how to back up and restore the Web server.

> **Important**   To complete the following procedures to back up and restore the Web server, you must use the Ntbackup.exe tool.

To back up to a file

1. Open **Accessories**, click **System Tools**, and then click **Backup**.

2. Click the **Advanced Mode** link on the Backup or Restore Wizard.

3. Click the **Backup** tab, and then on the **Job** menu, click **New**.

4. In the **Click to select the check box for any drive, folder, or file that you want to back up** text box, click the box next to **System State** and any other items you would like to backup. You should back up all boot and system volumes along with the System State.

5. In **Backup destination**, click **File** to back up files and folders to a file. This option is selected by default.

6. In **Backup media or file name**, type a path and file name for the backup (.bkf) file, or click the **Browse** button and navigate to a specific file.

7. Click **Tools**, and then click **Options** to select any backup options you want, such as the backup type and the log file type. When you have finished selecting backup options in the **Options** dialog box, click **OK**.

8. Click **Start Backup**, and then make any necessary changes to the **Backup Job Information** dialog box.

    Figure 6.4 shows the information for a backup job.

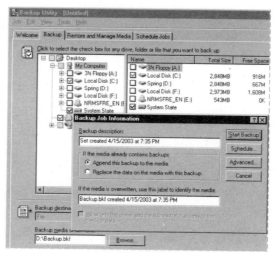

Figure 6.4   Backing Up the Target Server

9. Click the **Advanced** tab if you want to set advanced backup options such as data verification or hardware compression. When you have finished setting advanced backup options, click **OK**.

10. Click **Start Backup** to start the backup operation.

To restore the Web server from a file

1. Open **Accessories**, point to **System Tools**, and then click **Backup**.

2. Click the **Advanced Mode** link on the Backup or Restore Wizard.

3. Click the **Restore and Manage Media** tab, and then in **Expand the desired media item, then check the box for the items to restore**, double-click the media item that contains the backup file you want to use, and select the check box next to **System State** for that file. This will restore the System State data along with any other data you have selected for the current restore operation.

4. In **Restore files to**, do one of the following:

    ❑   Click **Original location** if you want the backed up files and folders to be restored to the folder or folders they were in when they were backed up. Skip to step 6.

-or-

❑   Click **Alternate location** if you want the backed up files and folders to be restored to a folder that you designate. This option will preserve the folder structure of the backed up data; all folders and subfolders will appear in the alternate folder you designate.
-or-

❑   Click **Single folder** if you want the backed up files and folders to be restored to a folder that you designate. This option will not preserve the folder structure of the backed up data; the files will appear only in the folder that you designate.

5.   If you selected **Alternate location** or **Single folder**, type a path for the folder under **Alternate location**, or click the **Browse** button to find the folder.

6.   On the **Tools** menu, click **Options**, click the **Restore** tab, and then do one of the following:

❑   Click **Do not replace the file on my computer** if you do not want the restore operation to copy over files that are already on your hard disk.
-or-

❑   Click **Replace the file on disk only if the file on disk is older** if you want the restore operation to replace older files on your disk with newer files from your backup.
-or-

❑   Click **Always replace the file on my computer** if you want the restore operation to replace files on your disk regardless of whether the backup files are newer or older.

7.   Click **OK** to accept the restore options you have set.

8.   Click **Start Restore**.

9.   Click the **Advanced** tab if you want to change any advanced restore options, such as restoring security settings and junction point data. When you are done setting advanced restore options, click **OK**.

10. Click **OK** to start the restore operation.

Enabling Client Access

After you have migrated your Web sites from the source server to the target server, you are ready to enable client access to the Web sites on the target server while maintaining the DNS entries to the source servers. After a period of time that meets your business needs, you can remove the DNS entries that point to the Web sites on the source server.

Enable client access to the Web sites that are on the target server by completing the following steps:

1. Create the appropriate DNS entries for the Web sites running on the target server.

    For more information about how to create DNS entries for your Web sites, see "Managing resource records" in Help and Support Center for Windows Server 2003.

2. Monitor client traffic to determine whether clients are successfully accessing the target server.

    For more information about how to monitor client traffic to Web sites on the target server, see "Verifying That Clients Are Not Accessing the Web Site" earlier in this chapter.

3. Establish a monitoring period, such as a few hours or a day, to confirm that clients accessing Web sites on the target server are experiencing response times and application responses that meet or exceed your requirements.

4. Remove the DNS entries that are pointing to the Web sites on the source server.

    For more information about how to remove DNS entries for your Web sites, see "Managing resource records" in Help and Support Center for Windows Server 2003.

5. Prevent new clients from accessing the Web sites on the source server by pausing the Web sites on the source server.

    For more information about how to pause Web sites on the source server, see "Verifying That Clients Are Not Accessing the Web Site" earlier in this chapter.

6. Monitor client traffic to the Web sites on the source server to determine when clients are no longer accessing the source server.

    For more information about how to monitor client traffic to Web sites on the source server, see "Verifying That Clients Are Not Accessing the Web Site" earlier in this chapter.

7. When clients are no longer accessing the Web sites on the source server, decommission the hardware for the source server.

Enhancing and Maintaining Web Site Security After Migration

To provide comprehensive security for your Web site, you must ensure that the entire Web server is protected from unauthorized access. To maintain the security of your server, you need to implement continuing security practices such as security monitoring, detection, and response. For more information about maintaining Web server security, see "Managing a Secure IIS Solution" in *Internet Information Services (IIS) 6.0 Resource Guide* of the *Microsoft® Windows Server™ 2003 Resource Kit* (or see "Managing a Secure IIS Solution" on the Web at http://www.microsoft.com/reskit).

Configuring Windows Server 2003 Security Settings

After installing Windows Server 2003, the security settings are configured so that the server is locked down. After installing IIS 6.0, evaluate the default security settings to determine whether they are sufficient for the Web sites that your Web server hosts. You might need more stringent security requirements for Web sites when the following is true:

■ Users on the Internet access the Web sites.

■ The Web sites contain confidential information.

Configure Windows Server 2003 to more restrictive security settings by completing the following steps:

1. Rename the Administrator account.

   The built-in account, Administrator, exists by default on every newly installed Web server. Potential attackers only have to guess the password for this well-known user account to exploit it. You can rename the Administrator user account to help protect your Web server from potential attackers. The Administrator account cannot be disabled.

> **Important** During the default installation of Windows Server 2003, the Guest account is disabled. Ensure that the Guest account has not been enabled since the installation.

2.   Convert all disk volumes to the NTFS file system.

From a security perspective, the primary reason for requiring that all disk volumes be converted to NTFS is that NTFS is the only file system supported by Windows Server 2003 that allows you to secure files and folders. FAT or FAT32 partitions cannot be secured.

Because the Web sites are stored as files and folders on the Web server, NTFS helps prevent unauthorized users from directly accessing or modifying the files and folders that make up your Web sites. For more information about the benefits of formatting disk volumes as NTFS on Web servers, see "NTFS Permissions" in IIS 6.0 Help, which is accessible from IIS Manager.

If any existing disk volumes are FAT or FAT32, convert the disk volumes to NTFS. Volumes converted to the NTFS file system cannot be converted back to FAT or FAT32.

The command-line tool **Convert.exe** converts FAT and FAT32 volumes to the NTFS file system.

3.   Remove NTFS permissions that are granted to the Everyone group on the root folder of all disk volumes.

By default, the Everyone group is granted Read and Execute permissions on the root folder of each disk volume. The default permissions can pose a potential security threat for any newly created folders on the volumes because, unless explicitly denied, these permissions are inherited in any new folders. To help prevent this potential security problem, remove all permissions that are granted to the Everyone group on the root folder of all disk volumes.

Important   The Administrators group still has full control on the root folder of each disk volume. In "Setting NTFS Permissions" later in this chapter, you will grant access to the Web site users by setting the appropriate NTFS permissions on the Web site content.

---

4.   Remove any compilers or development environments.

If compilers or development environments are installed on production Web servers, potential attackers can use them to upload source files to a malicious program and then use the Web server to compile the malicious program. In many instances, the source files might not be perceived as a threat, whereas an executable file would be. You can remove any compilers and development environments to help ensure that potential attackers cannot remotely compile a malicious program and then run that malicious program on the Web server.

Consult the documentation of the compiler or development environment for information about how to remove them.

5. Disable NetBIOS over TCP/IP.

To prevent attackers from executing the NetBIOS Adapter Status command on a server, and reveal the name of the user who is currently logged on, disable NetBIOS over TCP/IP on public connections of the server.

> **Important**   If you disable NetBIOS over TCP/IP, note the following conditions:
>
> You might not be able to connect to computers that are running operating systems other than Windows 2000, Windows XP, or a Windows Server 2003 operating system.
>
> You cannot use broadcast-based NetBIOS name resolution to resolve computer names to IP addressed for computers on the same network segment. Instead, you must install a DNS server and either having the computers register with DNS (or manually configure DNS records) or configure entries in the local Hosts file for each computer.

The following procedures explain how to configure Windows Server 2003 security settings.

To disable and rename the Administrator user account

1. In Control Panel, click **Administrative Tools**, and then click **Computer Management**.

2. In the console tree, double-click **Local Users and Groups**, and then click **Users**.

3. In the details pane, right-click **Administrator**, and then click **Properties**.

4. On the **General** tab, select the **Account is disabled** check box, and then click **OK**.

5. In the details pane, right-click **Administrator**, and then click **Properties**.

6. Type the new account name, and then press **Enter**.

To disable and rename the Guest user account

1. In Control Panel, click **Administrative Tools**, and then click **Computer Management**.

2. In the console tree, double-click **Local Users and Groups**, and then click **Users**.

3. In the details pane, right-click **Guest**, and then click **Properties**. Figure 6.5 shows how to disable the Guest user account.

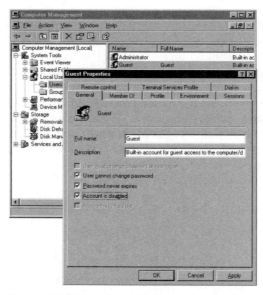

Figure 6.5   Disabling and Renaming the Guest User Account

4. In the **Guest Properties** dialog box, on the **General** tab, click the **Account is disabled** check box, and then click **OK**.

5. In the **Details** pane, right-click **Guest**, and then click **Rename**.

6. Type the new user name, and then press **Enter**.

> **Important**   To complete the following procedure and convert FAT and FAT32 volumes to NTFS, you must use the Convert.exe tool.

To convert FAT and FAT32 volumes to NTFS

■   In the **Run** dialog box, type **convert** followed by the appropriate syntax, and then click OK.

Syntax

```
convert [Volume] /fs:ntfs
```

Parameters

Volume

Specify the drive letter (followed by a colon), mount point, or volume name to convert to NTFS. Required if the volume to be converted is not the current volume.

```
/fs:ntfs
```

Required. Converts the volume to NTFS.

To secure the root of the system volume by removing permissions

The system volume must use the NTFS file system if you want to set file and folder permissions.

1.   Open Accessories, and then click **Windows Explorer**.

2.   In Windows Explorer, locate the root of the system volume (for example, C:\).

3.   Right-click the root of the system volume, click **Properties**, and then click the **Security** tab.

4.   In the **Group or user names** list box, click **Everyone**, and then click **Remove**.

5.   Click **OK**.

To disable NetBIOS over TCP/IP

1.   In Control Panel, click **Network Connections**, click the connection on which you want to disable NetBIOS over TCP/IP, and then click **Properties**.

2.   On the **General** tab (for a local area connection) or the **Networking** tab (for all other connections), click **Internet Protocol (TCP/IP)**, and then click **Properties**.

3.   Click **Advanced**, and then click the **WINS** tab.

4.   In the **NetBIOS setting** box, click **Disable NetBIOS over TCP/IP**, click **OK** three times, and then click **Close**.

Preventing Unauthorized Access to Web Sites

Each Web site and application in IIS 6.0 and Windows Server 2003 is stored as a grouping of folders and files. Unauthorized access to, or modification of, these files and folders can present a serious breach of security. You must ensure that only authorized users can access or modify the Web sites that are hosted on your Web server.

Storing Content on a Dedicated Disk Volume

Store the files and folders that comprise the content of your Web sites on a dedicated disk volume that does not contain the operating system. Doing this helps prevent *directory transversal attacks*. Directory transversal attacks occur when an attacker attempts to send the Web server a request for a file that is located in another directory structure.

For example, Cmd.exe exists in the *systemroot*\System32 folder. Without the appropriate security settings, an attacker might be able to make a request to *systemroot*\System32\Cmd.exe and invoke the command prompt. If the Web site content is stored on a separate disk volume, a directory transversal attack cannot work because Cmd.exe does not exist on the same disk volume. The default NTFS permissions for Windows Server 2003 prohibit anonymous users from executing or modifying any files in the systemroot folder and subfolders, so that only an unauthorized authenticated user can perform this type of attack.

In addition to security concerns, placing the content on a disk volume that is dedicated to Web site and application content makes administration tasks, such as backup and restore, easier. In cases where you store the content on a separate physical drive that is dedicated to the content, you will reduce the disk contention on the system volume and improve overall disk-access performance. Ensure that the dedicated disk volume is converted to NTFS.

To help protect your Web sites, store content on dedicated disk volumes by completing the following steps:

1.   Create a disk volume, or designate an existing disk volume, where the Web sites will be stored.

2. Configure the NTFS permissions on the root of the disk volume so that:

   ❑ The Administrators group has full control.

   ❑ All other permissions are removed.

3. Create a folder, or designate an existing folder, on the dedicated disk volume to hold the subfolders that will contain the Web sites.

4. Beneath the folder that you created, or designated, in the previous step, create a subfolder for each Web site or application that will be installed on the Web server.

5. Install the Web sites in the subfolders that you created in the previous step.

At this step in the deployment process, only members of the Administrators group have access to the content. You will grant access to the users who will access the Web sites in "Setting NTFS Permissions" later in this chapter.

Setting IIS Web Site Permissions

In IIS 6.0, you can set Web site permissions that allow you to control access to a Web site or virtual directory. IIS examines Web site permissions to determine which type of action can occur, such as accessing the source code of a script or browsing folders.

Use Web site permissions in conjunction with NTFS permissions, not in place of NTFS permissions. You can set Web site permissions for specific sites, directories, and files. Unlike NTFS permissions, Web site permissions affect everyone who tries to access your Web site.

> **Note**   If Web site permissions conflict with NTFS permissions for a directory or file, the more restrictive settings are applied.

Table 6.6 lists and describes the Web site permissions that are supported by IIS 6.0.

Table 6.6 **Web Site Permissions That Are Supported by IIS 6.0**

Permission	Description
Read	Users can view the content and properties of directories or files. This permission is set by default. This permission is required for Web sites that have static content. If all of your content is scripted, such as a Web site that only uses ASP content, you can remove the Read permission.
Write	Users can change content and properties of directories or files.
Directory browsing	Users can view file lists and collections.
Log visits	A log entry is created for each visit to the Web site. As an operational security practice, it is highly recommend that you enable logging.
Index this resource	Indexing Service can index this resource. This allows searches to be performed on the resource.
Execute	Users have the appropriate level of script execution: ■ **None**. Does not allow scripts or executables to run on the server. ■ **Scripts only**. Allows only scripts to run on the server. ■ **Scripts and Executables**. Allows both scripts and executables to run on the server.

Setting NTFS Permissions

NTFS permissions allow you to set permissions that are observed by IIS and by other Windows Server 2003 components. Windows Server 2003 examines NTFS permissions to determine the types of access a user, or a process, has on a specific file or folder.

Use NTFS permissions in conjunction with Web site permissions, not in place of Web site permissions. NTFS permissions affect only the accounts that have been granted or denied access to the Web site and application content. Web site permissions affect all of the users who access the Web site or application.

> **Note** If Web site permissions conflict with NTFS permissions for a directory or file, the more restrictive settings are applied.

You need to set NTFS permissions to allow the following situations:

■ Administrators can manage the content of the Web sites.

■ Users can, at a minimum, read the content of the Web sites.

Web sites can run under the identity of the following:

The user who is accessing the Web sites   When you want to restrict access to resources, such as specific Web pages or database content that is stored in SQL Server, run your Web site under the identity of the user. For example, Basic authentication can allow Web sites to pass through the identity of the user to other servers, such as a computer running SQL Server. By using this method, you can control the behavior of the Web site or application on a user-by-user basis.

Regardless of the identity that is used to run the Web site or application, you need to assign the appropriate NTFS permissions to the Web site or application so that it can run under the corresponding identity. Typically, these NTFS permissions are assigned to a group to which a number of users belong. Use this group when setting the permissions on the resources.

The primary disadvantage of restricting access by user accounts and NTFS permissions is that each user must have an account and must use that account to run the Web sites. For your Internet-based Web site, requiring users to have accounts might be impractical. However, for intranet Web sites you can use the existing accounts of users.

Explicitly deny access to anonymous accounts on the Web site when you want to prevent anonymous access. *Anonymous access* occurs when a user who has no authenticated credentials accesses system resources. Anonymous accounts include the built-in Guest account, the group Guests, and the IIS anonymous accounts.

In addition to explicitly denying access to anonymous accounts, eliminate write access permissions for all users except members of the Administrators group.

Tip   If IIS denies access to content, you can enable object access auditing to find out the account that was used to access the content. The failed access event is recorded in the Security event log. The event log entry specifies the account that was used in the failed access. After you identify the account used in the failed access, grant the appropriate NTFS permissions to the account.

Maintaining Web Site Security

After securing the Web sites on your Web server, you need to help ensure that the Web sites stay secure. You need to deploy Web servers that are easy to manage and operate. As you deploy the Web server, keep in mind the operations and processes that must be performed after the Web server is deployed.

For more detailed coverage of security operations processes, see "Managing a Secure IIS Solution" in *Internet Information Services (IIS) 6.0 Resource Guide* of the *Windows Server 2003 Resource Kit* (or see "Managing a Secure IIS Solution" on the Web at http://www.microsoft.com/reskit).

Obtaining and Applying Current Security Patches

You should always evaluate and apply the latest security updates to help ensure that your Web sites remain secure. These security updates are published as service packs or hotfixes. As new security vulnerabilities are discovered, Microsoft publishes updates to help mitigate any security risks they might cause. You need to apply these security updates to help ensure that your Web server is protected from the most current security risks.

Stay current with security updates by completing the following steps:

1. Obtain the current security updates by using any combination of the following:

   ❑ **Subscribe to the Microsoft Security Notification Service newsletter.** The Microsoft Security Notification Service newsletter is a free subscription-based service that sends notification e-mails about available security updates to administrators. To subscribe to the Microsoft Security Notification Service newsletter, see the Microsoft.com Profile Center link on the Web Resources page at http://www.microsoft.com/windows/reskits/webresources. There is no charge for registering to receive the newsletters.

   ❑ **Run Windows Update on a regular basis.** Windows Update is a service that runs on Windows-based computers. Windows Update scans the local computer and identifies any updates that are applicable for the software installed on the computer. Windows Update is installed on Windows Server 2003 by default. You must manually start Windows Update on the Web server from Help and Support Center for Microsoft® Windows Server 2003.

   For more information about running Windows Update, see "Windows Update" in Help and Support Center for Windows Server 2003.

❏ **Deploy Microsoft Software Update Services (SUS).** SUS is a service that acts as an intermediary between the Windows Update server on Microsoft.com and the Windows-based computers in your organization running Windows Update. By using SUS, you can download the latest updates to a server on your intranet, test the updates on test servers, select the updates that you want to deploy, and then deploy the updates to computers within your organization.

For more information about deploying SUS, see "Deploying Microsoft Software Update Services" in *Designing a Managed Environment* of the *Microsoft Windows Server 2003 Deployment Kit* (or see "Deploying Microsoft Software Update Services" on the Web at http://www.microsoft.com/reskit).

Table 6.7 lists the options for obtaining security updates, and describes the advantages and disadvantages of each option.

Table 6.7   Options to Obtain Security Updates

Option	Advantages	Disadvantages
Microsoft Security Notification Service Newsletter	■ Does not require Web servers to be directly connected to the Internet ■ Does not require a dedicated server ■ Free	■ Is not specific to a particular technology, such as IIS ■ Is not specific to a particular operating system version ■ Requires administrators to manually review newsletters for recommended updates
Windows Update	■ Provides automatic notification of available updates ■ Free	■ Requires the Web server to have Internet access.
SUS	■ Provides automatic notification of available updates	■ Requires a dedicated server to run properly ■ Requires the SUS server be able to access the Internet ■ Requires separate purchase of SUS

You can configure Windows Update and Automatic Updates in SUS to install updates automatically, with or without confirmation, based on the security rating of the update.

Table 6.8 lists the security ratings used by Windows Update and Automatic Updates, and provides a description of each rating.

Table 6.8   Security Ratings Used by Windows Update and Automatic Updates

Rating	Description
Critical	A vulnerability that, if exploited, might allow the propagation of an Internet worm without user action.
Important	A vulnerability that, if exploited, might result in a compromise of the confidentiality, integrity, or availability of users' data, or of the integrity or availability of processing resources.
Moderate	A vulnerability risk that can be mitigated by factors such as default configuration, auditing, or difficulty to exploit.
Low	A vulnerability that is extremely difficult to exploit, or that has minimal impact.

Enabling Windows Server 2003 Security Logs

Collecting information about the security aspects of the Web server is required to help ensure that the Web server stays secure. Windows Server 2003 uses security and system logs to store collected security events. The security and system logs are repositories for all events recorded on the Web server. Many management systems, such as Microsoft Operations Manager, periodically scan these logs and can report security problems to your operations staff.

If you audit or log too many events, the log files might become unmanageable and contain superfluous data. Before enabling the system and security logs, you need to enable auditing for the system log and establish the number of events that you want recorded in the security log. You cannot change the information that is logged in the system log: These events are preprogrammed into Windows Server 2003 services and applications. You can customize system log events by configuring *auditing*. Auditing is the process that tracks the activities of users and processes by recording selected types of events in the security log of the Web server. You can enable auditing based on categories of security events. At a minimum, enable auditing on the following categories of events:

- Any changes to user account and resource permissions
- Any failed attempts for user logon
- Any failed attempts for resource access
- Any modification to the system files

You can customize which types of events are recorded in the security log. The most common security events recorded by the Web server are associated with user accounts and resource permissions.

The following procedures explain how to enable security auditing.

> **Important**   To complete the following procedure and define auditing policy settings for an event category, you must use the Local Security Policy MMC snap-in.

To define or modify auditing policy settings for an event category on the local Web server

1. Open Administrative Tools, and then click **Local Security Policy**.

2. In the console tree, click **Local Policies**, and then click **Audit Policy**.

3. In the details pane, double-click an event category for which you want to change the auditing policy settings. Figure 6.6 shows how to define which policy settings you want to audit.

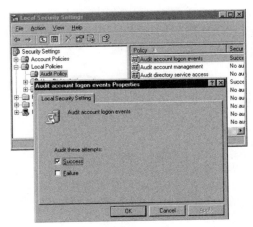

Figure 6.6   Defining Auditing Policy Settings for an Event Category

4. On the **Properties** page for the event category, do one or both of the following:

   ❑ To audit successful attempts, select the **Success** check box.

   ❑ To audit unsuccessful attempts, select the **Failure** check box.

5. Click **OK**.

To define or modify auditing policy settings for an event category within a domain or organizational unit, when the Web server is joined to a domain

This procedure is run on the domain controller.

1.   Open Administrative Tools, and then click **Active Directory Users and Computers**.

2.   Right-click the appropriate domain, site, or organizational unit and then click **Properties**.

3.   On the **Group Policy** tab, select an existing Group Policy object to edit the policy.

4.   In **Group Policy Object Editor**, in the console tree, double-click **Computer Configuration**, double-click **Windows Settings**, double-click **Security Settings**, double-click **Local policy**, and then click **Audit Policy**.

5.   In the details pane, double-click an event category for which you want to change the auditing policy settings.

6.   If you are defining auditing policy settings for this event category for the first time, select the **Define these policy settings** check box.

7.   Do one or both of the following:

 ❑   To audit successful attempts, select the **Success** check box.

 ❑   To audit unsuccessful attempts, select the **Failure** check box.

8.   Click **OK**.

Enabling File Access Auditing for Web Site Content

In addition to enabling Windows Server 2003 security logs, enable file access auditing for your Web site content. This is a separate step that must be completed to monitor any changes to the files and directories that contain your application and content.

You can enable auditing on a user-by-user basis for each file and directory. However, at a minimum, enable auditing for all users for any successful or failed attempts to do the following:

■   Modify or delete existing content.

■   Create new content.

> **Tip**   Beyond these minimal events, you can audit content for other purposes, such as forensic analysis of intruder detection.

Before you set up file access auditing for your Web site content, you must first enable object access auditing. This security setting determines whether to audit the event of a user accessing an object, such as a file, folder, or printer. You can enable object access auditing by defining auditing policy settings for the object access event category of the Audit Policies in Local Security Settings. After object access auditing is enabled, you can view the security log in Event Viewer to review the results of your changes. You can then set up file access auditing for Web site content.

> **Tip**   Because the security log is limited in size, carefully select the files and folders to be audited. In addition, consider the amount of disk space that you want to devote to the security log. The maximum size for the security log is defined in Event Viewer.

If file or folder auditing has been inherited from the parent folder, you will see one of the following:

■   In the **Auditing Entry for *File or Folder*** dialog box, in the **Access** box, the check boxes are unavailable.

■   In the **Advanced Security Settings for *File or Folder*** dialog box, the **Remove** button is unavailable.

> **Important**   To complete the following procedures and enable file access auditing for Web site content, the following must be true:
>
> ■   You are logged on as a member of the Administrators group or you have been granted the **Manage auditing and security log** right in Group Policy.
>
> ■   Windows Explorer is installed on the target server.
>
> ■   The disk volumes on which the Web site is stored use the NTFS file system.

To enable object access auditing

1.   Open Administrative Tools, and then click **Local Security Policy**.

2.   Double-click **Local Policies**, and then click **Audit Policy**.

3.   Right-click **Audit object access**, and then click **Properties**.

4.   Enable auditing by clicking one of the following:

❑   Click **Success** to generate an audit entry when a user success-fully accesses an object.

❑   Click **Failure** to generate an audit entry when a user unsuc-cessfully attempts to access an object.

❑   If you clear both check boxes, object access auditing is turned off.

5.   Click **OK**.

To apply or modify auditing policy settings for a local file or folder

1.   Open Accessories, and then click **Windows Explorer**.

2.   Right-click the file or folder for which you want to set audit policy settings, click **Properties**, and then click the **Security** tab.

3.   Click **Advanced**, and then click the **Auditing** tab.

4.   Do one of the following:

❑   To set up auditing for a new user or group, click **Add**. In **Enter the object name to select**, type the name of the user or group that you want to audit, and then click **OK**.

❑   To remove auditing for an existing group or user, click the group or user name, click **Remove**, click **OK**, and then skip the rest of this procedure.

❑   To view or change auditing for an existing group or user, click the name of the group or user, and then click **Edit**.

5.   In the **Apply onto** box, click the location where you want auditing to take place.

6.   In the **Access** box, indicate what actions you want to audit by select-ing the appropriate check boxes:

❑   To audit successful events, select the **Successful** check box.

❑   To stop auditing successful events, clear the **Successful** check box.

❑   To audit unsuccessful events, select the **Failed** check box.

❑   To stop auditing unsuccessful events, clear the **Failed** check box.

To stop auditing all events, click **Clear All**.

Figure 6.7 shows how to apply auditing policy settings to a local file or folder.

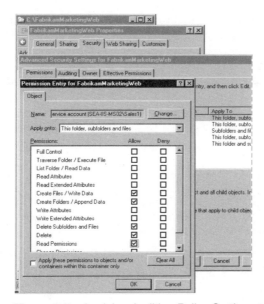

Figure 6.7   Applying Auditing Policy Settings to a Local File or Folder

7.   If you want to prevent subsequent files and subfolders of the original object from inheriting these audit entries, select the **Apply these auditing entries to objects and/or containers within this container only** check box.

Configuring IIS Logs

In addition to the Windows Server 2003 system and security logs, you should configure IIS to log site visits. When users access your server running IIS 6.0, IIS logs the information. The logs provide valuable information that you can use to identify any unauthorized attempts to compromise your Web server.

Depending on the amount of traffic to your Web site, the size of your log file (or the number of log files) can consume valuable disk space, memory resources, and CPU cycles. You might need to balance the gathering of detailed data with the need to limit files to a manageable size and number. If you are planning to put thousands of Web sites on one Web server with high traffic volumes and disk writes, you might want to use centralized binary logging to preserve server resources. Also, consider limiting log size by changing the frequency of log file creation. For more information, see "Saving Log Files" in IIS 6.0 Help, which is accessible from IIS Manager.

Logging information in IIS 6.0 goes beyond the scope of the event logging or performance monitoring features provided by Windows. The IIS logs can include information, such as who has visited your site, what the visitor viewed, and when the information was last viewed. You can use the IIS logs to identify any attempts to gain unauthorized access to your Web server.

IIS 6.0 supports different log formats for the IIS logs that you enable. Based on the characteristics of the Web site in this scenario, the following log formats are most applicable.

W3C Extended log file format   World Wide Web Consortium (W3C) Extended format is a customizable ASCII format with a variety of different properties. You can log properties that are important to you, while limiting log size by omitting unwanted property fields. Properties are separated by spaces. Time is recorded as Universal Time Coordinate (UTC).

For information about customizing this format, see "Customizing W3C Extended Logging" in IIS 6.0 Help, which is accessible from IIS Manager. For more information about the W3C Extended format specification, see the W3C World Wide Web Consortium link on the Web Resources page at http://www.microsoft.com/windows/reskits/webresources.

IIS log file format   IIS log file format is a *fixed* (meaning that it cannot be customized) ASCII format. This file format records more information than other log file formats, including basic items, such as the IP address of the user, user name, request date and time, service status code, and number of bytes received. In addition, IIS log file format includes detailed items, such as the elapsed time, number of bytes sent, action (for example, a download carried out by a **GET** command), and target file. The IIS log file is an easier format to read than the other ASCII formats because the information is separated by commas, while most other ASCII log file formats use spaces for separators. Time is recorded as local time.

For more information about the IIS log file format, see "About Logging Site Activity" in IIS 6.0 Help, which is accessible from IIS Manager.

NCSA Common log file format   National Center for Supercomputing Applications (NCSA) Common log file format is a fixed ASCII format that is available for Web sites, but not for FTP sites. This log file format records basic information about user requests, such as remote host name, user name, date, time, request type, HTTP status code, and the number of bytes sent by the server. Items are separated by spaces. Time is recorded as local time.

For more information about the NCSA Common log file format, see "About Logging Site Activity" in IIS 6.0 Help, which is accessible from IIS Manager.

For more information about the other logging formats supported by IIS, see the "Configuring IIS Logs" topic in "Securing Web Sites and Applications" in *Internet Information Services (IIS) 6.0 Deployment Guide* of the *Microsoft Windows Server 2003 Deployment Kit* (or see "Securing Web Sites and Applications" on the Web at http://www.microsoft.com/reskit) .

Enabling IIS Logging

IIS logging is enabled by default in IIS 4.0. If you disabled logging in IIS 4.0, the migration process will transfer the disabled setting to IIS 6.0 logging. If you want to a record of all Web site traffic, you must enable IIS 6.0 logging.

You can create separate logs for each Web site on the Web server and record events for each of those Web sites. After you enable logging for a Web site, all traffic to the Web site (including virtual directories) is written to the corresponding file for each site. You can also enable logging for specific virtual directories.

To enable logging on a Web site

1. In IIS Manager, double-click the local computer, double-click the **Web or FTP Sites** directory, right-click the Web site for which you want to enable logging, and then click **Properties**.

2. On the **Web Site** tab, select the **Enable logging** check box.

    Figure 6.8 displays the **Web Site** tab as it appears in IIS 6.0.

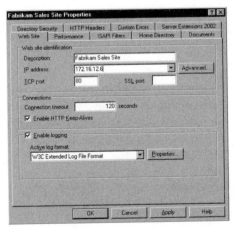

Figure 6.8 Enabling Logging on a Web Site

3. In the **Active log format** list box, click to choose a log format. By default, the format is **W3C Extended Log File Format**.

4.   Click **Apply**, and then click **OK**.

To enable logging for a specific virtual directory on a site

1.   In IIS Manager, double-click the local computer, double-click the **Web Sites** directory, right-click the virtual directory for which you want to enable logging, and then click **Properties**.

2.   On the **Virtual Directory** or **Directory** tab, select the **Log visits** check box if it is not already selected. By default, the check box is selected.

3.   Click **Apply**, and then click **OK**.

For more information about logging Web site activity, see "Logging Site Activity" in IIS 6.0 Help. For more information about managing IIS logs, see "Analyzing Log Files" in *Internet Information Services (IIS) 6.0 Resource Guide* of the *Microsoft Windows Server 2003 Resource Kit* (or see "Analyzing Log Files" on the Web at http://www.microsoft.com/reskit).

Reviewing Security Policies, Processes, and Procedures

As a part of maintaining the security of your Web server, you must perform periodic reviews of the security policies, processes, and procedures in use by your organization. Review your security practices for any changes that might affect the security of the Web server. These changes in security practices can include the following:

Ensuring that any recent security risks are mitigated   As new security risks are identified, such as new viruses, you need to ensure that your security practices help mitigate these risks. If your current security practices do not address the new risks, then modify them to help mitigate the risks.

Identifying changes in Web server configuration that can compromise security   Through the course of normal administration of the Web server, configuration changes are made. During this process, security settings might have been inadvertently changed. You need to periodically review the configuration of the Web server to ensure that it complies with the security requirements of your organization.

You can categorize these Web server security practices by their function, such as operating system security, security policies, firewall security, and router security. In addition, the frequency with which these processes and procedures are completed varies. Some security practices need to be completed continuously while others might be completed monthly.

Table 6.9, Table 6.10, Table 6.11, and Table 6.12 list examples of security policies, processes, and procedures for an ISP, grouped by categories. These examples are representative of the types of security practices that are required to maintain the security of your Web server. For more information about the security policies, processes, and procedures for your Web server, see "Managing a Secure IIS Solution" in *Internet Information Services (IIS) 6.0 Resource Guide* of the *Microsoft Windows Server 2003 Resource Kit* (or see "Managing a Secure IIS Solution" on the Web at http://www.microsoft.com/reskit).

Table 6.9   Windows Server 2003 Operating System Security

Security Policy, Process, or Procedure	Frequency
Limit user rights to only those that are required.	Constant
Limit any windows for vulnerabilities that can be exploited when deploying new servers.	Constant
Limit Terminal Services access to only necessary accounts.	Constant
Run a two-tier DNS structure to protect the identity of internal servers.	Constant
Run an intrusion detection system.	Constant
Scan the ports in use on your server addresses and addresses assigned to remote users.	Daily
Review event and IIS logs.	Weekly
Test firewalls from inside and outside by using port scanners and other appropriate tools.	Weekly

Table 6.10   Windows Server 2003 Policy Security

Security Policy, Process, or Procedure	Frequency
Explicitly deny interactive logon user right to all nonadministrative accounts.	Constant
Explicitly deny "Allow logon through Terminal Services" user right to all nonadministrative accounts.	Constant
Enable FULL (Success/Failure) auditing on domain Group Policy objects.	Constant
Send event notification when events like "User added to Domain Administrators" occur.	Constant
Allow only Administrators to have write permissions on all content servers.	Constant
Require strong passwords for all users	Constant
Require smart cards for all administrators.	Constant
Allow administrators to log on only to specific workstations.	Constant

Table 6.10   Windows Server 2003 Policy Security

Security Policy, Process, or Procedure	Frequency
Enable account lockout policies for failed logon attempts.	Constant
Audit the domain Group Policy object.	Monthly
Audit Active Directory user rights.	Monthly
Audit all servers to determine if nonessential services are running.	Monthly

Table 6.11   Firewall and RouterSecurity

Security Policy, Process, or Procedure	Frequency
Restrict the network segments where management traffic is allowed.	Constant
By default, deny IP traffic and log any failed attempts.	Constant
Ensure that the minimal firewall rules are enforced, including:	Constant

- Explicitly deny all traffic to the following:
    - TCP and UDP ports 135-139, 455 (NetBIOS/SMB)
    - TCP and UDP ports 3389 (Terminal Services)
    - Domain controllers
    - Internal DNS servers
- Permit traffic to TCP and UDP port 53 (DNS) to external DNS servers.

Table 6.12   Miscellaneous Security

Security Policy, Process, or Procedure	Frequency
Run virus scans on all servers.	Constant
Monitor security distribution lists and newsgroups for potential security issues.	Constant
During virus outbreaks, block any suspicious content (such as e-mail attachments).	Constant
Monitor the number of Non-Delivery mail reports generated (indicates e-mail spamming).	Weekly
Monitor SMTP relay attempts that are not valid (indicates e-mail spamming).	Weekly
Audit accounts to determine the users who are no longer employed at the organization, partner organizations, or customer organizations.	Monthly

Additional Resources

These resources contain additional information and tools related to this chapter.

Related Information

- "Migrating File and Print Servers to Windows Server 2003" in this book for information about migrating a file or print server.

- "Deploying Microsoft Software Update Services" in *Designing a Managed Environment* of *the Microsoft Windows Server 2003 Deployment Kit*(or "Deploying Microsoft Software Update Services" on the Web at http://www.microsoft.com/reskit) for information about deploying SUS.

- "Securing Web Sites and Applications" in *Internet Information Services (IIS) 6.0 Deployment Guide* of the *Microsoft Windows Server 2003 Deployment Kit* (or "Securing Web Sites and Applications" on the Web at http://www.microsoft.com/reskit) for more information about Web site security.

- "Upgrading an IIS Server to IIS 6.0" in *Deploying Internet Information Services (IIS) 6.0* of the *Microsoft Windows Server 2003 Deployment Kit* (or "Upgrading an IIS Server to IIS 6.0" on the Web at http://www.microsoft.com/reskit) for information about upgrading a Web server running IIS 4.0 to IIS 6.0.

- "Analyzing Log Files" in *Internet Information Services (IIS) 6.0 Resource Guide* of the *Microsoft® Windows Server™ 2003 Resource Kit* (or "Analyzing Log Files" on the Web at http://www.microsoft.com/reskit) for information about managing IIS logs.

- "Managing a Secure IIS Solution" in *Internet Information Services (IIS) 6.0 Resource Guide* of the *Microsoft Windows Server 2003 Resource Kit* (or "Managing a Secure IIS Solution" on the Web at http://www.microsoft.com/reskit) for information about maintaining Web server security.

- The *Hardware Compatibility List* on the product CD-ROM or the Hardware Compatibility List link on the Web Resources page at http://www.microsoft.com/windows/reskits/webresources for information about the hardware devices supported by Windows Server 2003.

■ The Microsoft.com Profile Center link on the Web Resources page at http://www.microsoft.com/windows/reskits/webresources for information about how to subscribe to the Microsoft Security Notification Service newsletter.

■ The SharePoint Team Services Administrator's Guide link on the Web Resources page at http://www.microsoft.com/windows/reskits/webresources for information about administering FrontPage 2002 Server Extensions.

■ The W3C World Wide Web Consortium link on the Web Resources page at http://www.microsoft.com/windows/reskits/webresources for information about the W3C Extended format specification.

■ The Windows Server 2003 link on the Web Resources page at http://www.microsoft.com/windows/reskits/webresources for the latest information about compatibility with Windows Server 2003.

Related IIS 6.0 Help Topics   ■ "About Certificates" in IIS 6.0 Help, which is accessible from IIS Manager, for information about configuring client certificates.

■ "About Logging Site Activity" in IIS 6.0 Help, which is accessible from IIS Manager, for information about log file formats.

■ "Metabase Edit-While-Running Feature" in IIS 6.0 Help, which is accessible from IIS Manager, for information about the edit-while-running feature.

■ "NTFS Permissions" in IIS 6.0 Help, which is accessible from IIS Manager, for information about the benefits of converting disk volumes to NTFS on Web servers.

■ "Saving Log Files" in IIS 6.0 Help, which is accessible from IIS Manager, for information about balancing the gathering of detailed data with the need to limit files to a manageable size and number.

■ "Troubleshooting" in IIS 6.0 Help, which is accessible from IIS Manager, for information about troubleshooting problems related to Web sites that are not functioning.

Related Windows Server 2003 Help topics

For best results in identifying Help topics by title, in Help and Support Center, under the **Search** box, click **Set search options**. Under **Help Topics**, select the **Search in title only** check box.

- "Windows Update" in Help and Support Center for Microsoft® Windows Server™ 2003 for information about using Windows Update.

- "Managing resource records" in Help and Support Center for Windows Server 2003 for information about how to create DNS entries for your Web sites.

Related Tools

- The *IIS 6.0 Migration Tool* on the *Microsoft Windows Server 2003 Deployment Kit* companion CD, or the Microsoft Download Center link on the Web Resources page at http://www.microsoft.com/windows/reskits/webresources for information about using the IIS 6.0 Migration Tool.

- The Windows Application Compatibility link on the Web Resources page at http://www.microsoft.com/windows/reskits/webresources to download the latest version of the Windows Application Compatibility Toolkit.

7

Migrating to Group Policy-Based Administration

This chapter discusses migrating from Windows NT® version 4.0 System Policy-based management to the more powerful and versatile Windows Server 2003 Group Policy-based management infrastructure. It then demonstrates a basic Group Policy configuration and deployment so you can begin using Group Policy to centrally manage users and computers on your Active Directory directory service-based network.

In This Chapter:

System Policy and Group Policy

System Policy is the policy mechanism used in Windows NT 4.0 and Windows 95/Windows 98. Note that Windows Millennium Edition (Me) does not support system policy.

System Policy is a set of registry settings that define the configuration settings available to a group of users or an individual. Similarly, *Group Policy* lets you manage settings for computers running the Microsoft® Windows® Server 2003 or Microsoft Windows® 2000 families of operating systems, or the Microsoft® Windows® XP Professional operating system. It can also manage secure configurations for users. Compared to System Policy, Group Policy greatly enhances your ability to provide the standardized functionality, security, and management control that your organization needs. When you use Group Policy in an Active Directory network, you take full advantage of all that Group Policy has to offer.

Group Policy is refreshed regularly and the settings you configure are easily removed or overwritten if you change your Group Policy design.

Group Policy Overview

If you have Windows 2000 or Windows Server 2003 and have created an Active Directory domain, you already have Group Policy installed and operational by default. This is because the creation of a domain also creates default settings for all users and computers in the domain, as well as an additional set of settings for domain controllers. You also already have replication between domain controllers, so your policy configurations can reach all users and computers in your network. All you need to do now is to build on this existing infrastructure.

You use Group Policy to define configurations for groups of users and computers, including policy settings for registry-based policies, software installation, scripts, folder redirection, Remote Installation Services, Internet Explorer maintenance, and security. You can also use Group Policy to help manage server computers—domain controllers or member servers—by configuring operational and security settings. The Group Policy settings that you configure to perform these tasks are contained in a Group Policy Object (GPO).

To see sample standard desktop configurations and the actual policy settings used for those configurations, see the Group Policy scenarios in the whitepaper at the Implementing Common Desktop Management Scenarios link on the Web Resources page at http://www.microsoft.com/windows/reskits/ webresources.

Group Policy can significantly boost user productivity and satisfaction by doing the following:

- Providing mobile or portable computer users uninterrupted access to their data in intermittently connected situations.

- Delivering a consistent computing environment to users who are not assigned use of a specific computer.

- Minimizing data loss by enabling centralized backup of user data and configuration files.

- Minimizing user downtime by enabling automated installation and repair of applications.

Implementing Group Policy also boosts administrative efficiency and reduces IT costs by doing the following:

- Enabling one-to-many management of users and computers throughout the organization.

- Automating enforcement of information-technology (IT) policies.

- Simplifying administrative tasks, such as application installations.

- Enabling rapid deployment of security settings across the enterprise.

- Efficiently implementing standard computing environments for groups of users.

- Eliminating the need to manually configure user settings, install applications, or transfer user files to provide users access to their computing environments on any computer.

- Enabling scenarios where users log in to any available computer in a pool.

- Easing the IT task of implementing centralized backup of user files.

- Reducing support costs by using Windows Installer to automatically repair broken application installations.

Comparing Group Policy with System Policy

There is no recommended "upgrade path" from System Policy-based management to Group Policy-based management. A new Group Policy infrastructure replaces System Policy. System Policy is designed for managing Windows NT and Windows 95/Windows 98, and Group Policy requires that the target be Windows 2000, Windows XP Professional, or Windows Server 2003.

Group Policy is not System Policy for Windows NT 4.0. Although Group Policy does include the functionality from Windows NT 4.0 System Policy, it also provides policy settings for scripts, software installation, security settings, Internet Explorer maintenance, folder redirection, and Remote Installation Services.

The following are examples of Group Policy and System Policy behavior in mixed environments:

- If a computer is part of a Windows NT 4.0 domain, and the user is part of an Active Directory domain, System Policy is processed for the computer when the user logs on. After logon, the User portion of Group Policy is applied.

- If both the computer and user are part of a Windows NT 4.0 domain, only System Policy is applied, regardless of operating system.

- If the computer is part of an Active Directory domain, and the user is part of a Windows NT 4.0 domain, the Computer portion of Group Policy is processed during startup. Then, when the user logs on, User System Policy is applied.

- If both the computer and user are part of an Active Directory domain, Group Policy is fully applied.

In Windows NT 4.0 (as well as Windows 95 and Windows 98), the System Policy settings:

- Affect those in domains, subject to the security group restrictions.

- May be further controlled by user membership in security groups.

- Are not secure.

- Persist in users' profiles (this is sometimes referred to as "tattooing" the registry). This means that after a registry setting is set using Windows NT 4.0 System Policy, the setting persists until the setting is specifically reversed or the user edits the registry.

- Are limited in scope and number.

In Windows 2000 and Windows Server 2003, Group Policy:

- Represents the primary method for enabling centralized change and configuration management. You use Group Policy to manage registry-based policy, software installation options, security settings, scripts (for computer startup and shutdown, and for user logon and logoff), Internet Explorer maintenance, folder redirection, and Remote Installation Services.

- Is implemented by linking GPOs to Active Directory sites, domains, and organizational units (OUs).

- Affects all users and computers in the specified Active Directory container (site, domain, or organizational unit) by default.

- May be further controlled by user or computer membership in security groups and, for Windows XP and Windows Server 2003, through WMI filters.

- Ensures that settings are secure.

- Settings do not persist in the registry. The Windows NT 4.0 effect of persistent registry settings can be problematic when a user's group membership is changed. An advantage of Group Policy is that this does not occur.

- Does not overwrite previously set configured user preferences. For example, if a GPO "goes out of scope" for a particular user, a user preference will have been retained.

- Can be used for tightly managed desktop configurations and to enhance the user's computing environment.

Administrative Templates

In Windows NT 4.0, the System Policy Editor uses files called administrative templates (.adm files) to determine which registry settings can be modified. These files define which settings are displayed by the System Policy Editor user interface. In Windows 2000 and Windows Server 2003, the Administrative Templates node of the Group Policy snap-in uses .adm files to define the registry settings that can be configured in a GPO.

Windows 2000 and Windows Server 2003 each come with a predefined set of Administrative template files. An .adm file is a template that provides the friendly name for the setting and an explanation, not the actual policy settings that are deployed to client operating systems; these settings are contained in the registry.pol file inside the GPO.

.Adm files are text-based Unicode files which consist of a hierarchy of categories and subcategories that define how the options are displayed through the Group Policy Object Editor user interface. They also indicate the registry locations where changes should be made if a particular selection is made, specify any options or restrictions (in values) that are associated with the selection, and in some cases, indicate a default value to use if a selection is activated.

The version of System Policy Editor for Windows 95 and Windows 98 is different than the version designed for Windows NT 4.0. While the System Policy Editor interface is similar, the different registry formats in Windows 95 and Windows 98 and Windows NT 4.0 prevent policy creation across these operating system platforms. One template, Common.adm, contains policy common to both the Windows NT 4.0 and Windows 95 and Windows 98 registry structures, as shown in Table 7.1. The administrative template files included in Windows 2000 and Windows Server 2003 are intended to configure policy in these later versions of the Windows registry.

Table 7.1   Administrative Templates in Windows Server 2003

Template File	Where the Template Is Used	Description
System.adm	The Group Policy Object Editor snap-in - loaded by default in Windows 2000 and Windows Server 2003	Contains all of the policy settings for the core operating system for users and computers
Inetres.adm	The Group Policy Object Editor snap-in - loaded by default in Windows 2000 and Windows Server 2003	Contains policy settings for Internet Explorer
Conf.adm	The Group Policy Object Editor snap-in - loaded by default in Windows 2000 and Windows Server 2003	Contains policy settings used to configure Microsoft NetMeeting
Wmplayer.adm	The Group Policy Object Editor snap-in - loaded by default in Windows 2000 and Windows Server 2003	Contains policy settings used to configure Windows Media Player
Wuau.adm	The Group Policy Object Editor snap-in - loaded by default in Windows Server 2003	Contains policy settings used to configure Windows Automatic Updates
Winnt.adm	Windows NT 4.0 System Policy Editor	Contains policy for Windows NT 4.0 clients

Table 7.1   Administrative Templates in Windows Server 2003

Template File	Where the Template Is Used	Description
Common.adm	Windows NT 4.0 or Windows 95 and Windows 98 System Policy Editor	Contains policy for Windows NT 4.0 and Windows 95 and Windows 98 clients
Windows.adm	Windows 95 and Windows 98 System Policy Editor	Contains policy for Windows 95 and Windows 98 clients

The Administrative Templates node in the Group Policy Object Editor includes all registry-based Group Policy information. This includes Group Policy for the Windows 2000, Windows XP Professional, and Windows Server 2003 operating systems and their components and applications.

By default, when a GPO is created, the .adm files loaded into the Group Policy snap-in are located in the %systemroot%\Inf folder on the computer where the snap-in is run. The .adm files are subsequently stored in a specific GPO folder on the SYSVOL volume of the domain controller to which the snap-in connects—by default, the Primary Domain Controller (PDC) Emulator—and this folder is replicated to other domain controllers. On subsequent editing of the GPO, the SYSVOL-based .adm files are used by the snap-in. This is the default behavior, but Group Policy settings are available to control the way .adm files are used. See KB article 816662 for more details.

The five templates that are loaded by default do not create persistent registry entries because they write registry changes under the \Software\Policies and \Software\Microsoft\Windows\CurrentVersion\Policies registry keys. The other .adm files located in the Inf folder do create persistent registry entries and are available primarily to support system policy (Config.pol and Ntconfig.pol). Therefore, do not use the other .adm files unless absolutely necessary.

It is also possible to create new, custom .adm files. For example, when an application adds Group Policy support, you might need to create a new .adm file to describe the location of the appropriate registry settings and the UI exposed by the Group Policy Object Editor. By using the Group Policy Object Editor, you can add additional .adm files to the GPO, which, by default, are then copied to the domain controller.

Distinguishing True Policies from Group Policy Preferences

In Windows 2000 and Windows Server 2003, all settings set registry entries and values in either the \Software\Policies (the preferred location for all new policies) or \Software\Microsoft\Windows\CurrentVersion\Policies trees, in either HKEY_CURRENT_USER or HKEY_LOCAL_MACHINE.

Group Policy settings that are stored in these specific locations of the registry are known as true policies. Because they are stored here, you have the following advantages:

■   These trees are secure and cannot be modified by a non-administrator.

■   When Group Policy changes, for any reason, these trees are cleaned, and any new settings—if they exist after the change—are then rewritten.

■   If a user has set a user preference for the setting—which is stored by the application outside of the Group Policy trees—when a Group Policy no longer affects the setting (for example, when a GPO is unlinked from an OU to which a user belongs), the user preference is returned. In short, Group Policy can override—but does not overwrite—a user preference.

This prevents the behavior that was present in Windows NT 4.0, where System Policy settings resulted in persistent settings in the user and computer registry (also known as "tattooing"). The policy remained in effect until the value was reversed, either by a counteracting policy or by editing the registry. These settings are stored outside the approved registry locations above and are known as preferences.

All the policy settings in the .adm files listed in Table 7.1, except the .adm files used for System Policy, describe registry settings in the Policies trees of the registry. This means that they clean up the registry when the GPO that applies them is no longer in effect. By default, only true policies are displayed in the Group Policy snap-in.

It is still possible for administrators to add additional .adm files that set registry values outside of the Windows 2000 and Windows Server 2003 Group Policy locations mentioned previously, and Internet Explorer settings can be managed in **Preference Mode**. These settings are more appropriately referred to as preferences because the user, application, or other parts of the system can also change them. In this case, the administrator ensures that this registry entry or value is set in a particular way, but a user can change this after Group Policy has configured the setting. Although it is possible to add any .adm file, if you use an .adm file from a previous version of Windows, the registry keys are unlikely to have an effect on Windows 2000, Windows XP Professional, and Windows Server 2003, or they actually set preference settings and mark the registry with these settings; that is, the registry settings persist.

In the Group Policy Object Editor, preferences are indicated by a red icon to distinguish them from true Group Policy settings, which are indicated by a blue icon. Note that, by default, they are not visible; you must set the UI preference first then they show up blue. To do so, clear the **Only show policy settings that can be fully managed** check box on the **Filtering** dialog box in the **View** menu of the Group Policy Object Editor. You need to clear this check box each time you need to see these preferences after restarting the Group Policy Object Editor.

You can manage advanced settings for Internet Explorer, such as setting a size limit for users' Temporary Internet files. In order to do this, you need to first enable **Preference Mode** for Internet Explorer Maintenance. By default, the **Preference Mode** option is hidden. You access this option by right-clicking **Internet Explorer Maintenance** node and selecting **Preference Mode** on the shortcut menu.

This adds an **Advanced** node to the results pane. This node contains settings for managing Temporary Internet files and other UI features. Note that switching to **Preference Mode** disables some of the Internet Explorer Maintenance nodes. If a setting name has **Preference Mode** appended to it, it can be used in that mode; otherwise, it means that setting is disabled. For example, the **Connection Settings (Preference Mode)** option under the **Connection** node can be used in **Preference Mode** as indicated by its labeling in the UI, whereas the **User Agent String** option (note the exclusion of **Preference Mode**) cannot be used in **Preference Mode**, and this is reflected in its labeling.

Use of non-Group Policy settings within the Group Policy infrastructure is strongly discouraged. To set registry settings on Windows NT 4.0, Windows 95, and Windows 98 clients, use the Windows NT 4.0 System Policy Editor tool, Poledit.exe.

Group Policy Management Console (GPMC)

GPMC is a new tool that unifies management of all aspects of Group Policy across multiple forests in an enterprise. GPMC allows you to manage all GPOs, Windows Management Instrumentation (WMI) filters, and Group Policy-related permissions in your network. Think of GPMC as your primary access point to Group Policy, with all the Group Policy management tools available in the GPMC interface. The information presented in this chapter is based on using GPMC for Group Policy deployment and ongoing management.

Before you begin planning your Group Policy design, install GPMC. It is available as a download from the Microsoft Web site. See the Group Policy Management Console link on the Web Resources page at http://www.microsoft.com/windows/reskits/webresources. This is a free download, and you are licensed to use this software if you have at least one licensed copy of Windows Server 2003 in your organization.

GPMC consists of an MMC-based user interface (UI) and a set of scriptable interfaces for managing Group Policy. The UI integrates all previous Group Policy tools into a unified Group Policy-management console.

You can use GPMC in an Active Directory network on computers that are running Windows Server 2003 or Windows XP Professional with Service Pack 1 and the Microsoft® .NET Framework.

This tool can manage both Windows Server 2003 and Windows 2000 Active Directory–based domains. Figure 7.1 shows the GPMC interface opened to the **Inheritance** tab.

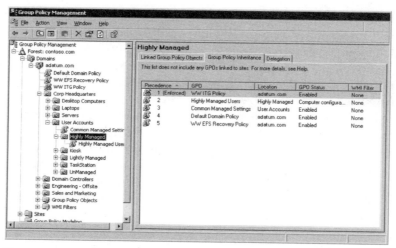

Figure 7.1 Group Policy Management Linking and Inheritance

GPMC provides the following:

■ A new user interface that integrates existing Group Policy functionality currently accessible by using various tools such as the Active Directory Users and Computers snap-in, the Active Directory Sites and Services snap-in, the Delegation of Control Wizard, the RSoP snap-in, the Delegation Wizard, and the ACL editor. The UI also simplifies inheritance and enforcement of GPOs.

■ Access to the Group Policy Object Editor.

■ Backing up and restoring GPOs.

■   Importing GPOs.

■   Copying and pasting GPOs, including across trusted domains.

■   Searching for existing GPOs.

■   Integration of Resultant Set of Policy (RSoP) capabilities:

❑   Group Policy Modeling allows you to simulate the application of Group Policy for specified combinations of computer and user accounts. This is valuable in planning Group Policy deployments prior to implementing in the production environment. The simulation occurs on a service running on a Windows Server 2003 domain controller. Note that although Windows 2000 does not support RSoP infrastructure, it is possible to simulate the application of Group Policy for Windows 2000 computers using Group Policy Modeling.

❑   Group Policy Results allows you to retrieve RSoP data for viewing GPO interaction and for troubleshooting Group Policy deployments. The computer from which this data is retrieved must be running either Windows XP Professional or Windows Server 2003.

■   Support cross-domain and cross-forest GPO import and copy operations.

■   Reporting GPO settings and RSoP data in HTML-based reports that you can save and print.

■   Scripting all operations that are available within the tool. To help you get started, the GPMC installation includes 32 sample scripts that use COM interfaces. You cannot, however, use scripts to edit individual policy settings in a GPO.

To create a GPO, use GPMC. To edit a new GPO, use the Group Policy Object Editor snap-in for the Microsoft Management Console (MMC), which you can start from GPMC. By using GPMC to link a GPO to selected Active Directory system containers — sites, domains, and organizational units (OUs) — you apply the policy settings in the GPO to the users and computers in those Active Directory containers.

For detailed, step-by-step information about using GPMC to deploy and manage your Group Policy infrastructure, see the online Help available in GPMC.

For more information about GPMC, read "Administering Group Policy with the Group Policy Management Console," available from the Group Policy

Management Console link on the Web Resources page at http://www.microsoft.com/windows/reskits/webresources. You can also find more information about using GPMC in "Troubleshooting Group Policy in Microsoft Windows Server 2003," available from the Troubleshooting Group Policy link on the Web Resources page at http://www.microsoft.com/windows/reskits/webresources.

Group Policy and Windows Operating Systems

You need to consider possible interoperability issues when planning a Group Policy implementation in a mixed environment, if you do not immediately plan to upgrade all your servers and/or clients. Group Policy only applies to computers running Windows 2000, Windows XP Professional, or Windows Server 2003.

Windows Server 2003 and Windows XP Professional include many new Group Policy settings that are not used on Windows 2000. However, even if the client and server computers in your organization mostly run Windows 2000, and you have any Windows Server 2003-based computers, you should use the Windows Server 2003 administrative templates (.adm files) because they are the most inclusive. If you apply a GPO with newer settings to a previous operating system that does not support the setting, it will not cause a problem. Destination computers that are running Windows 2000 or Windows XP Professional will simply ignore settings supported only in Windows Server 2003. To determine which settings apply to which operating systems, in the description for the setting, see the **Supported on** information in the Group Policy Object Editor Group Policy Object Editor, in either the Extended view or the setting's **Properties** page, which explains which operating systems can read the setting.

If you plan to deploy Group Policy in mixed environments, take the following Group Policy processing behavior into account.

■   If the destination computer is running Windows NT 4.0, Windows 95, or Windows 98, it uses System Policy rather than Group Policy. System Policy is a Windows NT 4.0-style policy based on registry settings specified by using the System Policy Editor, Poledit.exe.

■   If the destination computer is running Windows 2000, Windows XP Professional, or Windows Server 2003, and the computer account and the account for the logged-on user are both located in a Windows 2000 or Windows Server 2003 domain, both the computer and the user portions of a GPO are processed. If either the logged-on user account or the computer account is located in a Windows NT 4.0 domain, System Policy is processed for those accounts located in the domain.

You can also configure GPOs individually per computer by using local GPOs (LGPOs), on Windows 2000, Windows XP Professional, or Windows Server 2003 computers. LGPOs are processed before Active Directory-based GPOs, which means that if the computer or user is a member of a domain, the Active Directory-based GPOs will override the LGPOs if the same settings are configured in both.

Identifying and troubleshooting problems in a mixed environment where both System Policy and Group Policy apply can be complicated. When possible, move both the computer and the user account into a Windows 2000 or Windows Server 2003 domain.

For more information about migrating user and computer accounts from a Windows NT 4.0 domain to a Windows 2000 or Windows Server 2003 domain, see "Upgrading Windows NT 4.0 Domains to Windows Server 2003 Active Directory" in *Designing and Deploying Directory and Security Services* of the *Microsoft Windows® Server™ 2003 Deployment Kit.*

Using Group Policy

In this and in the subsequent sections, you will create and link a GPO to a test organizational unit (OU), edit that GPO, test it, and then copy the GPO to a production environment and link to an OU. These sections describe configuring a GPO with a single setting and then linking it—just keep adding new settings as you need them.

Note that this is an example only, and you should read the complete Resource Kit and white-paper documentation when you begin to build your own Group Policy infrastructure. You can find links to this documentation in the "Additional Resources" section at the end of this chapter.

Creating and Linking a GPO to a Test OU

In an Active Directory environment, you assign Group Policy settings by linking GPOs to sites, domains, or OUs. Typically, most GPOs are assigned at the organizational unit level, so be sure your OU structure supports your Group Policy-based management strategy. You might also apply some Group Policy settings at the domain level, particularly those such as password policies, which only effect domain accounts if applied at the domain level. In general, very few policy settings are likely to be applied at the site level.

A GPO is a "virtual object"– it is stored in both Active Directory and in the Sysvol folder on each domain controller. These locations have different replication mechanisms—using Active Directory replication and the File Replication Service (FRS), respectively. These two replication technologies ensure that the GPO is replicated to all domain controllers throughout the domain. In general, the underlying Active Directory and FRS infrastructure will handle this replication, but you should be aware of the way in which GPOs are replicated.

A well-designed OU structure, reflecting the administrative structure of your organization and taking advantage of GPO inheritance, is the first step toward the successful application of Group Policy. For example, it can prevent needing to duplicate certain settings so that the policies can be applied to different parts of the organization, or having to link the same GPO to multiple Active Directory containers to achieve your objectives. If possible, create OUs to delegate administrative authority as well as to help implement Group Policy. An OU is the lowest-level Active Directory container to which you can assign Group Policy settings.

Applying Group Policy to New User and Computer Accounts   By default, all new computer or user accounts are created in the Computer or User containers, respectively. Because these are not OUs, it is not possible to link GPOs to them. However, you can specify that all new accounts will be created in specific OUs. You do this by first creating OUs for new user and computer accounts and then running Redirusr.exe (for user accounts) and/or Redircmp.exe (for computer accounts) once for each domain. From this point, all new user and computer accounts will be placed in the targeted OUs. These tools are included with Windows Server 2003. You can run either of these tools or both of them.

For more details, see article 324949, "Redirecting the Users and Computers Containers in Windows Server 2003 Domains," in the Microsoft Knowledge Base.

Important   For all procedures in this chapter, you must log on to the domain with a domain administrator account.

To create a test OU

1. Using the Active Directory Users and Computers MMC snap-in, create a test OU as described in the "Upgrading to Windows Server 2003 Active Directory" chapter of this book. Use **TestGP** for the new OU name.

2. Right-click the OU named **TestGP**, point to **New**, and then click **User**.

3. Complete the user information for a fictitious user account.

4. Repeat steps 2 and 3 to create additional fictitious user accounts (you should probably create about ten fictitious user accounts for test purposes).

5. Close the **Active Directory Users and Computers** snap-in.

To create and link a GPO

In GPMC, right-click a domain or OU item, and then click **Create and Link a GPO here**. This option is equivalent to clicking **New** on the **Group Policy** tab that was available in the Active Directory Users and Computers snap-in, prior to installing GPMC. In the **New GPO** dialog box, type a name for the new GPO, and then click **OK**. Although this operation is presented in GPMC as one action to the user, there are actually two steps taking place. First, a GPO is created in the domain, and second, the new GPO is linked to the domain or OU.

To create a GPO and link it to a site (as opposed to a domain or OU), you must first create the GPO in the domain, and then link it.

1. To open GPMC, click **Start**, point to **Administrative Tools**, and then click **Group Policy Management**.

2. Expand your domain, and then expand the **TestGP** OU.

3. Right-click **TestGP,** and then click **Create and Link a GPO Here**. When prompted for the **New GPO** name, type **NoRunMenu**, and then click **OK**.

Group Policy inheritance and precedence determine where you link GPOs. By default, options set in GPOs linked to higher levels of Active Directory containers — sites, domains, and OUs — are inherited by all containers at lower levels, though inheritance does not occur across domains. However, inherited policy can be overridden by a GPO that is linked at a lower level. For example, you might use a GPO linked at a high level OU for assigning standard desktop wallpaper, but want a certain OU to get different wallpaper. To do so, you can link a second GPO to that specific lower-level OU. Because lower-level

GPOs apply last, the second GPO overrides the domain-level GPO and provides that specific lower-level OU with a different set of Group Policy settings. You can also modify this default inheritance behavior by using the **Block Inheritance** and **Enforced** Group Policy link configuration options.

Always fully test your GPOs in safe (non-production) environments prior to deployment in your production environment. Your tests should closely simulate your production environment. GPMC's backup, copy, and import options can be of considerable value here. The more you plan, design, and test GPOs prior to deployment, the easier it is to create, implement, and maintain an optimal Group Policy solution. The importance of testing and pilot deployments in this context cannot be overemphasized.

Consider an iterative implementation of Group Policy. That is, rather than deploying one hundred new Group Policy settings at once, stage and then initially deploy only a few settings to validate that the Group Policy infrastructure is working well.

Configuring a GPO

You configure and edit GPOs by using the Group Policy Object Editor MMC snap-in. You can open this tool from within GPMC. The following sections describe configuring a single setting in your new GPO using the Group Policy Object Editor.

Configuring the "Disable the Run menu" GPO Setting

A common GPO setting administrators configure is **Disable the Run menu**. This procedure shows you how to configure a setting in your new GPO.

To Disable the Run menu in the NoRunCmd GPO

1.   In the GPMC console tree, right-click the GPO named **NoRunMenu**, and then click **Edit**. This starts Group Policy Object Editor.

2.   In the Group Policy Object Editor console tree, expand **User Configuration**.

3.   Under User Configuration, expand **Administrative Templates**.

4.   Click **Start Menu and Taskbar**.

5.   In the right pane, double-click **Remove Run menu from Start menu**. Click **Enabled** and then click **OK**.

6.   Close Group Policy Object Editor.

7. Restart a client computer and log on as one of the fictitious users that you created in the TestGP OU. Click **Start** and verify that the Run command is not listed on the Start menu.

Verifying That Your GPO Works

Before deploying your Group Policy solution, it is critical that you assess it to determine the effects of applying the various policy settings that you select, individually and in combination. The primary mechanism for assessing your Group Policy deployment is to create a staging environment and log on using a test account. This is the best way to understand the impact and interaction of all the applied GPO settings.

For Active Directory networks with at least one Windows Server 2003 domain controller, you can use Group Policy Modeling in GPMC to simulate the deployment of GPOs to any destination computer running Windows 2000 Server or Professional, Windows XP Professional, or Windows Server 2003.

The primary tool for viewing the actual application of GPOs is Group Policy Results in GPMC. Note that Group Policy Results can only be retrieved from computers running Windows XP Professional or Windows Server 2003 (this feature does not exist on computers running Windows 2000 operating systems).

Using Group Policy Modeling to Simulate Resultant Set of Policy

The built-in Group Policy Modeling Wizard calculates the simulated net effect of GPOs. Group Policy Modeling can also simulate such things as security group membership, WMI filter evaluation, and the effects of moving user or computer objects to a different Active Directory container. The simulation is performed by a service that runs on domain controllers running Windows Server 2003, though you can simulate RSoP for a Windows 2000 computer, even though Windows 2000 doesn't include RSoP. These calculated settings are reported in HTML and are displayed in GPMC on the **Settings** tab in the details pane for the selected GPO. To expand and contract the settings under each item, click **hide** or **show all** so that you can see all the settings, or only a few. To perform a Group Policy Modeling analysis you must have the **Perform Group Policy Modeling analyses** permission on the domain or organizational unit that contains the objects on which you want to run the query. By default, only Domain Administrators and Enterprise Administrators have this permission.

To run a Group Policy Modeling analysis

1. To simulate the results, right-click **Group Policy Modeling**, and then click **Group Policy Modeling Wizard**.

2. On the **User and Computer Selection** page, click the **User** option button, and then click **Browse**.

3. Click **Locations**, type in **Users**, and then click **OK**. The **Users** OU will be displayed in the Locations text box.

4. Click **Advanced**, and then click **OK** to display all users in this group. Select a user.

5. Select **Skip to the final page of this wizard without collecting additional data**, and then click **Next**.

     The **Summary of Selections** page displays the criteria that the wizard will use to process the simulation.

6. Click **Next**, and then click **Finish**.

7. To view all settings, click **show all**.

To run the wizard, right-click **Group Policy Modeling** (or an Active Directory container), and then click **Group Policy Modeling Wizard.** If you run it from an Active Directory container, the wizard fills in the **Container** fields for user and computer with the LDAP distinguished name of that container.

When you have answered all the questions in the wizard, your answers are displayed as if they were from a single GPO. They are also saved as a query represented by a new item under the **Group Policy Modeling** item. The display also shows which GPO is responsible for each setting, under the heading **Winning GPO**. You can also see more detailed precedence information (for example, which GPOs attempted to set the settings, but did not succeed). To do so, right-click the item, and then click **Advanced View**. This starts the traditional RSoP snap-in. Each setting has a **Precedence** tab.

Keep in mind that modeling does not include evaluating any local GPOs (LGPOs). Because of this, in some cases you might see a difference between the simulation and the actual results.

To save the results of the modeling, right-click the query, and then click **Save Report**.

Using Group Policy Results to Determine Resultant Set of Policy

Use the Group Policy Results Wizard to see what Group Policy settings are actually in effect for a user or computer by gathering RSoP data from the destination computer. In contrast to Group Policy Modeling, Group Policy Results reveals the actual Group Policy settings that were applied to the destination computer. The target must be running Windows XP Professional or Windows Server 2003 and the computer from which you run GPMC must have network connectivity to the target.

The settings are reported in HTML and are displayed in a GPMC browser window on the **Summary** and **Settings** tabs in the details pane for the selected GPO. To remotely access Group Policy Results data for a user or computer, you must have the **Remotely access Group Policy Results data** permission on the domain or organizational unit that contains the user or computer, or you must be a member of a local Administrator's group on the appropriate computer and must have network connectivity to the destination computer. To delegate Group Policy Results, you need the Windows Server 2003 schema in your Active Directory, which you receive by default when you create a clean Windows Server 2003 domain. If not, to update your schema, run the **ADPrep /forestprep** command on the domain controller that performs the schema operations master role.

To run a Group Policy Results analysis

1. In GPMC, right-click **Group Policy Results**, and then click **Group Policy Results Wizard**.

2. On the **Computer Selection** page, click **This Computer**.

3. On the **User Selection** page, select a user from the Users OU. The Group Policy Results report in the right pane displays the combined settings for this computer and the selected user.

When you have answered all the questions in the wizard, GPMC creates a report that shows the resultant set of policy for the user and computer you entered in the wizard. The display shows which GPO is responsible for each setting on the **Settings** tab, under the heading **Winning GPO**. You can save the results by right-clicking the query and choosing **Save Report**.

Now, by simply configuring new settings in your newly deployed GPO, testing that GPO in your test OU, and then verifying that it works as expected by running Group Policy Modeling and Group Policy Results analyses, you can expand the scope and power of your centralized management. You need not understand all the hundreds of available settings when you first deploy a GPO; build your management solution in clear and simple stages.

Linking a Complete and Tested GPO to a Production OU

To apply the settings of a GPO to the users and computers of a domain, site, or OU, you now need to add a link for that GPO to your production environment. Do this by using GPMC in a similar manner to creating and linking the GPO to your test OU. You can add one or more GPO links to each domain, site, or OU by using GPMC. Keep in mind that creating and linking GPOs is a privilege that should be delegated only to administrators who are trusted and understand Group Policy.

Most GPOs are normally linked to the OU structure because this provides the most flexibility and manageability:

- You can move users and computers into and out of OUs.

- OUs can be easily rearranged if necessary.

- You can work with smaller groups of users who have common administrative requirements.

- You can organize users and computers based on which administrators manage them.

Organizing GPOs into user- and computer-oriented GPOs can help make your Group Policy environment easier to understand and can simplify trouble-shooting.

The following procedure shows you how to move your GPO from your test OU to your production environment.

To link a GPO to your production OUs

1. In GPMC, right-click the **Users** OU.

2. Click **Link an Existing GPO**. Select the GPO named **NoRunMenu**, and then click **OK**.

This assumes that your test OUs exist in the same domain as the production OUs. Although separate test and production domains are recommended, if your GPOs are linked to OUs only, you might have adequate "separation" if you use a distinct set of OUs for test and production in the same domain.

Even though GPOs can be linked across domains, it is not recommended because of performance reasons. Also, many Group Policy settings, including software distribution and folder redirection, are not applied by default in slow-link situations (slower than 500 kilobits per second, by default).

If you want to use a GPO from another domain, you can use the GPMC copy/paste feature to copy a GPO across *trusted* domains, and then link this new GPO to the OU. The following procedure shows you how to copy a GPO.

To copy a GPO

1. In the GPMC console tree, right-click the GPO that you want to copy, and then click **Copy**.

   ❑ To place the copy of the GPO in the *same* domain as the source GPO, right-click the **Group Policy Objects** container, and then click **Paste**.

   ❑ To place the copy of the GPO in a *different* domain (either in the same or a different forest), expand the destination domain, right-click the **Group Policy Objects** container, and then click **Paste**.

2. If you are copying within a domain, click **Use the default DACL for new GPOs** or **Preserve the existing DACL**, and then click **OK**.

3. If you are copying to or from another domain, answer all the questions in the cross-domain copying wizard that appears, and then click **Finish**.

Your pre-configured GPO from another domain is now ready to use in the new domain and can be customized as needed. Then link it to the new domain as described previously. For more information about copying GPOs, see the "Migrating GPOs Across Domains by Using GPMC" whitepaper link on the Web Resources page at http://www.microsoft.com/windows/reskits/webresources.

Additional Resources

These resources contain additional information related to this chapter.

Related Information

■ "Deploying a Simple Managed Environment" in *Designing a Managed Environment* of the *Microsoft Windows Server 2003 Deployment Kit* (or see "Deploying a Simple Managed Environment" on the Web at http://www.microsoft.com/reskit).

■ "Deploying Security Policy" in *Designing a Managed Environment* of the *Microsoft Windows Server 2003 Deployment Kit* (or see "Deploying Security Policy" on the Web at http://www.microsoft.com/reskit).

■ "Deploying a Managed Software Environment" in *Designing a Managed Environment* of the *Microsoft Windows Server 2003 Deployment Kit* (or see "Deploying a Managed Software Environment" on the Web at http://www.microsoft.com/reskit).

- "Staging Group Policy Deployments," in *Designing a Managed Environment* of the *Microsoft Windows Server 2003 Deployment Kit* (or see "Staging Group Policy Deployments" on the Web at http://www.microsoft.com/reskit).

- "Designing the Active Directory Logical Structure" in *Designing and Deploying Directory and Security Services* in the *Microsoft Windows Server 2003 Deployment Kit* (or see "Designing the Active Directory Logical Structure" on the Web at http://www.microsoft.com/reskit).

- "Upgrading Windows NT 4.0 Domains to Windows Server 2003 Active Directory" in *Designing and Deploying Directory and Security Services* of the *Microsoft Windows Server 2003 Deployment Kit* (or "Upgrading Windows NT 4.0 Domains to Windows Server 2003 Active Directory" on the Web at http://www.microsoft.com/reskit).

- "Designing and Deploying File Servers" in *Planning Server Deployments* in the *Microsoft Windows Server 2003 Deployment Kit* (or see "Deploying a Simple Managed Environment" on the Web at http://www.microsoft.com/reskit).

- "Planning an Active Directory Deployment Project" in *Designing and Deploying Directory and Security Services* in the *Microsoft Windows Server 2003 Deployment Kit* (or see "Planning an Active Directory Deployment Project" on the Web at http://www.microsoft.com/reskit).

- "Deploying Distributed Security Services" in *Designing and Deploying Directory and Security Services* in the *Microsoft Windows Server 2003 Deployment Kit* (or see "Deploying Distributed Security Services" on the Web at http://www.microsoft.com/reskit).

- The Implementing Common Desktop Management Scenarios link on the Web Resources page at http://www.microsoft.com/windows/reskits/webresources for information about using the sample Group Policy objects included on the Windows Server 2003 Deployment Kit companion CD.

- The Best Practice Active Directory Design for Managing Windows Networks link on the Web Resources page at http://www.microsoft.com/windows/reskits/webresources.

- The Group Policy Management Console link on the Web Resources page at http://www.microsoft.com/windows/reskits/webresources.

- The Troubleshooting Group Policy link on the Web Resources page at http://www.microsoft.com/windows/reskits/webresources.

- The Migrating GPOs Across Domains by Using GPMC link on the Web Resources page at http://www.microsoft.com/windows/reskits/webresources.

Related Help Topics

For best results in identifying Help topics by title, in Help and Support Center, under the **Search** box, click **Set search options**. Under **Help Topics,** click to select the **Search in title only** check box.

- "Group Policy" in Help and Support Center for Windows Server 2003.

- Online Help in GPMC for detailed information about using GPMC to help deploy Group Policy and troubleshoot your deployment.

- Help for specific Group Policy settings in the default **Extended** view in Group Policy Object Editor (select a Group Policy setting to see detailed information for that setting).

- Command-line reference A-Z in Help and Support Center for Windows Server 2003, for more information about command-line tools such as Dcgpofix.exe.

- Type **hh <*help file name>*.chm** at the command line to see the full description of Group Policy settings; for example, system.chm is the Help file for the largest built-in .adm file. If you open this Help file on a Windows XP Professional–based computer, you will only see settings for Windows 2000 and Windows XP Professional; if you open this Help file on a computer running Windows Server 2003, you will see settings for Windows 2000, Windows XP Professional, and Windows Server 2003.

Glossary

Symbols

.msi The file name extension for Windows Installer package files.

A

access control list (ACL) A list of security protections that apply to an entire object, a set of the object's properties, or an individual property of an object. There are two types of access control lists: discretionary and system.

Accessibility Wizard An interactive tool that makes it easier to set up commonly used accessibility features by specifying options by type of disability, rather than by numeric value changes.

Active Directory The Windows-based directory service. Active Directory stores information about objects on a network and makes this information available to users and network administrators. Active Directory gives network users access to permitted resources anywhere on the network using a single logon process. It provides network administrators with an intuitive, hierarchical view of the network and a single point of administration for all network objects. See also domain; forest.

Active Directory Installation Wizard The tool that is used to install and remove Active Directory. See also Active Directory.

Active Directory replication The synchronization of Active Directory partition replicas between domain controllers. Replication automatically copies the changes that originate on a writable directory partition replica to all other domain controllers that hold the same directory partition replica. More specifically, a destination domain controller pulls these changes from the source domain controller. See also Active Directory; domain controller; global catalog.

Active Directory Service Interfaces (ADSI) A directory service model and a set of Component Object Model (COM) interfaces. ADSI enables Windows applications and Active Directory clients to access several network directory services, including Active Directory. ADSI is supplied as a software development kit (SDK). See also Active Directory; Component Object Model (COM).

Active Directory Users and Computers   An administrative tool used by an administrator to perform day-to-day Active Directory administration tasks. The tasks that can be performed with this tool include creating, deleting, modifying, moving, and setting permissions on objects stored in the directory. Examples of objects in Active Directory are organizational units, users, contacts, groups, computers, printers, and shared file objects. See also Active Directory; permission.

ActiveX   A set of technologies that allows software components to interact with one another in a networked environment, regardless of the language in which the components were created.

administrative credentials   Logon information that is used to identify a member of an administrative group. Groups that use administrative credentials include Administrators, Domain Admins, and DNS Admins. Most system-wide or domain-wide tasks require administrative credentials. See also Administrators group; group.

administrator account   On a local computer, the first account that is created when you install an operating system on a new workstation, stand-alone server, or member server. By default, this account has the highest level of administrative access to the local computer, and it is a member of the Administrators group.

In an Active Directory domain, the first account that is created when you set up a new domain by using the Active Directory Installation Wizard. By default, this account has the highest level of administrative access in a domain, and it is a member of the Administrators, Domain Admins, Domain Users, Enterprise Admins, Group Policy Creator Owners, and Schema Admins groups.

See also Active Directory; Administrators group; local computer; member server; user account.

Administrators group   On a local computer, a group whose members have the highest level of administrative access to the local computer. Examples of administrative tasks that can be performed by members of this group include installing programs; accessing all files on the computer; auditing access control; and creating, modifying, and deleting local user accounts.

In an Active Directory domain, a group whose members have the highest level of administrative access in the domain. Examples of administrative tasks that can be performed by members of this group include setting domain policy; assigning and resetting domain user account passwords; setting up and managing domain controllers; and creating, modifying, and deleting domain user accounts.

See also Active Directory; auditing; domain; domain controller; group; local computer; user account.

Advanced Configuration and Power Interface (ACPI)   An open industry specification that defines power management on a wide range of mobile, desktop, and server computers and peripherals. ACPI is the foundation for the OnNow industry initiative that allows system manufacturers to deliver computers that start at the touch of a keyboard. ACPI design is essential to take full advantage of power management and Plug and Play. See also Plug and Play.

advertise   In Windows 2000, Windows XP, the Windows Server 2003 family, and Systems Management Server (SMS), to make a program available to members of a group.

advertisement   In Systems Management Server, a notification sent by the site server to the client access points (CAPs) specifying that a software distribution program is available for clients to use. In Windows 2000 and Windows XP, the Software Installation snap-in generates an application advertisement script and stores this script in the appropriate locations in Active Directory and the Group Policy object.

Anonymous access   An authentication mechanism by which users who are able to connect to an Internet site without credentials are assigned to the IUSR_*ComputerName* account and granted the access rights that are assigned to that account. See also Anonymous authentication.

Anonymous authentication   An authentication mechanism that does not require user accounts and passwords. Anonymous authentication grants remote users the identity IUSR_*ComputerName*. Anonymous authentication is used on the Internet to grant visitors restricted access to predefined public resources. See also Anonymous access; user account.

answer file   A text file used to automate Setup or other installation processes. Using this text file, you can provide custom answers to Setup-related questions. Typically, you must point the Setup program to use the answer file at the same time Setup is started. Answer files can only be used on applications and operating systems that support them. See also Setup; Unattend.txt.

application   A computer program, such as a word processor or electronic spreadsheet, or a group of Active Server Pages (ASP) scripts and components that perform such tasks.

application isolation   The separation of applications by process boundaries that prevent the applications from affecting one another. Application isolation is configured differently for each of the two Internet Information Services (IIS) isolation modes. See also IIS 5.0 isolation mode; worker process isolation mode.

application pool   A grouping of one or more URLs served by a worker process.

application programming interface (API)   A set of routines that an application uses to request and carry out lower-level services performed by a computer's operating system. These routines usually carry out maintenance tasks such as managing files and displaying information.

assigning   In Windows 2000, Windows XP, the Windows Server 2003 family, and Systems Management Server (SMS), to deploy a program to members of a group, where installation of the program is mandatory.

auditing   The process that tracks the activities of users by recording selected types of events in the security log of a server or a workstation.

authentication   The process Windows uses to verify that the detected device is the same device you want to communicate with. Windows uses a passkey, also known as a personal identification number (PIN), for authentication. If the passkey entered by the user matches the passkey of the detected device, authentication succeeds; if the passkeys do not match, authentication fails. However, some devices allow communication without authentication.

authorization   The process that determines what a user is permitted to do on a computer system or network.

auto-static updates   The process of adding static routes to the routing table automatically. When you configure an interface to use auto-static update mode, the router sends a request to other routers and inherits routes. The routes are saved in the routing table as auto-static routes and are kept even if the router is restarted or the interface goes down. Auto-static updates are supported in Routing Information Protocol (RIP) for Internet Protocol (IP) and in RIP for Internetwork Packet Exchange (IPX), but they are not available for use with Open Shortest Path First (OSPF). See also Open Shortest Path First (OSPF); routing.

automated installation   An unattended setup using one or more of several methods such as Remote Installation Services, bootable CD, and Sysprep. See also Remote Installation Services (RIS); Sysprep.

Automatic Private IP Addressing (APIPA)   A TCP/IP feature in Windows XP and Windows Server 2003 that automatically configures a unique IP address from the range 169.254.0.1 through 169.254.255.254 with a subnet mask of 255.255.0.0 when the TCP/IP protocol is configured for dynamic addressing and a DHCP server is not available. The APIPA range of IP addresses is reserved by the Internet Assigned Numbers Authority (IANA) for use on a single subnet, and IP addresses within this range are not used on the Internet. See also Dynamic Host Configuration Protocol (DHCP); IP address; Transmission Control Protocol/Internet Protocol (TCP/IP).

availability   A level of service provided by applications, services, or systems. Highly available systems have minimal downtime, whether planned or unplanned. Availability is often expressed as the percentage of time that a service or system is available, for example, 99.9 percent for a service that is down for 8.75 hours a year.

B

b-node   A NetBIOS implementation that uses broadcast NetBIOS name queries for name registration and resolution. See also network basic input/output system (NetBIOS).

backup domain controller (BDC)   A domain controller running Windows NT Server 4.0 or earlier that receives a read-only copy of the directory database for the domain. The directory database contains all account and security policy information for the domain. See also Active Directory; primary domain controller (PDC).

Backup Operators group   A type of local or global group that contains the user rights you need to back up and restore files and folders. Members of the Backup Operators group can back up and restore files and folders regardless of ownership, permissions, encryption, or auditing settings. See also auditing; global group; local group.

backup set   A collection of files, folders, and other data that has been backed up and stored in a file or on one or more tapes.

baseline   A range of measurements derived from performance monitoring that represents acceptable performance under typical operating conditions.

Basic authentication   An authentication mechanism that is supported by most browsers, including Internet Explorer. Basic authentication encodes user name and password data before transmitting it over the network. Note that *encoding* is not the same as *encryption*. Also known as *plaintext authentication*. See also Anonymous authentication; Digest authentication.

basic input/output system (BIOS)   On x86-based computers, the set of essential software routines that test hardware at startup, start the operating system, and support the transfer of data among hardware devices. The BIOS is stored in read-only memory (ROM) so that it can be executed when you turn on the computer. Although critical to performance, the BIOS is usually invisible to computer users.

bootable CD   A CD-ROM that can be used to start a computer. An automated installation uses a bootable CD to start a computer. See also automated installation.

BOOTP   See definition for bootstrap protocol (BOOTP).

bootstrap protocol (BOOTP)   A protocol used primarily on TCP/IP networks to configure diskless workstations. RFCs 951 and 1542 define this protocol. DHCP is a later boot configuration protocol that uses this protocol. The Microsoft DHCP service provides limited support for BOOTP service. See also Dynamic Host Configuration Protocol (DHCP); Transmission Control Protocol/Internet Protocol (TCP/IP).

bottleneck   A condition, usually involving a hardware resource, that causes a computer to perform poorly.

browser   Software that interprets the markup of files in HTML, formats them into Web pages, and displays them to the end user. Some browsers also permit end users to send and receive e-mail, read newsgroups, and play sound or video files embedded in Web documents.

built-in groups   The default security groups installed with the operating system. Built-in groups have been granted useful collections of rights and built-in abilities.

   In most cases, built-in groups provide all the capabilities needed by a particular user. For example, members of the built-in Backup Operators group can back up and restore files and folders. To provide a needed set of capabilities to a user account, assign it to the appropriate built-in group.

   See also group.

C

cache   A special memory subsystem in which frequently used data values are duplicated for quick access.

certificate   A digital document that is commonly used for authentication and to secure information on open networks. A certificate securely binds a public key to the entity that holds the corresponding private key. Certificates are digitally signed by the issuing certification authority (CA), and they can be issued for a user, a computer, or a service. See also certification authority (CA); private key; public key.

certification authority (CA)   An entity responsible for establishing and vouching for the authenticity of public keys belonging to subjects (usually users or computers) or other certification authorities. Activities of a certification authority can include binding public keys to distinguished names through signed certificates, managing certificate serial numbers, and certificate revocation. See also certificate; public key.

child domain   For DNS and Active Directory, a domain located in the namespace tree directly beneath another domain (the parent domain). For example, *example.microsoft.com* would be a child domain of the parent domain *microsoft.com*. Also known as a *subdomain*. See also Active Directory; domain; Domain Name System (DNS); parent domain.

class A category of objects that share a common set of characteristics. Each object in the directory is an instance of one or more classes in the schema. See also schema.

clean installation The process of installing an operating system on a clean or empty partition of a computer's hard disk.

client Any computer or program connecting to, or requesting the services of, another computer or program. Client can also refer to the software that enables the computer or program to establish the connection.

For a local area network (LAN) or the Internet, a computer that uses shared network resources provided by another computer (called a *server*).

See also server.

client authentication A method of authentication by which the client in a client-server communication proves its identity to the server. See also client; server.

client request A service request from a client computer to a server computer or a cluster of server computers. See also client; server.

cluster In data storage, the smallest amount of disk space that can be allocated to hold a file. All file systems used by Windows organize hard disks based on clusters, which consist of one or more contiguous sectors. The smaller the cluster size, the more efficiently a disk stores information. If no cluster size is specified during formatting, Windows picks defaults based on the size of the volume. These defaults are selected to reduce the amount of space that is lost and the amount of fragmentation on the volume. Also called an *allocation unit*.

In computer networking, a group of independent computers that work together to provide a common set of services and present a single-system image to clients. The use of a cluster enhances the availability of the services and the scalability and manageability of the operating system that provides the services.

See also availability; client; scalability.

cluster storage Storage where one or more attached disks hold data used either by server applications running on the cluster or by applications for managing the cluster. Each disk on the cluster storage is owned by only one node of the cluster. The ownership of disks moves from one node to another when the disk group fails over or moves to the other node. See also cluster; failover.

Cmdlines.txt A text file that GUI-mode Setup executes when installing optional components, such as applications.

collection In Systems Management Server, a set of resources in a site defined by membership rules. Collections are used to distribute software, view inventory on clients, and access clients for remote tool sessions.

COM+ An extension of the COM (Component Object Model) programming architecture that includes a runtime or execution environment and extensible services, including transaction services, security, load balancing, and automatic memory management. See also Component Object Model (COM).

Component Object Model (COM) An object-based programming model designed to promote software interoperability; it allows two or more applications or components to easily cooperate with one another, even if they were written by different vendors, at different times, in different programming languages, or if they are running on different computers running different operating systems. OLE technology and ActiveX are both built on top of COM. See also ActiveX.

Connection Manager A client dialer used to obtain Internet access.

Connection Manager Administration Kit (CMAK) A tool for creating, editing, and managing Connection Manager profiles. The Connection Manager is a client dialer. See also Connection Manager.

connection object An Active Directory object that represents a replication connection from one domain controller to another. The connection object is a child of the replication destinations NTDS Settings object and identifies the replication source server, contains a replication schedule, and specifies a replication transport. Connection objects are created automatically by the Knowledge Consistency Checker (KCC), but they can also be created manually. Automatically generated connections must not be modified by the user unless they are first converted into manual connections. See also Active Directory.

console A framework for hosting administrative tools, such as Microsoft Management Console (MMC). A console is defined by the items in its console tree, which might include folders or other containers, World Wide Web pages, and other administrative items. A console has windows that can provide views of the console tree and the administrative properties, services, and events that are acted on by the items in the console tree. See also console tree; details pane; Microsoft Management Console (MMC).

console tree The left pane in Microsoft Management Console (MMC) that displays the items contained in the console. The items in the console tree and their hierarchical organization determine the capabilities of a console. See also details pane; Microsoft Management Console (MMC).

consolidate To eliminate Windows NT or Active Directory domains by merging their contents with that in other domains. See also Active Directory; domain.

container object An object that can logically contain other objects. For example, a folder is a container object. See also Active Directory.

credentials   In general, a set of information that includes identification and proof of identification that is used to gain access to local and network resources. Examples of credentials are user names and passwords, smart cards, and certificates.

For Microsoft Provisioning Framework (MPF), a domain, name, and password for an account. A procedure can be configured to use specific credentials to temporarily elevate a user's privileges so that a user can execute the procedure.

D

debug   To detect, locate, and correct logical or syntactical errors in a program.

default gateway   A configuration item for the TCP/IP protocol that is the IP address of a directly reachable IP router. Configuring a default gateway creates a default route in the IP routing table. See also Internet Protocol (IP); IP address; routing table; Transmission Control Protocol/Internet Protocol (TCP/IP).

delegation   An assignment of administrative responsibility to a user, computer, group, or organization.

For Active Directory, an assignment of responsibility that allows users without administrative credentials to complete specific administrative tasks or to manage specific directory objects. Responsibility is assigned through membership in a security group, the Delegation of Control Wizard, or Group Policy settings.

For DNS, an assignment of responsibility for a DNS zone. Delegation occurs when a name server (NS) resource record in a parent zone lists the DNS server that is authoritative for a child zone.

See also Active Directory; administrative credentials; DNS server; Domain Name System (DNS); Group Policy; security group; zone.

delegation wizard   A wizard used to distribute precise elements of the administrator's workload to others.

deployment   The process of distributing and installing a software program throughout an entire organization. A deployment is not the same as a "pilot," which is where you provide the software application to a smaller group of users to identify and evaluate problems that might occur during the actual deployment.

destination computer   The computer on which you preinstall Windows that will be distributed to customers. You can either run Setup on the destination computer or copy a master installation onto a destination computer.

details pane   The right pane in Microsoft Management Console (MMC) that displays details for the selected item in the console tree. The details can be a list of items or they can be administrative properties, services, and events that are acted on by a snap-in. See also console tree; Microsoft Management Console (MMC); service; snap-in.

device driver   A program that enables a specific device, such as a modem, network adapter, or printer, to communicate with the operating system. Although a device might be installed on your system, Windows cannot use the device until you have installed and configured the appropriate driver. Device drivers load automatically (for all enabled devices) when a computer is started, and thereafter they run invisibly.

DFS path   The combination of a Distributed File System (DFS) root and a DFS link. An example of a DFS path is *server**dfs**a**b**c**link*, where *server**dfs* is the DFS root, and *a**b**c*\\ is the DFS link. See also DFS root; Distributed File System (DFS).

DFS root   The starting point of the Distributed File System (DFS) namespace. The root is often used to refer to the namespace as a whole. A root maps to one or more root targets, each of which corresponds to a shared folder on a server. See also Distributed File System (DFS).

DHCP option   Address configuration parameters that a DHCP service assigns to clients. Most DHCP options are predefined, based on optional parameters defined in Request for Comments (RFC) 1542, although extended options can be added by vendors or users. See also Dynamic Host Configuration Protocol (DHCP).

DHCP/BOOTP Relay Agent   The agent program or component responsible for relaying Dynamic Host Configuration Protocol (DHCP) and bootstrap protocol (BOOTP) broadcast messages between a DHCP server and a client across an Internet Protocol (IP) router. A DHCP relay agent supports DHCP/BOOTP message relay as defined in RFCs 1541 and 2131. The DHCP Relay Agent routing protocol component is managed using the Routing and Remote Access snap-in. See also bootstrap protocol (BOOTP); Dynamic Host Configuration Protocol (DHCP).

dial-up connection   The connection to your network if you use a device that uses the telephone network. This includes modems with a standard telephone line, ISDN cards with high-speed ISDN lines, or X.25 networks.

   If you are a typical user, you might have one or two dial-up connections, for example, to the Internet and to your corporate network. In a more complex server situation, multiple network modem connections might be used to implement advanced routing.

Digest authentication   An authentication mechanism that hashes user name, password, and other data before transmitting it over the network. See also Basic authentication.

directory   An information source that contains information about users, computer files, or other objects. In a file system, a directory stores information about files. In a distributed computing environment (such as a Windows domain), the directory stores information about objects such as printers, fax servers, applications, databases, and other users. See also domain.

directory browsing   A feature that automatically provides a default Web page of available directories and files to browsers that submit a Uniform Resource Locator (URL) that does not specify a particular file.

directory tree   A hierarchy of objects and containers in a directory that can be viewed graphically as an upside-down tree, with the root object at the top. Endpoints in the tree are usually single (leaf) objects, and nodes in the tree, or branches, are container objects. A tree shows how objects are connected in terms of the path from one object to another. A simple tree is a single container and its objects. A contiguous subtree is any unbroken path in the tree, including all the members of any container in that path.

DirectX   An extension of the Microsoft Windows operating system. DirectX technology helps games and other programs use the advanced multimedia capabilities of your hardware.

Distributed Component Object Model (DCOM)   The Microsoft Component Object Model (COM) specification that defines how components communicate over Windows-based networks. Use the DCOM Configuration tool to integrate client/server applications across multiple computers. DCOM can also be used to integrate robust Web browser applications. See also Component Object Model (COM).

Distributed File System (DFS)   A service that allows system administrators to organize distributed network shares into a logical namespace, enabling users to access files without specifying their physical location and providing load sharing across network shares. See also service.

distribution folder   The folder created on the distribution server to contain the Setup files.

distribution point   In Systems Management Server, a site system with the distribution point role that stores package files received from a site server. Systems Management Server clients contact distribution points to obtain programs and files after they detect that an advertised application is available from a client access point.

distribution point group   In Systems Management Server, a set of distribution points that can be managed as a single entity. See also distribution point; Systems Management Server (SMS).

distribution share   A network folder that contains the source files for Windows products that you install. It may also contain additional device drivers and application files. This folder can be created manually or by using Setup Manager.

DNS server   A server that maintains information about a portion of the DNS database and that responds to and resolves DNS queries. See also Domain Name System (DNS); server.

DNS suffix   For DNS, a character string that represents a domain name. The DNS suffix shows where a host is located relative to the DNS root, specifying a host's location in the DNS hierarchy. Usually, the DNS suffix describes the latter portion of a DNS name, following one or more of the first labels of a DNS name. See also domain name; Domain Name System (DNS).

domain   In Active Directory, a collection of computer, user, and group objects defined by the administrator. These objects share a common directory database, security policies, and security relationships with other domains.

In DNS, any tree or subtree within the DNS namespace. Although the names for DNS domains often correspond to Active Directory domains, DNS domains should not be confused with Active Directory domains.

See also Active Directory; Domain Name System (DNS).

domain consolidation   The process of combining two or more domains into a larger domain.

domain controller   In an Active Directory forest, a server that contains a writable copy of the Active Directory database, participates in Active Directory replication, and controls access to network resources. Administrators can manage user accounts, network access, shared resources, site topology, and other directory objects from any domain controller in the forest. See also Active Directory; directory; forest.

domain local group   A security or distribution group that can contain universal groups, global groups, other domain local groups from its own domain, and accounts from any domain in the forest. Domain local security groups can be granted rights and permissions on resources that reside only in the same domain where the domain local group is located. See also forest; global group; security group; universal group.

domain migration   The process of moving accounts, resources, and their associated security objects from one domain structure to another.

domain name   The name given by an administrator to a collection of networked computers that share a common directory. Part of the DNS naming structure, domain names consist of a sequence of name labels separated by periods. See also domain; Domain Name System (DNS); label.

domain name label   Each part of a full DNS domain name that represents a node in the domain namespace tree. Domain names are made up of a sequence of labels, such as the three labels ("noam," "reskit," and "com") that make up the DNS domain name "noam.reskit.com." Each label used in a DNS name must have 63 or fewer characters.

Domain Name System (DNS) A hierarchical, distributed database that contains mappings of DNS domain names to various types of data, such as IP addresses. DNS enables the location of computers and services by user-friendly names, and it also enables the discovery of other information stored in the database. See also domain name; IP address; ping; service; Transmission Control Protocol/Internet Protocol (TCP/IP).

domain namespace The database structure used by DNS. See also Domain Name System (DNS).

domain restructure The process of reorganizing one domain structure into another that typically results in the accounts, groups, and trusts being altered.

driver Kernel-mode code used either to control or emulate a hardware device.

dynamic disk A physical disk that provides features that basic disks do not, such as support for volumes that span multiple disks. Dynamic disks use a hidden database to track information about dynamic volumes on the disk and other dynamic disks in the computer. You convert basic disks to dynamic by using the Disk Management snap-in or the DiskPart command-line tool. When you convert a basic disk to dynamic, all existing basic volumes become dynamic volumes. See also dynamic volume.

Dynamic Host Configuration Protocol (DHCP) A TCP/IP service protocol that offers dynamic leased configuration of host IP addresses and distributes other configuration parameters to eligible network clients. DHCP provides safe, reliable, and simple TCP/IP network configuration, prevents address conflicts, and helps conserve the use of client IP addresses on the network.

DHCP uses a client/server model where the DHCP server maintains centralized management of IP addresses that are used on the network. DHCP-supporting clients can then request and obtain lease of an IP address from a DHCP server as part of their network boot process.

See also IP address; lease; service; Transmission Control Protocol/Internet Protocol (TCP/IP).

dynamic page A Hypertext Markup Language (HTML) document that contains animated GIFs, Java applets, ActiveX Controls, or dynamic HTML (DHTML). Also, a Web page that is created automatically, based on information that is provided by the user, or that is generated "on the fly" with Active Server Pages (ASP).

dynamic update An update to the Domain Name System (DNS) standard that permits DNS clients to dynamically register and update their resource records in zones. See also DNS server; Domain Name System (DNS); zone.

dynamic volume   A volume that resides on a dynamic disk. Windows supports five types of dynamic volumes: simple, spanned, striped, mirrored, and RAID-5. A dynamic volume is formatted by using a file system, such as file allocation table (FAT) or NTFS, and has a drive letter assigned to it. See also dynamic disk; mirrored volume; RAID-5 volume.

dynamic-link library (DLL)   An operating system feature that allows executable routines (generally serving a specific function or set of functions) to be stored separately as files with .dll extensions. These routines are loaded only when needed by the program that calls them.

E

enumeration   The means by which Windows learns about a device. Enumerator, a concept used in Windows Plug and Play, is a property of a device.

event   Any significant occurrence in the system or an application that requires users to be notified or an entry to be added to a log.

Event Log service   A service that records events in the system, security, and application logs. The Event Log service is located in Event Viewer. See also event; event logging; Event Viewer; service.

event logging   The process of recording an audit entry in the audit trail whenever certain events occur, such as services starting and stopping or users logging on and off and accessing resources. See also auditing; event; Event Viewer; service.

Event Viewer   A component you can use to view and manage event logs, gather information about hardware and software problems, and monitor security events. Event Viewer maintains logs about program, security, and system events. See also event; event logging.

exclusion range   A small range of one or more IP addresses within a DHCP scope excluded from the DHCP service. Exclusion ranges ensure that these scope addresses will never be offered to clients by the DHCP server. See also scope.

Extensible Authentication Protocol (EAP)   An extension to the Point-to-Point Protocol (PPP) that allows for arbitrary authentication mechanisms to be employed for the validation of a PPP connection. See also Point-to-Point Protocol (PPP).

Extensible Markup Language (XML)   A meta-markup language that provides a format for describing structured data. This facilitates more precise declarations of content and more meaningful search results across multiple platforms. In addition, XML enables a new generation of Web-based data viewing and manipulation applications. See also Hypertext Markup Language (HTML).

F

factory mode   A mode of running Sysprep that postpones Windows Welcome or Mini-Setup and allows you to install additional drivers and applications and test the Windows installation. To run Sysprep in factory mode, use the command line **Sysprep -factory**.

failover   In server clusters, the process of taking resource groups offline on one node and bringing them online on another node. When failover occurs, all resources within a resource group fail over in a predefined order; resources that depend on other resources are taken offline before, and are brought back online after, the resources on which they depend. See also server cluster.

FAT   See definition for file allocation table (FAT).

FAT32   A derivative of the file allocation table (FAT) file system. FAT32 supports smaller cluster sizes and larger volumes than FAT, which results in more efficient space allocation on FAT32 volumes. See also file allocation table (FAT).

fault tolerance   The ability of computer hardware or software to ensure data integrity when hardware failures occur. Fault-tolerant features appear in many server operating systems and include mirrored volumes, RAID-5 volumes, and server clusters. See also cluster; mirrored volume; RAID-5 volume.

file allocation table (FAT)   A file system used by MS-DOS and other Windows operating systems to organize and manage files. The file allocation table is a data structure that Windows creates when you format a volume by using FAT or FAT32 file systems. Windows stores information about each file in the file allocation table so that it can retrieve the file later. See also FAT32; NTFS file system.

File Replication service (FRS)   A service that provides multimaster file replication for designated directory trees between designated servers running Windows Server 2003. The designated directory trees must be on disk partitions formatted with the version of NTFS used with the Windows Server 2003 family. FRS is used by Distributed File System (DFS) to automatically synchronize content between assigned replicas and by Active Directory to automatically synchronize content of the system volume information across domain controllers. See also Active Directory; NTFS file system; service.

File Transfer Protocol (FTP)   A member of the TCP/IP suite of protocols, used to copy files between two computers on the Internet. Both computers must support their respective FTP roles: one must be an FTP client and the other an FTP server. See also Transmission Control Protocol/Internet Protocol (TCP/IP).

filter   For Indexing Service, software that extracts content and property values from a document to index them.

For Internet Protocol security (IPSec), a specification of Internet Protocol (IP) traffic that provides the ability to trigger security negotiations for a communication based on the source, destination, and type of IP traffic.

For Internet Information Services (IIS), a feature of Internet Server Application Programming Interface (ISAPI) that allows preprocessing of requests and post-processing of responses, permitting site-specific handling of Hypertext Transfer Protocol (HTTP) requests and responses.

In IP and Internetwork Packet Exchange (IPX) packet filtering, a definition in a series of definitions that indicates to the router the type of traffic allowed or disallowed on each interface.

See also Internet Information Services (IIS); Internet Protocol (IP); Internet Protocol security (IPSec); Internet Server Application Programming Interface (ISAPI); Internetwork Packet Exchange (IPX).

firewall   A combination of hardware and software that provides a security system for the flow of network traffic, usually to prevent unauthorized access from outside to an internal network or intranet. Also called a *security-edge gateway*. See also proxy server.

forest   One or more Active Directory domains that share the same class and attribute definitions (schema), site and replication information (configuration), and forest-wide search capabilities (global catalog). Domains in the same forest are linked with two-way, transitive trust relationships. See also Active Directory; domain; global catalog; schema.

forest root domain   The first domain created in a new forest. The forest-wide administrative groups, Enterprise Admins and Schema Admins, are located in this domain. As a best practice, new domains are created as children of the forest root domain. See also child domain; domain; forest.

fully qualified domain name (FQDN)   A DNS name that has been stated to indicate its absolute location in the domain namespace tree. In contrast to relative names, an FQDN has a trailing period (.) to qualify its position to the root of the namespace (*host.example.microsoft.com.*). See also domain name; Domain Name System (DNS); domain namespace.

G

global catalog A directory database that applications and clients can query to locate any object in a forest. The global catalog is hosted on one or more domain controllers in the forest. It contains a partial replica of every domain directory partition in the forest. These partial replicas include replicas of every object in the forest, as follows: the attributes most frequently used in search operations and the attributes required to locate a full replica of the object.

In Microsoft Provisioning System, the Exchange server maintains a list of global catalogs, and it maintains a load balance across global catalogs.

See also Active Directory; domain controller; forest.

global group A security or distribution group that can contain users, groups, and computers from its own domain as members. Global security groups can be granted rights and permissions for resources in any domain in the forest. See also group; local group; member server; permission; user account.

group A collection of users, computers, contacts, and other groups. Groups can be used as security or as e-mail distribution collections. Distribution groups are used only for e-mail. Security groups are used both to grant access to resources and as e-mail distribution lists. See also domain; global group; local group.

group memberships The groups to which a user account belongs. Permissions and rights granted to a group are also provided to its members. In most cases, the actions a user can perform in Windows are determined by the group memberships of the user account to which the user is logged on. See also group; user account.

Group Policy The infrastructure within Active Directory directory service that enables directory-based change and configuration management of user and computer settings, including security and user data. You use Group Policy to define configurations for groups of users and computers. With Group Policy, you can specify policy settings for registry-based policies, security, software installation, scripts, folder redirection, remote installation services, and Internet Explorer maintenance. The Group Policy settings that you create are contained in a Group Policy object (GPO). By associating a GPO with selected Active Directory system containers—sites, domains, and organizational units—you can apply the GPO's policy settings to the users and computers in those Active Directory containers. To create an individual GPO, use the Group Policy Object Editor. To manage Group Policy objects across an enterprise, you can use the Group Policy Management console. See also Active Directory; Group Policy object (GPO).

Group Policy object (GPO)   A collection of Group Policy settings. GPOs are essentially the documents created by the Group Policy Object Editor. GPOs are stored at the domain level, and they affect users and computers that are contained in sites, domains, and organizational units. In addition, each computer has exactly one group of policy settings stored locally, called the *local Group Policy object*. See also Group Policy.

Guest account   A built-in account used to log on to a computer running Windows when a user does not have an account on the computer or domain or in any of the domains trusted by the computer's domain. See also domain; user account.

H

handle   In the user interface, an interface added to an object that facilitates moving, sizing, reshaping, or other functions pertaining to an object. In programming, a pointer to a pointer, that is, a token that lets a program access an identified resource.

Hardware Compatibility List (HCL)   A hardware list that Microsoft compiled for specific products, including Windows 2000 and earlier versions of Windows. The list for a specific product, such as Windows 2000, includes the hardware devices and computer systems that are compatible with that version of the product. For products in the Windows Server 2003 family, you can find the equivalent information on the Windows Catalog Web site.

hardware configuration   Resource settings that have been allocated for a specific device. Each device on your computer has a hardware configuration, which can consist of interrupt request (IRQ) lines, direct memory access (DMA), an input/output (I/O) port, or memory address settings.

heaps   A portion of memory reserved for a program to use for the temporary storage of data structures whose existence or size cannot be determined until the program is running.

Help and Support Center   A unified place where a user can access all Help and Support content and services from both Microsoft and the OEM.

home directory   The root directory for a Web site, where the content files are stored. Also called a document root or Web root. In Internet Information Services (IIS), the home directory and all its subdirectories are available to users by default. Also, the root directory for an IIS service. Typically, the home directory for a site contains the home page. See also home page.

home page   In the context of Internet Explorer, the home page is the first page users see when they start the browser. "Home page" is also a more general term for the main page of a Web site, which usually contains a main menu or table of contents with links to other pages within the site.

host   Any device on a TCP/IP network that has an Internet Protocol (IP) address. Examples of hosts include servers, workstations, network-interface print devices, and routers. Sometimes used to refer to a specific network computer that is running a service used by network or remote clients.

For Network Load Balancing, a cluster consists of multiple hosts connected over a local area network (LAN).

See also client; cluster; local area network (LAN); server; service; Transmission Control Protocol/Internet Protocol (TCP/IP).

host name   The DNS name of a device on a network. These names are used to locate computers on the network. To find another computer, its host name must either appear in the Hosts file or be known by a DNS server. For most Windows-based computers, the host name and the computer name are the same. See also DNS server; Domain Name System (DNS).

hub   A common connection point for devices in a network. Typically used to connect segments of a local area network (LAN), a hub contains multiple ports. When data arrives at one port, it is copied to the other ports so that all segments of the LAN can see the data. See also local area network (LAN).

Hypertext Markup Language (HTML)   A simple markup language used to create hypertext documents that are portable from one platform to another. HTML files are simple ASCII text files with codes embedded (indicated by markup tags) to denote formatting and hypertext links.

Hypertext Transfer Protocol (HTTP)   The protocol used to transfer information on the World Wide Web. An HTTP address (one kind of Uniform Resource Locator (URL)) takes the following form: http://www.microsoft.com. See also protocol.

I

IIS 5.0 isolation mode   Internet Information Services (IIS) 6.0 isolation mode that simulates the IIS 5.0 Web process model.

in-memory metabase   An image of the Internet Information Services (IIS) metabase that has been loaded from disk into the computer's RAM memory and is used while IIS is running. See also metabase.

in-process Internet Server API (ISAPI) extensions that are hosted in the worker process address space. See also Internet Server Application Programming Interface (ISAPI).

independent software vendor (ISV) A third-party software developer; an individual or an organization that independently creates computer software.

install When referring to software, to add program files and folders to your hard disk and related data to your registry so that the software runs properly. Installing contrasts with upgrading, where existing program files, folders, and registry entries are updated to a more recent version.

When referring to hardware, to physically connect the device to your computer, to load device drivers onto your computer, and to configure device properties and settings.

See also device driver; registry; upgrade.

IntelliMirror A set of change and configuration management features based on Active Directory that enables management of user and computer data and settings, including security data. IntelliMirror also provides limited ability to deploy software to Windows 2000 and later workstations or servers. See also Active Directory.

interface In networking, a logical device over which packets can be sent and received. In the Routing and Remote Access administrative tool, it is a visual representation of the network segment that can be reached over the LAN or WAN adapters. Each interface has a unique name.

Interior Gateway Routing Protocol (IGRP) A distance vector IP routing protocol developed by Cisco Systems, Inc. See also Internet Protocol (IP).

Internet Authentication Service (IAS) The Microsoft implementation of a Remote Authentication Dial-In User Service (RADIUS) server, which provides authentication and accounting for network access, and proxy, which provides forwarding of RADIUS messages. See also Remote Authentication Dial-In User Service (RADIUS); service; virtual private network (VPN).

Internet Control Message Protocol (ICMP) A required maintenance protocol in the TCP/IP suite that reports errors and provides simple diagnostic capabilities. ICMP is used by the Ping tool to perform TCP/IP troubleshooting. See also Internet Protocol (IP); protocol; Transmission Control Protocol/Internet Protocol (TCP/IP).

Internet Engineering Task Force (IETF) An open community of network designers, operators, vendors, and researchers concerned with the evolution of Internet architecture and the smooth operation of the Internet. Technical work is performed by working groups organized by topic areas (such as routing, transport, and security) and through mailing lists. Internet standards are developed in IETF Requests for

Comments (RFCs), which are a series of notes that discuss many aspects of computing and computer communication, focusing on networking protocols, programs, and concepts.

Internet Group Management Protocol (IGMP)   A protocol used by Internet Protocol version 4 (IPv4) hosts to report their multicast group memberships to any immediately neighboring multicast routers. See also protocol.

Internet Information Services (IIS)   Software services that support Web site creation, configuration, and management, along with other Internet functions. Internet Information Services include Network News Transfer Protocol (NNTP), File Transfer Protocol (FTP), and Simple Mail Transfer Protocol (SMTP). See also File Transfer Protocol (FTP).

Internet Key Exchange (IKE)   A protocol that establishes the security association and shared keys necessary for two parties to communicate by using Internet Protocol security (IPSec). See also Internet Protocol security (IPSec); protocol.

Internet Protocol (IP)   A routable protocol in the TCP/IP protocol suite that is responsible for IP addressing, routing, and the fragmentation and reassembly of IP packets. See also packet; Transmission Control Protocol/Internet Protocol (TCP/IP).

Internet Protocol security (IPSec)   A set of industry-standard, cryptography-based protection services and protocols. IPSec protects all protocols in the TCP/IP protocol suite except Address Resolution Protocol (ARP). For virtual private network (VPN) connections, IPSec is used in conjunction with Layer Two Tunneling Protocol (L2TP). See also Layer Two Tunneling Protocol (L2TP); protocol; Transmission Control Protocol/Internet Protocol (TCP/IP); virtual private network (VPN).

Internet Server Application Programming Interface (ISAPI)   An application programming interface (API) that resides on a server computer for initiating software services tuned for Windows operating systems.

In Microsoft Provisioning System, ISAPI resides on the Web server.

See also application programming interface (API).

Internet service provider (ISP)   A company that provides individuals or companies access to the Internet and the World Wide Web. An ISP provides a telephone number, a user name, a password, and other connection information so users can connect their computers to the ISP's computers. An ISP typically charges a monthly or hourly connection fee.

Internetwork Packet Exchange (IPX)   A network protocol native to NetWare that controls addressing and routing of packets within and between local area networks (LANs). IPX does not guarantee that a message will be complete (no lost packets). See also local area network (LAN).

intranet   A network within an organization that uses Internet technologies and protocols, but is available only to certain people, such as employees of a company. Also called a *private network*. See also network.

IP address   For Internet Protocol version 4 (IPv4), a 32-bit address used to identify an interface on a node on an IPv4 internetwork. Each interface on the IP internetwork must be assigned a unique IPv4 address, which is made up of the network ID, plus a unique host ID. This address is typically represented with the decimal value of each octet separated by a period (for example, 192.168.7.27). You can configure the IP address statically or dynamically by using Dynamic Host Configuration Protocol (DHCP).

For Internet Protocol version 6 (IPv6), an identifier that is assigned at the IPv6 layer to an interface or set of interfaces and that can be used as the source or destination of IPv6 packets.

See also Dynamic Host Configuration Protocol (DHCP); Internet Protocol (IP); scope.

K

kernel   The core of layered architecture that manages the most basic operations of the operating system and the computer's processor. The kernel schedules different blocks of executing code, called threads, for the processor to keep it as busy as possible and coordinates multiple processors to optimize performance. The kernel also synchronizes activities among Executive-level subcomponents, such as I/O Manager and Process Manager, and handles hardware exceptions and other hardware-dependent functions. The kernel works closely with the hardware abstraction layer.

kernel mode   A highly privileged mode of operation where program code has direct access to all memory, including the address spaces of all user-mode processes and applications, and to hardware. Also known as *supervisor mode*, *protected mode*, or *Ring 0*.

Key   In Registry Editor, a folder that appears in the left pane of the Registry Editor window. A key can contain subkeys and entries. For example, Environment is a key of **HKEY_CURRENT_USER**.

In IP security (IPSec), a value used in combination with an algorithm to encrypt or decrypt data. Key settings for IPSec are configurable to provide greater security.

See also Internet Protocol security (IPSec); registry; subkey.

key pair   A private key and its related public key. See also private key; public key.

L

label   In DNS, each part of a DNS domain name that represents a node in the domain namespace tree. For example, the three labels *example*, *microsoft*, and *com* make up the DNS domain name *example.microsoft.com*. Each label used in a DNS name cannot exceed 63 octets, 255 bytes including the terminating dot, for the fully qualified domain name (FQDN). See also domain name; Domain Name System (DNS); fully qualified domain name (FQDN).

Layer Two Tunneling Protocol (L2TP)   An industry-standard Internet tunneling protocol that provides encapsulation for sending Point-to-Point Protocol (PPP) frames across packet-oriented media. For IP networks, L2TP traffic is sent as User Datagram Protocol (UDP) messages. In Microsoft operating systems, L2TP is used in conjunction with Internet Protocol security (IPSec) as a virtual private network (VPN) technology to provide remote access or router-to-router VPN connections. L2TP is described in RFC 2661. See also Internet Protocol security (IPSec); Point-to-Point Protocol (PPP); tunnel.

lease   The length of time for which a DHCP client can use a dynamically assigned IP address configuration. Before the lease time expires, the client must either renew or obtain a new lease with DHCP. See also Dynamic Host Configuration Protocol (DHCP); IP address.

Lightweight Directory Access Protocol (LDAP)   The primary access protocol for Active Directory. LDAP is an industry-standard protocol, established by the Internet Engineering Task Force (IETF), that allows users to query and update information in a directory service. Active Directory supports both LDAP version 2 and LDAP version 3. See also Active Directory; Internet Engineering Task Force (IETF); protocol.

Lmhosts file   A local text file that maps network basic input/output (NetBIOS) names (commonly used for computer names) to IP addresses for hosts that are not located on the local subnet. In this version of Windows, this file is stored in the *systemroot*\System32\Drivers\Etc folder. See also host; IP address; network basic input/output system (NetBIOS); systemroot.

local area network (LAN)   A communications network connecting a group of computers, printers, and other devices located within a relatively limited area (for example, a building). A LAN enables any connected device to interact with any other on the network. See also network basic input/output system (NetBIOS); virtual local area network (VLAN).

local computer   The computer that you are currently logged on to as a user. More generally, a local computer is a computer that you can access directly without using a communications line or a communications device, such as a network adapter or a modem.

local group   A security group that can be granted rights and permissions on only resources on the computer on which the group is created. Local groups can have any user accounts that are local to the computer as members, as well as users, groups, and computers from a domain to which the computer belongs. See also global group; member server; user account.

log file   A file that stores messages generated by an application, service, or operating system. These messages are used to track the operations performed. For example, Web servers maintain log files listing every request made to the server. Log files are usually plain text (ASCII) files and often have a .log extension.

In Backup, a file that contains a record of the date the tapes were created and the names of files and directories successfully backed up and restored. The Performance Logs and Alerts service also creates log files.

See also service.

logon script   A file, typically a batch file, that runs automatically every time a user logs on to a computer or network. It can be used to configure a user's working environment whenever a user logs on, and it allows an administrator to influence a user's environment without managing all aspects of it. A logon script can be assigned to one or more user accounts. See also user account.

long name   A folder name or file name longer than the 8.3 file name standard (up to eight characters followed by a period and an extension of up to three characters) of the file allocation table (FAT) file system. This version of Windows supports file names up to 255 characters and automatically translates long names of files and folders to 8.3 names for MS-DOS and Windows 3.*x* users. In a Macintosh environment, users can assign names up to 31 characters, excluding colons, to files and folders. See also file allocation table (FAT).

M

m-node   A NetBIOS node type that uses a mix of b-node and p-node communications to register and resolve NetBIOS names. M-node first uses broadcast resolution; then, if necessary, it uses a server query. See also network basic input/output system (NetBIOS).

master installation   A customized installation of Windows that you duplicate onto one or more destination computers.

master properties   In Internet Information Services (IIS), properties that are set at the computer level that become default settings for all Web or File Transfer Protocol (FTP) sites on that computer.

member server   A server that is joined to a domain but is not a domain controller. Member servers typically function as file servers, application servers, database servers, Web servers, certificate servers, firewalls, or remote access servers. See also domain; domain controller.

Message Queuing   A message queuing and routing system for Windows that enables distributed applications running at different times to communicate across heterogeneous networks and with computers that may be offline. Message Queuing provides guaranteed message delivery, efficient routing, security, and priority-based messaging. Formerly known as *MSMQ*.

metabase   A hierarchical store of configuration information and schema that is used to configure Internet Information Services (IIS). The metabase performs some of the same functions as the system registry, but it uses less disk space. In physical terms, the metabase is a combination of the MetaBase.xml and MBSchema.xml files and the in-memory metabase.

metabase configuration file   A file that stores Internet Information Services (IIS) configuration settings to disk. This file is named MetaBase.xml by default. When IIS is started or restarted, the configuration settings are read from MetaBase.xml into the IIS cache in memory, which is called the in-memory metabase.

metabase schema   The master configuration file (MBSchema.xml) supplied with Internet Information Services (IIS) that contains all of the predefined properties from which metabase entries are derived.

metadata   Data about data. For example, the title, subject, author, and size of a file constitute the file's metadata.

Microsoft Challenge Handshake Authentication Protocol version 2 (MS-CHAP v2)   An encrypted authentication mechanism for PPP connections that provides stronger security than CHAP and MS-CHAP v1. MS-CHAP v2 provides mutual authentication and asymmetric encryption keys. See also Point-to-Point Protocol (PPP).

Microsoft Management Console (MMC)   A framework for hosting administrative tools called *snap-ins*. A console might contain tools, folders or other containers, World Wide Web pages, and other administrative items. These items are displayed in the left pane of the console, called a *console tree*. A console has one or more windows that can provide views of the console tree. The main MMC window provides commands and tools for authoring consoles. The authoring features of MMC and the console tree itself might be hidden when a console is in User Mode. See also console tree; details pane; snap-in.

Microsoft Point-to-Point Encryption (MPPE)   A 128-bit key or 40-bit key encryption algorithm using RSA RC4. MPPE provides for packet confidentiality between the remote access client and the remote access or tunnel server, and it is useful where Internet Protocol security (IPSec) is not available. MPPE 40-bit keys are used to satisfy current North American export restrictions. MPPE is compatible with Network Address Translation. See also remote access server.

migrate   In file management, to move files or programs from an older file format or protocol to a more current format or protocol. For example, WINS database entries can be migrated from static WINS database entries to dynamically registered DHCP entries.

In Active Directory, to move Active Directory accounts, resources, and their associated security objects from one domain to another.

In Windows NT, to change the domain controller operating system from Windows NT to an operating system with Active Directory, such as Windows 2000 or Windows Server 2003. A migration from Windows NT can include in-place domain upgrades, domain restructuring, or both.

In Remote Storage, to copy an object from local storage to remote storage.

See also Active Directory; Dynamic Host Configuration Protocol (DHCP); Windows Internet Name Service (WINS).

migration   See definition for migrate.

Mini-Setup wizard   A wizard that starts the first time a computer boots from a hard disk that has been duplicated. The wizard gathers any information that is needed for the newly duplicated hard disk.

mirror set   A fault-tolerant partition created with Windows NT 4.0 or earlier that duplicates data on two physical disks. Windows XP and the Windows Server 2003 family do not support mirror sets. In the Windows Server 2003 family, you must create mirrored volumes on dynamic disks. See also dynamic disk; mirrored volume.

mirrored volume   A fault-tolerant volume that duplicates data on two physical disks. A mirrored volume provides data redundancy by using two identical volumes, which are called *mirrors*, to duplicate the information contained on the volume. A mirror is always located on a different disk. If one of the physical disks fails, the data on the failed disk becomes unavailable, but the system continues to operate in the mirror on the remaining disk. You can create mirrored volumes only on dynamic disks on computers running the Windows 2000 Server or Windows Server 2003 families of operating systems. You cannot extend mirrored volumes. See also dynamic disk; dynamic volume; fault tolerance; RAID-5 volume.

mounted drive   A drive attached to an empty folder on an NTFS volume. Mounted drives function the same as any other drive, but are assigned a label or name instead of a drive letter. The mounted drive's name is resolved to a full file system path instead of just a drive letter. Members of the Administrators group can use Disk Management to create mounted drives or reassign drive letters. See also NTFS file system.

Multicast Address Dynamic Client Allocation Protocol (MADCAP)   An extension to the DHCP protocol standard used to support dynamic assignment and configuration of IP multicast addresses on TCP/IP-based networks. See also Dynamic Host Configuration Protocol (DHCP); multicasting; Transmission Control Protocol/Internet Protocol (TCP/IP).

multicast scope   A range of multicast group IP addresses in the Class D address range that are available to be leased or assigned to multicast DHCP clients by DHCP. See also Dynamic Host Configuration Protocol (DHCP); IP address; lease; multicasting.

multicasting   The process of sending a message simultaneously to more than one destination on a network.

multihomed computer   A computer that has multiple network adapters or that has been configured with multiple IP addresses for a single network adapter. See also IP address; network adapter.

N

name resolution   The process of having software translate between names that are easy for users to work with and numerical IP addresses, which are difficult for users but necessary for TCP/IP communications. Name resolution can be provided by software components such as DNS or WINS. See also Domain Name System (DNS); Transmission Control Protocol/Internet Protocol (TCP/IP); Windows Internet Name Service (WINS).

namespace   A naming convention that defines a set of unique names for resources in a network. For DNS, a hierarchical naming structure that identifies each network resource and its place in the hierarchy of the namespace. For WINS, a flat naming structure that identifies each network resource using a single, unique name. See also Domain Name System (DNS); Windows Internet Name Service (WINS).

NetBIOS Node Type   A designation of the exact mechanisms by which network basic input/output system (NetBIOS) names are resolved to IP addresses. See also Internet Protocol (IP); IP address; network basic input/output system (NetBIOS).

NetBIOS over TCP/IP (NetBT)   A feature that provides the NetBIOS programming interface over the TCP/IP protocol. It is used for monitoring routed servers that use NetBIOS name resolution.

Netsh   A command-line and scripting tool for networking components for local or remote computers running Windows 2000, Windows XP Professional, or Windows Server 2003.

network   A group of computers and other devices, such as printers and scanners, connected by a communications link, enabling all the devices to interact with each other. Networks can be small or large, permanently connected through wires or cables, or temporarily connected through phone lines or wireless transmissions. The largest network is the Internet, which is a worldwide group of networks. See also network adapter.

network access server (NAS)   The device that accepts Point-to-Point Protocol (PPP) connections and places clients on the network that the NAS serves. See also Point-to-Point Protocol (PPP).

network adapter   A device that connects your computer to a network. Sometimes called an *adapter card* or *network interface card*.

network address translator (NAT)   An IP router defined in RFC 1631 that can translate IP addresses and Transmission Control Protocol/User Datagram Protocol (TCP/UDP) port numbers as packets are forwarded. See also Internet Protocol (IP); IP address; Transmission Control Protocol/Internet Protocol (TCP/IP).

network basic input/output system (NetBIOS)   An application programming interface (API) that can be used by programs on a local area network (LAN). NetBIOS provides programs with a uniform set of commands for requesting the lower-level services required to manage names, conduct sessions, and send datagrams between nodes on a network. See also application programming interface (API); basic input/output system (BIOS); local area network (LAN); service.

Network Load Balancing   A component of Windows 2000 Server that provides high availability and scalability of servers by using a cluster of two or more host computers working together. Clients access the cluster using a single IP address. See also cluster.

Network Monitor   A packet capture and analysis tool used to view network traffic. See also packet.

Network News Transfer Protocol (NNTP)   A protocol that is used to distribute network news messages to NNTP servers and to NNTP clients (news readers) on the Internet. NNTP provides for the distribution, inquiry, retrieval, and posting of news articles by using a reliable, stream-based transmission of news on the Internet. NNTP is designed in such a way that news articles are stored on a server in a central database, so that users can select specific items to read. Indexing, cross-referencing, and expiration of old messages are also provided. NNTP is defined in RFC 977.

network service Services such as file and printer sharing on your computer or automatic backup to a network server.

NTFS file system An advanced file system that provides performance, security, reliability, and advanced features that are not found in any version of file allocation table (FAT). For example, NTFS guarantees volume consistency by using standard transaction logging and recovery techniques. If a system fails, NTFS uses its log file and checkpoint information to restore the consistency of the file system. NTFS also provides advanced features, such as file and folder permissions, encryption, disk quotas, and compression. See also FAT32; file allocation table (FAT).

O

on-demand installation An installation option that gives software the ability to install new features on first use rather than when the application is first installed.

Open Shortest Path First (OSPF) A routing protocol used in medium-sized and large networks. This protocol is more complex than Routing Information Protocol (RIP), but it allows better control and is more efficient in propagation of routing information. See also protocol; routing; Routing Information Protocol (RIP).

organizational unit An Active Directory container object used within domains. An organizational unit is a logical container into which users, groups, computers, and other organizational units are placed. It can contain objects only from its parent domain. An organizational unit is the smallest scope to which a Group Policy object (GPO) can be linked, or over which administrative authority can be delegated. See also Active Directory; container object; Group Policy object (GPO); parent domain.

original equipment manufacturer (OEM) A company that typically purchases computer components from other manufacturers, uses the components to build a personal computer, preinstalls Windows onto that computer, and then sells the computer to the public.

out-of-process For IIS 5.0 isolation mode, ISAPI extensions that are hosted in a surrogate process called DLLHOST.exe, which is managed by COM+. See also IIS 5.0 isolation mode.

P

package   An icon that represents embedded or linked information. That information may consist of a complete file, such as a Paint bitmap, or part of a file, such as a spreadsheet cell. When you choose the package, the application used to create the object either plays the object (for example, a sound file) or opens and displays the object. If you change the original information, linked information is automatically updated. However, you must manually update embedded information.

package distribution   In Systems Management Server, the process of placing a decompressed package image on distribution points, sharing that image, and making it accessible to clients. This process occurs when you specify distribution points for a package. See also distribution point.

packet   An Open Systems Interconnection (OSI) network layer transmission unit that consists of binary information representing both data and a header containing an identification number, source and destination addresses, and error-control data.

packet filtering   Prevents certain types of network packets from either being sent or received. This can be employed for security reasons (to prevent access from unauthorized users) or to improve performance by disallowing unnecessary packets from going over a slow connection. See also packet.

parent domain   For DNS and Active Directory, domains that are located in the namespace tree directly above other derivative domain names (child domains). For example, *microsoft.com* would be the parent domain for *example.microsoft.com*, a child domain. See also Active Directory; child domain; domain; Domain Name System (DNS).

parent object   An object in which another object resides. For example, a folder is a parent object in which a file, or child object, resides. An object can be both a parent and a child object. For example, a subfolder that contains files is both the child of the parent folder and the parent folder of the files.

perimeter network   An Internet Protocol (IP) network segment that contains resources, such as Web servers and virtual private network (VPN) servers, that are available to Internet users. Also known as *screened subnet* or *demilitarized zone (DMZ)*. See also Internet Authentication Service (IAS); Internet Protocol (IP); virtual private network (VPN).

peripheral   A device, such as a disk drive, printer, modem, or joystick, that is connected to a computer and is controlled by the computer's microprocessor.

permission   A rule associated with an object to regulate which users can gain access to the object and in what manner. Permissions are assigned or denied by the object's owner.

ping   A utility that verifies connections to one or more remote hosts. The **ping** command uses Internet Control Message Protocol (ICMP) echo request and echo reply packets to determine whether a particular Internet Protocol (IP) system on a network is functional. **Ping** is useful for diagnosing IP network or router failures. See also host; Internet Control Message Protocol (ICMP); Internet Protocol (IP); packet.

pixel   Short for picture element, one spot in a rectilinear grid of thousands of such spots that form an image produced on the screen by a computer or on paper by a printer. A pixel is the smallest element that display or print hardware and software can manipulate to create letters, numbers, or graphics. Also called a *pel*.

plaintext   Data that is not encrypted. Sometimes also called *cleartext*.

platform   A type of client, such as Windows 2000, Windows NT 4.0, Windows Millennium Edition, Windows 98, Windows 3.*x*, Macintosh, or UNIX.

Plug and Play   A set of specifications developed by Intel Corporation that enables a computer to detect and configure a device automatically and install the appropriate device drivers. See also universal serial bus (USB).

Point-to-Point Protocol (PPP)   An industry standard suite of protocols for the use of point-to-point links to transport multiprotocol datagrams. PPP is documented in RFC 1661. See also Transmission Control Protocol/Internet Protocol (TCP/IP).

Point-to-Point Tunneling Protocol (PPTP)   Networking technology that supports multiprotocol virtual private networks (VPNs), enabling remote users to access corporate networks securely across the Internet or other networks by dialing into an Internet service provider (ISP) or by connecting directly to the Internet. PPTP tunnels, or encapsulates, Internet Protocol (IP) or Internetwork Packet Exchange (IPX) traffic inside IP packets. This means that users can remotely run applications that depend on particular network protocols. PPTP is described in RFC 2637. See also Internet Protocol (IP); Internetwork Packet Exchange (IPX); packet; tunnel; virtual private network (VPN).

pooled out-of-process   For IIS 5.0 isolation mode, a special Web Application Manager (WAM) package that hosts all out-of-process ISAPI extensions that are set to medium isolation within the same DLLHOST.exe process. See also IIS 5.0 isolation mode; out-of-process; Web Application Manager (WAM).

port number   A number that identifies a certain Internet application. For example, the default port number for the WWW service is 80.

PostScript A page-description language (PDL), developed by Adobe Systems for printing on laser printers. PostScript offers flexible font capability and high-quality graphics. It is the standard for desktop publishing because it is supported by imagesetters, the high-resolution printers used by printing services for commercial typesetting. See also service.

preshared key An Internet Protocol security (IPSec) technology in which a shared, secret key is used for authentication in IPSec policy. See also Internet Protocol security (IPSec); key.

primary domain controller (PDC) In a Windows NT domain, a domain controller running Windows NT Server 4.0 or earlier that authenticates domain logon attempts and updates user, computer, and group accounts in a domain. The PDC contains the master read-write copy of the directory database for the domain. A domain has only one PDC.

   In a Windows 2000 or Windows Server 2003 domain, the PDC emulator master supports compatibility with client computers that are not running Windows 2000 or Windows XP Professional.

   See also Active Directory; backup domain controller (BDC).

private key The secret half of a cryptographic key pair that is used with a public key algorithm. Private keys are typically used to decrypt a symmetric session key, digitally sign data, or decrypt data that has been encrypted with the corresponding public key. See also public key.

process isolation Running an application or component out of process.

protocol A set of rules and conventions for sending information over a network. These rules govern the content, format, timing, sequencing, and error control of messages exchanged among network devices. See also Internet Protocol (IP); Transmission Control Protocol/Internet Protocol (TCP/IP).

proxy server A firewall component that manages Internet traffic to and from a local area network (LAN) and that can provide other features, such as document caching and access control. A proxy server can improve performance by supplying frequently requested data, such as a popular Web page, and it can filter and discard requests that the owner does not consider appropriate, such as requests for unauthorized access to proprietary files. See also firewall; local area network (LAN).

public key The nonsecret half of a cryptographic key pair that is used with a public key algorithm. Public keys are typically used when encrypting a session key, verifying a digital signature, or encrypting data that can be decrypted with the corresponding private key. See also key; private key.

public key infrastructure (PKI)   The laws, policies, standards, and software that regulate or manipulate certificates and public and private keys. In practice, it is a system of digital certificates, certification authorities, and other registration authorities that verify and authenticate the validity of each party involved in an electronic transaction. Standards for PKI are still evolving, even though they are being widely implemented as a necessary element of electronic commerce. See also certificate; certification authority (CA); public key.

published application   An application that is available to users managed by a Group Policy object. Each user decides whether or not to install the published application by using **Add or Remove Programs** in Control Panel. See also Group Policy object (GPO).

pull partner   A WINS component that requests replication of updated WINS database entries from its push partner. See also push partner; Windows Internet Name Service (WINS).

push partner   A WINS component that notifies its pull partner when updated WINS database entries are available for replication. See also pull partner; Windows Internet Name Service (WINS).

R

RAID-5 volume   A fault-tolerant volume with data and parity striped intermittently across three or more physical disks. Parity is a calculated value that is used to reconstruct data after a failure. If a portion of a physical disk fails, Windows recreates the data that was on the failed portion from the remaining data and parity. You can create RAID-5 volumes only on dynamic disks on computers running the Windows 2000 Server or Windows Server 2003 families of operating systems. You cannot mirror or extend RAID-5 volumes. In Windows NT 4.0, a RAID-5 volume was known as a *striped set with parity*. See also dynamic disk; dynamic volume; fault tolerance.

Redundant Array of Independent Disks (RAID)   A method used to standardize and categorize fault-tolerant disk systems. RAID levels provide various mixes of performance, reliability, and cost. Some servers provide three of the RAID levels: Level 0 (striping), Level 1 (mirroring), and Level 5 (RAID-5). See also fault tolerance; RAID-5 volume.

registry   A database repository for information about a computer's configuration. The registry contains information that Windows continually references during operation, such as:

- Profiles for each user

- The programs installed on the computer and the types of documents that each can create

- Property settings for folders and program icons

- What hardware exists on the system

- Which ports are being used

The registry is organized hierarchically as a tree, and it is made up of keys and their subkeys, hives, and entries.

See also key; subkey.

registry key   An identifier for a record or group of records in the registry. See also registry.

remote access policy   A set of conditions and connection parameters that define the characteristics of the incoming connection and the set of constraints imposed on it. Remote access policy determines whether a specific connection attempt is authorized to be accepted.

remote access server   A Windows-based computer running the Routing and Remote Access service and configured to provide remote access.

Remote Authentication Dial-In User Service (RADIUS)   A security authentication protocol based on a client/server model and widely used by Internet service providers (ISPs). RADIUS is the most popular means of authenticating and authorizing dial-up, virtual private network (VPN), wireless, and authenticating switch clients today. A RADIUS client is included in the Routing and Remote Access service that ships with the Windows Server 2003 family. A RADIUS server and proxy, named Internet Authentication Service (IAS), is included in Windows Server 2003, Standard Edition; Windows Server 2003, Enterprise Edition; and Windows Server 2003, Datacenter Edition. See also authorization; Internet Authentication Service (IAS); tunnel; virtual private network (VPN).

Remote Boot Floppy Generator (Rbfg.exe)   A tool that generates a Remote Installation Services (RIS) boot floppy disk. A RIS boot floppy disk is used by RIS client computers to initiate a network boot to a RIS server for remote operating system installation on clients that cannot use Pre-Boot eXecution Environment (PXE). See also Remote Installation Services (RIS).

Remote Installation Preparation wizard (RIPrep.exe)   A component in Remote Installation Services that is used to create operating system images and to install them on the RIS server. See also Remote Installation Services (RIS).

Remote Installation Services (RIS)   Software services that allow an administrator to set up new client computers remotely, without having to visit each client. The target clients must support remote booting.

Remote Installation Services setup (RISetup.exe)   A component in Remote Installation Services that is used to set up the RIS server. See also Remote Installation Services (RIS).

repackaging   The process of converting an earlier version of an application to take advantage of many Windows Installer features, including the ability to advertise the application to users, the ability of the software to repair itself if essential files are deleted or corrupted, and the ability of users to install the application with elevated privileges.

replica   In Active Directory replication, one instance of a logical Active Directory partition that is synchronized by means of replication between domain controllers that hold copies of the same directory partition. *Replica* can also refer to an instance of an object or attribute in a distributed directory.

In the File Replication service (FRS), a computer that has been included in the configuration of a specific replica set.

reservation   A specific IP address within a scope permanently reserved for leased use to a specific DHCP client. Client reservations are made in the DHCP database using DHCP Manager and based on a unique client device identifier for each reserved entry. See also Dynamic Host Configuration Protocol (DHCP); IP address; lease; scope.

resource   For Resource Manager in Microsoft Provisioning Framework (MPF), a consumable entity such as disk space, IP addresses, or mailboxes that can be assigned to a consumer.

restructure   To change an Active Directory forest infrastructure. Restructuring implies that Active Directory objects are migrated between domains or forests. See also Active Directory; forest; migrate.

RIS   See definition for Remote Installation Services (RIS).

rollback   The removal of the updates performed by one or more partially completed transactions. Rollbacks are required to restore the integrity of a database after an application, database, or system failure.

root   The highest or uppermost level in a hierarchically organized set of information. The root is the point from which further subsets are branched in a logical sequence that moves from a broad or general focus to narrower perspectives. See also DFS root; root hints; root target.

root domain   The beginning of the DNS namespace. In Active Directory, the initial domain in an Active Directory tree. Also, the initial domain of a forest. See also Active Directory; domain; Domain Name System (DNS); forest; namespace.

root hints   DNS data stored on a DNS server that identifies the authoritative DNS servers for the root zone of the DNS namespace. The root hints are stored in the file Cache.dns, located in the *systemroot*\System32\Dns folder. See also DNS server; Domain Name System (DNS); systemroot.

root target   The mapping destination of a DFS root, which corresponds to a shared folder on a server. See also DFS root; target.

router   A device or computer that forwards packets between interfaces based on a network layer destination address. For example, an Internet Protocol (IP) router forwards IP packets based on the destination IP address in the IP header. Routers typically use a routing table, which contains a series of entries for destinations and the corresponding next-hop address and interface to use to forward a packet to its eventual destination. See also local area network (LAN); routing; wide area network (WAN).

routing   The process of forwarding a packet through an internetwork from a source host to a destination host. See also host; packet.

Routing Information Protocol (RIP)   An industry standard, distance vector routing protocol used in small- to medium-sized Internet Protocol (IP) and Internetwork Packet Exchange (IPX) internetworks. See also Internet Protocol (IP); Internetwork Packet Exchange (IPX); protocol.

routing protocol   Any of several protocols that enable the exchange of routing table information between routers. Typically, medium- to large-sized TCP/IP internetworks implement routing protocols to simplify the administration of routing tables. See also router; routing; routing table.

routing table   A database of routes containing information on network destinations, next-hop addresses and interfaces, and metrics for reachable network segments on an internetwork.

S

scalability   A measure of how well a computer, service, or application can grow to meet increasing performance demands. For server clusters, the ability to incrementally add one or more systems to an existing cluster when the overall load of the cluster exceeds its capabilities. See also server cluster.

schema   The set of definitions for the universe of objects that can be stored in a directory. For each object class, the schema defines which attributes an instance of the class must have, which additional attributes it can have, and which other object classes can be its parent object class. See also parent object.

scope   A range of IP addresses that are available to be leased or assigned to DHCP clients by the DHCP service. See also Dynamic Host Configuration Protocol (DHCP); IP address; lease.

script   A type of program consisting of a set of instructions to an application or tool program. A script usually expresses instructions by using the application's or tool's rules and syntax, combined with simple control structures such as loops and if/then expressions. "Batch program" is often used interchangeably with "script" in the Windows environment.

secure dynamic update   The process in which a DNS client submits a dynamic update request to a DNS server and the DNS server performs the update only if the client is authenticated. See also DNS server; dynamic update.

Secure Sockets Layer (SSL)   A protocol that supplies secure data communication through data encryption and decryption. SSL uses RSA public-key encryption for specific TCP/IP ports. It is intended for handling commerce payments. An alternative method is Secure-HTTP (S-HTTP), which is used to encrypt specific Web documents, rather than the entire session. SSL is a general-purpose encryption standard. SSL can also be used for Web applications that require a secure link, such as e-commerce applications, or for controlling access to Web-based subscription services.

security   On a network, protection of a computer system and its data from harm or loss, implemented especially so that only authorized users can gain access to shared files. See also authorization.

security group   A group that can be listed in discretionary access control lists (DACLs) used to define permissions on resources and objects. A security group can also be used as an e-mail entity. Sending an e-mail message to the group sends the message to all the members of the group. See also group.

server   In general, a computer that provides shared resources to network users. See also client.

server certificate   A unique digital identification that forms the basis of a Web server's Secure Sockets Layer (SSL) security features. Server certificates are obtained from a mutually trusted, third-party organization, and they provide a way for users to authenticate the identity of a Web site.

server cluster   A group of computers, known as *nodes*, working together as a single system to ensure that mission-critical applications and resources remain available to clients. A server cluster presents the appearance of a single server to a client. See also cluster.

service   A program, routine, or process that performs a specific system function to support other programs, particularly at a low (close to the hardware) level. When services are provided over a network, they can be published in Active Directory, facilitating service-centric administration and usage. Some examples of services are the Security Accounts Manager service, File Replication service, and Routing and Remote Access service. See also File Replication service (FRS).

Service Pack   A software upgrade to an existing software distribution that contains updated files consisting of patches and hot fixes.

Setup   The program that installs Windows. Also known as *unattended installation*, *Winnt32.exe*, and *Winnt.exe*.

shared folder   A folder on another computer that has been made available for other people to use on the network.

shortcut   A link to any item accessible on your computer or on a network, such as a program, file, folder, disk drive, Web page, printer, or another computer. You can put shortcuts in various areas, such as on the desktop, on the **Start** menu, or in specific folders.

Simple Mail Transfer Protocol (SMTP)   A TCP/IP protocol for sending messages from one computer to another on a network. This protocol is used on the Internet to route e-mail.

Simple Network Management Protocol (SNMP)   A network protocol used to manage TCP/IP networks. In Windows, the SNMP service is used to provide status information about a host on a TCP/IP network. See also protocol; service; Transmission Control Protocol/Internet Protocol (TCP/IP).

site   One or more well-connected (highly reliable and fast) TCP/IP subnets. A site allows administrators to configure Active Directory access and replication topology to take advantage of the physical network. See also Active Directory; subnet; Transmission Control Protocol/Internet Protocol (TCP/IP).

smart card   A credit card–sized device that is used with an access code to enable certificate-based authentication and single sign-on to the enterprise. Smart cards securely store certificates, public and private keys, passwords, and other types of personal information. A smart card reader attached to the computer reads the smart card.

SMS   See definition for Systems Management Server (SMS).

snap-in   A type of tool that you can add to a console supported by Microsoft Management Console (MMC). A stand-alone snap-in can be added by itself; an extension snap-in can be added only to extend the function of another snap-in. See also Microsoft Management Console (MMC).

sniffer   An application or device that can read, monitor, and capture network data exchanges and read network packets. If the packets are not encrypted, a sniffer provides a full view of the data inside the packet. See also packet.

software metering   The process by which SMS monitors program usage on client computers.

static page   A Hypertext Markup Language (HTML) page that is prepared in advance of a request for it and that is sent to the client upon request. This page takes no special action when it is requested. See also dynamic page.

stripe set   A volume that stores data in stripes on two or more physical disks. A stripe set is created by using Windows NT 4.0 or earlier. Windows XP and Windows Server 2003 do not support stripe sets. Instead, you must create a striped volume on dynamic disks. See also dynamic disk.

subkey   An element of the registry that contains entries or other subkeys. A tier of the registry that is immediately below a key or a subtree (if the subtree has no keys). See also key; registry.

subnet   A subdivision of an Internet Protocol (IP) network. Each subnet has its own unique subnetted network ID. See also Internet Protocol (IP).

subnet mask   A 32-bit value that enables the recipient of Internet Protocol version 4 (IPv4) packets to distinguish the network ID and host ID portions of the IPv4 address. Typically, subnet masks use the format 255.*x.x.x*. IPv6 uses network prefix notations rather than subnet masks. See also IP address.

superscope   An administrative grouping feature that supports a DHCP server's ability to use more than scope for each physical interface and subnet. Superscopes are useful under the following conditions: If more DHCP clients must be added to a network than were originally planned, if an Internet Protocol (IP) network is renumbered, or if two or more DHCP servers are configured to provide scope redundancy and fault-tolerant design DHCP service for a single subnet. Each superscope can contain one or more member scopes (also known as *child scopes*). See also fault tolerance; scope; subnet.

switch   A computer or other network-enabled device that controls routing and operation of a signal path. In clustering, a switch is used to connect the cluster hosts to a router or other source of incoming network connections.

Syspart   A process that executes through an optional parameter of Winnt32.exe. Used for clean installations to computers that have dissimilar hardware. This automated installation method reduces deployment time by eliminating the file-copy phase of Setup.

Sysprep   A tool that prepares the hard disk on a source computer for duplication to destination computers and then runs a non-Microsoft disk-imaging process. This automated installation method is used when the hard disk on the master computer is identical to those of the target computers. See also destination computer.

system volume   The volume that contains the hardware-specific files that are needed to load Windows on x86-based computers with a basic input/output system (BIOS). The system volume can be, but does not have to be, the same volume as the boot volume. See also basic input/output system (BIOS).

systemroot   The path and folder name where the Windows system files are located. Typically, this is C:\Windows, although you can designate a different drive or folder when you install Windows. You can use the value %systemroot% to replace the actual location of the folder that contains the Windows system files. To identify your systemroot folder, click **Start**, click **Run**, type **%systemroot%**, and then click **OK**.

Systems Management Server (SMS)   A Microsoft product that includes inventory collection, software deployment, and diagnostic tools. SMS automates the task of upgrading software, allows remote problem solving, provides asset management information, and monitors software usage, computers, and networks.

T

target   The mapping destination of a DFS root or link, which corresponds to a physical folder that has been shared on the network. See also DFS root; Distributed File System (DFS).

Time to Live (TTL)   For Internet Protocol (IP), a field in the IP header of an IP packet that indicates the maximum number of links over which the packet can travel before being discarded by a router.

For DNS, TTL values are used in resource records within a zone to determine how long requesting clients should cache and use this information when it appears in a query response answered by a DNS server for the zone.

See also DNS server; Domain Name System (DNS); Internet Protocol (IP); packet; Transmission Control Protocol/Internet Protocol (TCP/IP); zone.

topology   The physical layout of computers, cables, switches, routers, and other components of a network. *Topology* also refers to the underlying network architecture, such as Ethernet or Token Ring.

In Active Directory replication, the set of connections that domain controllers use to replicate information among themselves.

See also Active Directory replication; domain controller.

Transmission Control Protocol/Internet Protocol (TCP/IP)   A set of networking protocols widely used on the Internet that provides communications across interconnected networks of computers with diverse hardware architectures and various operating systems. TCP/IP includes standards for how computers communicate and conventions for connecting networks and routing traffic. See also Internet Protocol (IP); protocol.

trust relationship   A logical relationship established between domains to allow pass-through authentication, in which a trusting domain honors the logon authentications of a trusted domain. User accounts and global groups defined in a trusted domain can be given rights and permissions in a trusting domain, even though the user accounts or groups don't exist in the trusting domain's directory. See also domain; global group; group; permission; user account.

tunnel   A logical connection over which data is encapsulated. Typically, both encapsulation and encryption are performed, and the tunnel is a private, secure link between a remote user or host and a private network. See also host.

U

Unattend.txt   The generic name for the Windows Setup answer file. In the CD boot installation method, Unattend.txt must be named Winnt.sif.

unattended Setup   An automated, hands-free method of installing Windows. During installation, unattended Setup uses an answer file to supply data to Setup instead of requiring that an administrator or end user interactively provide the answers. See also Setup.

Uniform Resource Locator (URL) A naming convention that uniquely identifies the location of a computer, directory, or file on the Internet. A URL also specifies the appropriate Internet protocol, such as Hypertext Transfer Protocol (HTTP) or File Transfer Protocol (FTP). An example of a URL is http://www.microsoft.com.

universal group A security or distribution group that can contain users, groups, and computers from any domain in its forest as members.

Universal security groups can be granted rights and permissions on resources in any domain in the forest.

See also domain; forest; security group.

Universal Naming Convention (UNC) A convention for naming files and other resources beginning with two backslashes (\\), indicating that the resource exists on a network computer. UNC names conform to the *servername**sharename* syntax, where *servername* is the server's name and *sharename* is the name of the shared resource. The UNC name of a directory or file can also include the directory path after the share name, by using the following syntax: *servername**sharename**directory**filename*.

universal serial bus (USB) An external bus that supports Plug and Play installation. Using USB, you can connect and disconnect devices without shutting down or restarting your computer. You can use a single USB port to connect up to 127 peripheral devices, including speakers, telephones, CD-ROM drives, joysticks, tape drives, keyboards, scanners, and cameras. A USB port is usually located on the back of your computer near the serial port or parallel port. See also Plug and Play.

upgrade When referring to software, to update existing program files, folders, and registry entries to a more recent version. Upgrading, unlike performing a new installation, leaves existing settings and files in place. See also install; registry.

user account In Active Directory, an object that consists of all the information that defines a domain user, which includes user name, password, and groups in which the user account has membership. User accounts can be stored in either Active Directory or on your local computer.

For computers running Windows XP Professional and member servers running Windows Server 2003, use Local Users and Groups to manage local user accounts. For domain controllers running Windows Server 2003, use Active Directory Users and Computers to manage domain user accounts.

See also Active Directory; group; member server.

user class   An administrative feature that allows DHCP clients to be grouped logically according to a shared or common need. For example, a user class can be defined and used to allow similar DHCP leased configuration for all client computers in a specific building or site location. See also Dynamic Host Configuration Protocol (DHCP); lease.

user profile   A file that contains configuration information for a specific user, such as desktop settings, persistent network connections, and application settings. Each user's preferences are saved to a user profile that Windows uses to configure the desktop each time a user logs on.

V

vendor class   An administrative feature that allows DHCP clients to be identified and leased according to their vendor and hardware configuration type. For example, assigning a vendor class of *HP* to a printer vendor such as Hewlett-Packard would allow all Hewlett-Packard printers to be managed as a single unit so they could all obtain a similar DHCP leased configuration. See also Dynamic Host Configuration Protocol (DHCP); lease.

virtual cluster   A Network Load Balancing cluster that you create by assigning specific port rules to specific virtual IP addresses. With virtual clusters, you can use different port rules for different Web sites or applications hosted on the cluster, provided each Web site or application has a different virtual IP address.

virtual directory   A directory name, used in an address, that corresponds to a physical directory on the server. Sometimes called URL mapping.

virtual local area network (VLAN)   A logical grouping of hosts on one or more local area networks (LANs) that allows communication to occur between hosts as if they were on the same physical LAN. See also host; local area network (LAN).

virtual private network (VPN)   The extension of a private network that encompasses encapsulated, encrypted, and authenticated links across shared or public networks. VPN connections typically provide remote access and router-to-router connections to private networks over the Internet. See also routing; tunnel.

virtual server   A virtual computer that resides on a Hypertext Transfer Protocol (HTTP) server but appears to the user as a separate HTTP server. Several virtual servers can reside on one computer, each capable of running its own programs and each with individualized access to input and peripheral devices. Each virtual server has its own domain name and IP address, and each appears to the user as an individual Web site or File Transfer Protocol (FTP) site. Some Internet service providers (ISPs) use virtual servers for those clients who want to use their own domain names. Also called a Web site.

volume set   A volume that consists of disk space on one or more physical disks. A volume set is created by using basic disks and is supported only in Windows NT 4.0 or earlier. Volume sets were replaced by spanned volumes, which use dynamic disks. See also dynamic disk.

W

W3SVC   See definition for World Wide Web Publishing Service (WWW service).

Web application   A software program that uses Hypertext Transfer Protocol (HTTP) for its core communication protocol and that delivers Web-based information to the user in the Hypertext Markup Language (HTML) language. Also called a Web-based application.

Web Application Manager (WAM)   For IIS 5.0 isolation mode, a COM+ application package that works with DLLHOST.exe to host out-of-process ISAPI extensions. Provides communication between DLLHOST.exe and INETINFO.exe. See also IIS 5.0 isolation mode.

Web Distributed Authoring and Versioning (WebDAV)   An extension to the Hypertext Transfer Protocol (HTTP) 1.1 standard that facilitates access to files and directories through an HTTP connection. Remote authors can add, search, delete, or change directories and documents and their properties.

Web farm   A Network Load Balancing cluster of IIS servers that support client Web site requests.

Web garden   An application pool served by more than one worker process.

Web page   A World Wide Web document. A Web page typically consists of a Hypertext Markup Language (HTML) file, with associated files for graphics and scripts, in a particular directory on a particular computer. It is identified by a Uniform Resource Locator (URL).

Web server   In general, a computer that is equipped with server software that uses Internet protocols such as Hypertext Transfer Protocol (HTTP) and File Transfer Protocol (FTP) to respond to Web client requests on a TCP/IP network.

Web service extensions   ISAPIs and CGIs that extend Internet Information Services (IIS) functionality beyond serving static pages.

wide area network (WAN)   A communications network connecting geographically separated locations that uses long-distance links of third-party telecommunications vendors. See also local area network (LAN).

Winbom.ini   An .ini file that provides a bill-of-materials to incorporate into the Windows installation. Winbom.ini can control different points of the installation and configuration process: for example, it can control Sysprep during Factory mode, Windows preinstallation when starting from the Windows Preinstallation Environment (WinPE), or Windows XP configuration during Windows Welcome.

Windows Installer   An operating system service that enables the operating system to manage the installation process. Windows Installer technologies are divided into two parts that work in combination: a clientside installer service (Msiexec.exe) and a package (.msi) file. Windows Installer uses the information contained within a package file to install the application.

Windows Internet Name Service (WINS)   A Windows name resolution service for network basic input/output system (NetBIOS) names. WINS is used by hosts running NetBIOS over TCP/IP (NetBT) to register NetBIOS names and to resolve NetBIOS names to Internet Protocol (IP) addresses. See also IP address; network basic input/output system (NetBIOS); service.

Windows Management Instrumentation (WMI)   A management infrastructure in Windows that supports monitoring and controlling system resources through a common set of interfaces and provides a logically organized, consistent model of Windows operation, configuration, and status.

WINS lookup   A process by which a Domain Name System (DNS) server queries Windows Internet Name Service (WINS) to resolve names it does not find in its authoritative zones. See also DNS server; Domain Name System (DNS); Windows Internet Name Service (WINS); zone.

WMI provider   In Windows Management Instrumentation (WMI), a set of interfaces that provide programmatic access to management information in a system. Internet Information Services (IIS) implements a WMI provider in the namespace called MicrosoftIISv2to provide programmatic access to metabase properties and system settings.

worker process   The implementation of the core Web server in Internet Information Services (IIS). Worker processes run in W3wp.exe.

worker process isolation mode   The new Web process model for Internet Information Services (IIS) 6.0.

World Wide Web (WWW)   A set of services that run on top of the Internet and provide a cost-effective way of publishing information, supporting collaboration and workflow, and delivering business applications to connected users all over the world. The Web is a collection of Internet host systems that make these services available on the Internet, using the Hypertext Transfer Protocol (HTTP). Web-based information is usually delivered in the form of hypertext and hypermedia, using Hypertext

Markup Language (HTML). The most graphical service on the Internet, the Web also has the most sophisticated linking abilities.

World Wide Web Consortium (W3C) An international industry consortium that is jointly hosted by the Massachusetts Institute of Technology Laboratory for Computer Science (MIT/LCS) in North America, by the Institut National de Recherche en Informatique et en Automatique (INRIA) in Europe, and by the Keio University Shonan Fujisawa Campus in Asia. W3C was founded in 1994 to develop common standards for the World Wide Web. Initially, the W3C was established in collaboration with CERN, where the Web originated, with support from the Defense Advanced Research Projects Agency (DARPA) and the European Commission.

World Wide Web Publishing Service (WWW service) The service that manages the Internet Information Services (IIS) core components that process HTTP requests and configure and manage Web applications. Formerly known as W3SVC.

Z

ZAP (.zap) file Zero Administration Windows application package file. A text file (similar to an .ini file) that describes how to install an application (which command line to use); the properties of the application (name, version, and language); and what entry points the application should automatically install (for file name extension, CLSID, and ProgID). A .zap file is generally stored in the same location on the network as the setup program it references. See also package.

zone In the Macintosh environment, a logical grouping that simplifies browsing the network for resources, such as servers and printers.

In a DNS database, a manageable unit of the DNS database that is administered by a DNS server. A zone stores the domain names and data of the domain with a corresponding name, except for domain names stored in delegated subdomains.

See also DNS server; domain; Domain Name System (DNS).

Index

In-depth, daily administration guides
for Microsoft Windows Server 2003

Microsoft® Windows® Server 2003 Administrator's Companion
ISBN 0-7356-1367-2

The in-depth, daily operations guide to planning, deployment, and maintenance. Here's the ideal one-volume guide for the IT professional who administers Windows Server 2003. This ADMINISTRATOR'S COMPANION offers up-to-date information on core system-administration topics for Windows, including Active Directory® services, security, disaster planning and recovery, interoperability with NetWare and UNIX, plus all-new sections about Microsoft Internet Security and Acceleration (ISA) Server and scripting. Featuring easy-to-use procedures and handy workarounds, this book provides ready answers for on-the-job results.

Microsoft Windows Server 2003 Security Administrator's Companion
ISBN 0-7356-1574-8

The in-depth, daily operations guide to enhancing security with the network operating system. With this authoritative ADMINISTRATOR'S COMPANION—written by an expert on the Windows Server 2003 security team—you'll learn how to use the powerful security features in the latest network server operating system. The guide describes best practices and technical details for enhancing security with Windows Server 2003, using the holistic approach that IT professionals need to grasp to help secure their systems. The authors cover concepts such as physical security issues, internal security policies, and public and shared key cryptography, and then drill down into the specifics of key security features of Windows Server 2003.

learn more about the full line of Microsoft Press® products for IT professionals, please visit:

microsoft.com/mspress/IT

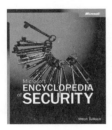

Get a **Free**
e-mail newsletter, updates,
special offers, links to related books,
and more when you
register online!

Register your Microsoft Press® title on our Web site and you'll get a FREE subscription to our e-mail newsletter, *Microsoft Press Book Connections.* You'll find out about newly released and upcoming books and learning tools, online events, software downloads, special offers and coupons for Microsoft Press customers, and information about major Microsoft® product releases. You can also read useful additional information about all the titles we publish, such as detailed book descriptions, tables of contents and indexes, sample chapters, links to related books and book series, author biographies, and reviews by other customers.

Registration is easy. Just visit this Web page and fill in your information:

http://www.microsoft.com/mspress/register

Microsoft®

- -